PRAISE FOR JORDAN P. BARNES

"One Hit Away is a gripping, startling account into addiction, compassion and ultimate salvation. It is powerful because of its honesty. Raw without being sensationalistic, this harrowing account of Jordan's journey provides insight and compassion into the struggle of addiction. It is an important, engrossing book that is hard to put down."

ANNIE GRACE, AUTHOR, THIS NAKED MIND:
CONTROL ALCOHOL, FIND FREEDOM, DISCOVER
HAPPINESS & CHANGE YOUR LIFE

"Raw, brutal, and jaw dropping. Jordan P. Barnes exposes his readers to the dark abyss that is heroin addiction. His transparency brings a level of understanding and empathy to anyone who has ever been touched by addiction."

KYLIE LEBLANC, AUTHOR & CURATOR,
ADDICTSRIPPLE.COM

"One Hit Away takes you on a journey you won't forget. An honest expression of such a common and hardcore reality is so necessary. This memoir is a work of art for both truth and healing on a level that many of us have yet to encounter."

KAYLEON DORTCH-ELLIOTT, AUTHOR, ONE DAY AT A
TIME: REMAINING IN STEP, MY SENTIMENTS EXACTLY
PODCAST

"Barnes' beautifully written memoir takes one by the hand and invites them into the hell of addiction—the suffocation, the trap, and the never-ending fear that one is doomed. His story is honest, raw, and tugs at the heart. More importantly, he delivers a story of hope—that for even the worst addict, if they want help, happiness can be found. Kudos to Jordan P. Barnes for such profound service through his beautiful words."

"Jordan's memoir is a heartrending true story of his journey from being hopelessly addicted—always chasing the next high—to battling his way to sobriety, marriage, and the joys of fatherhood. This is an unflinching story about how it is possible to transcend the darkness of addiction and live a life of happiness."

"Authentic and inspiring, One Hit Away is more than just a transparent, real life story of the tragedies of addiction—it's a heartfelt message filled with hope and salvation. We all know someone who has struggled with addiction. However, if you had the pleasure of meeting Jordan, you'd never know he fought those demons on the bitter, cold, and dangerous streets of Portland—only that he's an example of how anything is possible in recovery."

"As an addict in recovery, I approve this message. Chee huu."

"Jordan P. Barnes' One Hit Away takes the reader on a traumatizing yet moving narrative that hits you in the gut from the first chapter on. It's an emotional tale—a survival rollercoaster of habit and helplessness that exposes the harsh reality of the struggle for sobriety. A naked and honest look inside the perilous road of recovery and rehabilitation, it's a must-read for anyone wishing to understand the power of addiction as well as the hope for redemption."

ONE HIT AWAY

ONE HIT AWAY

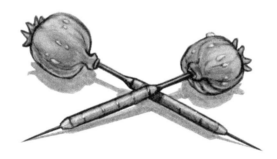

A MEMOIR OF RECOVERY BY
JORDAN P. BARNES

Island Time Press, LLC
P.O. Box 630
Kailua, HI 96734

Designed by @Jordan_P_Barnes
www.JordanPBarnes.com
Cover art and sketches by @Wadsworthink
www.KateWadsworth.com
Edited by @Jessey_Mills
www.JesseyMills.com
Audiobook Narrated by @RyanHaugenVA
www.RyanHaugen.com

DEDICATION

This memoir is dedicated to my mother and father, who never gave up on me even after I had long given up on myself.

I also owe my life as I know it to the team and staff at Sand Island Treatment Center, Honolulu, Hawai'i, where men and women dedicate their lives to giving fellow addicts and alcoholics a fighting chance.

JONATHAN COLBY BARNES

APRIL 22ND, 1983 - MAY 13TH, 2019

In loving memory of my brother.

Jonathan was a brilliant mind who read light-years beyond his age as a child. His favorite books were Dune, Ender's Game, The Hitchhiker's Guide to the Galaxy and Watership Down.

At a point in my life when I needed it most, Jonathan sent me a copy of Papillon by Henri Charrière and insisted I read it. That book had an immediate and lasting impact, and the message resonates still: escape from whatever prison is eating you alive by any means necessary.

You are sorely missed.

"We are not creatures of circumstance; we are *creators* of circumstance."

BENJAMIN DISRAELI

CONTENTS

AUTHOR'S NOTE

This book is an informational resource intended to educate the public on addictions and addictive substances. It is not intended as a substitute for the medical advice of physicians. The reader should consult a physician in matters relating to his/her health and particularly with respect to any symptoms that may require diagnosis or medical attention.

This is a true story. All incidents and people are real, though some names and identifying characteristics have been changed to preserve anonymity of those depicted. Though conversations in this book are written from my best-efforts recollection and memory to capture the essence, meaning and sentiment of what was said, all errors of fact or interpretation are my own. Wherever possible, references have been made to interviews, journals, medical records, court logs, emails and recordings.

It's important to note that though it is not my intent to "drug-a-log" or glorify drug use, this book is ultimately a true story of recovery based on actual events. Light shines brightest in the darkness, and as such, this text contains more than its fair share of scenes and references to drug use that some may find uncomfortable.

Therefore, please proceed with caution if you're easily triggered, in a fragile state of mind or new to recovery. If you need help, know that resources are available to you and you are never alone.

www.aa.org
www.na.org
www.al-anon.org
www.nar-anon.org

ONE HIT AWAY

1

CARRIED AWAY

Sprawled across the side entryway to Beth Israel Congregation, I roll onto my side and wipe a palmful of dew off my clammy face. Everything about this morning is brittle, cold and still. Suspended in limbo, I'm drained from squirming all night on the slick ground like a caterpillar in a cocoon. As first light swirls around me and creeps into the shadows, I'm in no rush to greet it —there's no point jump-starting the engines until the street dealers kick off their rounds. Having suffered through too many of Portland's sunrises in recent years, the art on the horizon has either lost its beauty or I'm too jaded to see in color anymore.

Peeling my head away from an uncomfortable makeshift pillow made of rolled-up sweatpants, I see that both Simon and the surrounding streets are sleeping in. We're nestled in darkness, lit only by the headlights of an occasional car that turns down Flanders Street. My sleeping bag is bunched under my hip to help relieve the pressure from the cold stone beneath me, but it's not the only reason I had a hard time sleeping last night.

A few hours ago, I woke up to the alarm of Simon snoring and rattling away in his sleep—it was an eerie and guttural sound like an empty spray-paint can being shaken. I was still fighting to fall back asleep, long after his sputtering faded and drifted away with the breeze. So, while he put another day behind him, I was reminded that long nights take a toll and this life never pays.

We both went to sleep with full bellies and a shot, so we're fortunate that neither one of us will be dope sick. It's nice to catch a break now and then and wake up without wishing I would die already. But it's never enough—I'm still skeptical about how hard Simon crashed out and wonder if he's holding out on me. Though if I were in his shoes, there's no doubt I'd do the same. Riding high comes naturally in a free-for-all where everyone looks out for themselves. We all have it—a grizzly survival instinct to take what we can, when we can and figure tomorrow out if it comes.

This isn't our land, but we periodically come here to stake a claim in the covered alcove guarding the ornate entryway. If unoccupied, I prefer this location because it's a reasonably safe place to hang my boots. Not only is there protection overhead from the frequent rain that tends to ruin a good night's sleep, but it's also set back from the street enough that being noticed, roused and moved by the police is a rarity.

The groundskeeper here is a man of quiet compassion. It isn't in him to run us off outside of business hours, and he refuses to call the police on us. For the most part, we are often gone before he would have to step over our bodies to open the temple doors. Scattering like roaches, we are sent packing by an internal alarm that forces us to get up at first light and attend to our bad habits.

Simon is still asleep. He's had it easy after spending all day yesterday collecting free doses from every street dealer he could pin down. This is common for any junkie recently released from a stint in jail. Any time after I've been arrested, all I have to do is show one of my dealers my booking paperwork and they'll set me right. A freebie from them is a cheap investment in their own job security, reigniting the habit that was broken by an unpleasant jailhouse detox. Our dealers also need us back up and running again, racking up goods and on our best game. It's no secret that a dope sick junkie is unprofitable.

I pull myself together and pack with purpose, grabbing the dope kit I stashed in a tree nearby and then my shredded shoes that I left out to dry. I often struggle to tell whether my insoles are wet or merely cold, but when water oozes out of my shoelaces as I double-knot them, I take note that at some point today I need to steal fresh socks.

"Time to go," I call out.

Simon, in one of the few ways that he is needy, often depends on me rousing him. He's never been a morning person and is still sound asleep, his face buried in his sleeping bag.

"Come on, get up." I spin in place and scan the ground to make sure I'm not forgetting anything. Eager to start the day, I nudge him with my toe a bit harder than I intended to.

When that doesn't wake him, I reach down to shake his shoulder and feel an unnatural resistance. Something, everything, is wrong. His whole body feels stiff, and as I pull harder, Simon keels over, his rigid limbs creaking out loud like a weathered deck. There is lividity in his face—his nose is dark purple and filled with puddled blood. A pair of lifeless, open eyes stare through me and into nothingness. Instinctively, my hand snaps back and Simon sinks away.

I stumble back and try to make sense of my surroundings. Nobody is around yet, but soon, the world will rise.

"No, no, no." I lose control of the volume of my voice and squeeze my throat. "Don't be dead, please, don't do this to me," I chant as I drop to my knees, pleading over his corpse.

My hands hover over him as if trying to draw warmth from a smothered fire. I desperately grasp for a way to fix this. My heart is racing as though I just sent a speedball its way, but the surge doesn't stop. A decision needs to be made, and fast, but before I can make sense of anything, a wisp of breath rolls down my collar and an invisible hand clutches my cheeks, forcing me to stare down death.

I snap the clearest picture in my mind and my eyes sting. Even though I know a lot of junkies who walk these streets with no life left in them, this is the first dead body I've ever seen. Looking down at Simon, I finally understand how pathetic this existence is and how lonely this life will always be. I see nothing beyond this moment for Simon, other than being hauled away like trash on the curb. We are forever trapped here, alone and useless, likely remembered only for our crimes, selfishness and former selves. Heaven is out of the picture, and because of that, I am okay with what I have to do next. I know the act is irreversible and unforgivable, but then again, if God has abandoned us, he's not around to judge me.

Dropping my sleeping bag onto the ground, I slide my backpack off my shoulders and let it fall like a hammer. I kneel over Simon's body, steal one last look around and wince as I rummage through the front pocket of his jeans. I know he always keeps a wake-up hit on him. His pocket is tight and fights my hand as I dip into them. My fingers scratch around but keep coming up empty-handed. Time is running out and traffic is increasing.

I reach into his back pocket and soon realize the dope isn't in his wallet either. The longer I search, the more determined I am, but I can't bring myself to roll him over and disturb him further. By the time I give up, I sit back on my heels. I can't believe what I've become.

"I'm so sorry, Simon."

Please stop looking at me. I can't take it. Pulling my sweater cuff over my palm, I reach out with a shaky hand to close his eyes. My hand gets close, then backs off as I turn my head away to exhale. When my hand reaches forward once again, my palm lands on his face but fails to brush his frozen eyelids closed. Backing away, I grab my belongings and shrink into the distance.

My legs give out less than a block away. Hunched over a fire pit of a stomach, I can barely breathe. On the surface, I know this isn't something I should run from—this is not who I am. I have to go back but I don't know what that means. If I turn my back on Simon and keep running, it won't be hard for the police to identify me once they start asking around. Nobody I know will protect me.

All my life, I only seem to make matters worse, but this is bigger than me. I can't leave my friend there alone—he deserves better. Stashing anything potentially incriminating in the nearest bush, I turn toward the synagogue and in the distance, see the groundskeeper making his morning rounds.

"Pierce! Please, *help us!*" My feet scuffle toward him and I cast my hands toward the alcove. I witness his heartbreak when he discovers how we've repaid his compassion. He fumbles for his phone, strikes three numbers and asks for the police. While he talks to the operator, he stares me down until I look away. His kindness doesn't deserve this ultimate betrayal. My eyes chase his words as he describes the scene to the dispatcher. He respectfully approaches and leans over the body to make a clearly hesitant observation.

"Yes, it appears the young man is deceased," he says. "1972 North Flanders Street. Yes. Correct. Seven. Two. Please hurry, and oh my, we have a bat mitzvah scheduled today!"

Both of us stand by the body in silence until an ambulance arrives, followed by police and detectives. Paramedics apologize for our loss and announce the time of death before handing over the scene to the medical examiner. Detectives keep me around throughout the photography process and body bagging, burning the image into my mind. Pacing back and forth, I hold myself together until I am finally questioned.

I tell them everything I know and don't catch my breath until they rule out homicide. I steal a glance at the Investigation Report and wonder how a drug overdose can be classified as a natural death.

As the detectives comb over the body, they recover a small amount of dope folded inside a torn piece of plastic. A lump of coal ignites in my stomach. I need that more than ever. Simon made the fatal mistake of assuming his opioid tolerance was the same as it was before his incarceration.

The bat mitzvah is beginning, and a short procession of young teenagers—accompanied by their parents—walk by the scene. Some look confused and scared while others are talking among themselves, understandably curious. One boy pulls out his phone and lifts it up to take a picture.

"Take a picture of my friend like this and I'll fucking kill you." My warning flashes through gritted teeth.

The cop glances at me, letting my threat pass as the boy smirks. I'm sure they're all judging me and they keep coming. There is nowhere to hide while they surround us. Pierce steps forth to intervene, but his body isn't large enough to block the tragedy behind him. He directs the families toward the main entrance around the corner, begging the parents to lead by example.

"One . . . two . . . *three.*"

I turn around in time to catch Simon's covered body being slid onto a stretcher. Death has always seemed so close but never so set in stone. I picture myself inside the body bag which isn't hard since I've overdosed twice before. That could easily have been me. The only difference between me and where Simon is laying now is that the EMT's reached me in time to reverse my past opioid overdoses with a shot of Narcan.

Narcan. If only I had some on me last night, and that I wasn't so used to tuning out my surroundings while I slept. There once was a time when I wouldn't leave home without the small vial that lived inside my dope kit. That was back when I had a home and before I hawked what remained in my bottle for a meager dime bag of dope. I can only imagine how many lives could be saved were it not such a controversial drug. I think back to a night that I'll never forget, where my ex-fiancée overdosed in my dorm room. I wouldn't be here today had I not had Narcan on me to save her life, which isn't to say that this is a good place to be. It's a painful memory to recall, so I lock it away.

I provide what little contact information I have for his family to the detectives. I think he's from Florida. He once mentioned his parents are separated, but I never caught their names. I am handed a police report number and a card with a name and number to call for a follow-up within a few days. For now, I am free to go, but the medical examiner—having loaded the gurney into his truck—peels off his gloves, closes the door and motions for me to hold on for a second. As he approaches, he looks into my eyes with the care of a father talking to a son.

"Sorry you had to go through that. I'm Deputy Medical Examiner Bellant. You're Jordan, right?"

I nod.

"Jordan what?"

"Barnes."

"Do you have a family, Mr. Barnes?"

I nod again, though I'm not being completely truthful. There was a time when I had a family.

"What about a phone?"

The instant I start to shake my head, he reaches into his pocket and plucks out some loose change.

"Here, take this." A couple of quarters drop into my palm. "Do me a favor and give them a call. Tell them you love them, before it's too late." He takes one last look around at the scene. "Oh, and Jordan. Don't take this the wrong way, but I hope I never see you again. You understand?"

As he pulls away, I'm left with his words ringing in my ears like so many other junkies who must have received a similar warning. Down the road is a pay phone that's calling my name. Holding the quarters on edge, I drop them into the slot and punch a familiar number. He picks up on the first ring, which means he's working.

"Hello? Who's this?" the voice asks.

I pull the receiver off my ear and press it to my forehead. I have to choose my next words carefully.

"Hello?" he asks again.

"Hey, it's Jordan."

"What do you want?"

"I need to meet up with—"

"Nah, man," he says, cutting me off. "It's too early to trade. Call me later—I don't want to be carrying your shit around with me all day."

"Wait! I have money!" It's a lie, but I know that as long as I can get him to meet me, he'll show pity and either help me out or pay me to disappear. This detective's business card will also prove my story. "Hello? You still there? I have forty bucks." I stand straight up, knowing I can't afford for him to hang up on me.

"Bullshit. You never have cash."

"No, I promise!" I lie again and double down. "Trust me, it's been a good morning." I look down and hold my breath. Simon would forgive me for this, for using his death as leverage. He would understand where I'm coming from. He would do the same.

The voice on the line pauses for a second. "Okay, okay. Northwest Fourth and Flanders. But hurry up, man. I'm almost sold out."

"I'm on my way. Give me fifteen minutes." I slam the phone down and take off running, thanking God he's within reach.

2

ESCAPE ROOM

As if reading tea leaves, I stare at my half-digested lunch pooling in the sink and question my future. Wetting my hands, I wipe off my lips and spit out more chunks of vomit. Lately—it seems that every few weeks—I remind myself that I can't drink normally after yet another painful lesson I failed to learn from.

The water level is slowly rising, so I cut off the faucet, tug on my sleeve and thrust my hand into the clammy chum to clear the clog. I give the drain screen a back massage until the blockage is cleared and scoop out the remaining contents over the side of the sink and into a trashcan below. Rinsing off my hands, I shake them like a wet dog, skip the towel and blindly reach for one more beer from the mini-fridge.

One of the benefits of not having a roommate is that the sink in my dorm room often doubles as a urinal, which allows me to make the most of my hideout. Outside the door is a gauntlet of a hallway that leads to the men's bathroom where half the residents share community toilets and showers.

My stomach cramps and I wish there was a portal to transport me directly into a toilet stall. I don't want to be seen in my present condition. Ready to get this over with, I down the last sip of my beer, carefully rise to my feet, twist the cold knob and prepare to step out into the shared space.

Montgomery Hall is a beautiful four-story dormitory, built from red clay brick that decapitates 10th Street like a monolithic sanctuary. My room faces the interior courtyard where the outer walls are overgrown with lush vines that creep into my open window. Now and then, when new life from outside puts out feelers, I stuff the tendrils back out of the window, refusing to accept that nature will always persevere.

Since my social life is a vacuum, I live out my days like a cooped-up hermit in this cluttered room with only the bare necessities. It's an odd feeling to be a fifth-year super-senior in college once again living back on campus, but I didn't have many options after I lost my job due to my drinking. I finally ran out of excuses when calling in sick and eventually agreed with my boss that it was never going to work out.

Still trying to hold it together, my anxieties shoot through the roof whenever I'm forced to slip out for classes, so I tend to register for courses where attendance isn't a consideration and grades consist of only a midterm and final. The greatest lesson college has taught me was to manage occasional bouts of sobriety, though it's a restless struggle that is always short-lived.

In the hall, it's apparent the dorm is shockingly alive, with real people living real lives. Every other door is cracked, purposefully left open to allow music to ooze out and battle in the corridor. Students are coming and going, stoking a life with a purpose and investing in their future. Not wanting to be seen, I stick close to the wall, keeping my eyes tracked on the worn-out carpet and let my shoulder bump off the drywall to help me toe the line. Wandering past a slightly cracked open door, I hear my name called and freeze in fear. The door creaks open to a dark room as a familiar Radiohead song bleeds into the hallway.

"Well, fuck me—he lives!" a nasally voice commentates.

I empty my lungs. "If you could call it that." I wobble at the threshold and steady myself by bracing my hands against thin air. Standing in place, my feet shuffle beneath me.

"You know, I was just thinking of checking on you." Jared steps out into the light and places a fragile hand against the door jamb. He is thin and pale, with eyes that dance and vibrate rapidly as he speaks. His sweatpants are riddled with cigarette holes—close calls from falling asleep while smoking. He scans me up and down. "Jesus, Jordan. You look like shit."

I swallow hard while my eyelids dangle halfway open. Upstairs in my mind, the lights are on, but nobody's home.

He steps forward and his breath tickles my cheek. "How many days has it been now?" Jared asks.

I rack my brain, close my eyes and recap through a blur, talking to myself until something clicks. "Two weeks, I think. Something like that."

"Damn, that's rough. I keep telling you man, these binges of yours . . . " Jared drops his shaking head and lets the silence speak. "They're not getting any better. I hate to see you, or anyone for that matter, fucked up like this. You know it doesn't have to be this way."

I rock backward on my heels, trying to find a balance. He actually thinks I have a choice.

"I want to help you." He sniffles and smears a drop of mucus off his nose. "If you'll let me. My offer still stands. If you're ready for something that makes you feel a hell of a lot better than alcohol, just say the word." Jared raises both palms sky high like a saint.

I don't even bother thinking about it. Without a word, I dip my head under his arm and slide into his cave, taking a seat by his desk. He closes the door behind me, turns around and unfolds a small sheet of foil that crumbles black ash onto the carpet.

"This stays between us, okay?"

Curious, I nod.

With little fanfare, I watch as he flicks a lighter beneath the foil, heating a sticky brown substance on the surface above. With a straw ready in his mouth, his cheeks collapse while he inhales the smoke. He showcases the mesmerizing technique as the drug slips across the foil like a comet, the tail end burning a crumbled labyrinth on the surface. With a slight angle of his wrist, he lets gravity slide the black glob near the edge of the foil before he adjusts the angle once more to return it the way it came.

Like Three-card Monte, I watch his sleight of hand intently. Our eyes lock in silence. He forcefully exhales a cloud of smoke in my face and pulls the straw out of his mouth. Drool cascades down his lower lip as his eyes become lazy. "Ever heard of 'chasing the dragon?'" His thumb taps the foil. "It's basically smoking opium," he says. Using his pants, he wipes his slobber off the straw and hands it over. "Here, take this and let me light it for you."

As I bite on the straw, I drunkenly recall every other remedy that has failed me in the past. Alcoholics Anonymous, counseling, probation, hollow promises, ultimatums—none of them worked. My back has been against the wall for so long I have become spineless, so as I stare down the barrel of a shaking straw, I don't fear the fallout. With nothing to lose, I inhale the sweet smoke, my lungs inflating my chest cavity until I wave my hand to signal I'm out of breath.

"Hold it in, hold it in," he coaches.

First a peep escapes, followed by an endless cloud of smoke as I let the hit out. I trade fresh air for a comfort blanket that tucks in my brain and puts it to sleep on ice. My mind floods with relaxation and expedited enlightenment—everything is everything.

This is precisely what I've been looking for as far back as I can remember. I open my eyes to see Jared's chapped lips caked together and smiling. Without a word, he snaps his lighter once more and an orange glow enshrines my face. As he nods toward the foil, my newly polished soul turns golden and expands past the walls of this room. Any pressure to relieve myself dissipates and I smoke until I'm blue in the face. When I finally get up to stumble back to my bed, I see the world in a new light, free of anxiety and fears and the promise of being burned time and time again.

My spiral into homelessness was a torturous death by a thousand cuts, leaving me to bleed out helplessly on the sidewalk and be stepped over by pedestrians. My saving grace is that I have been in this situation before and know how to handle myself. As a troubled youth, I spent a few months as a runaway, living out of my car or on friends' couches when their parents would allow. And when I did return home, I would argue for emancipation until my mother couldn't stand the word. The cops classified me "beyond parental control" and my poor parents did everything in their power to reel me in short of prosecuting me. By seventeen, I had developed the foundation for a life of heavy drinking along with a taste for cocaine and an enthusiasm for hallucinogens. I was smart enough to steer clear from meth, but ironically—all things considered—weed was the only substance that made me paranoid.

Being homeless was my decision then, just like it is my decision now. Fortunately, I have found a comfortable baseball dugout near the 60th Avenue Transit Station that I claim as my own every night after sunset. It's protected, and every time I hop the fence coming or going, it rocks as if it will finally topple over. Not only is it in a good neighborhood, but it's safer than sleeping on the street, where the main concern is being randomly attacked by some violent drunk or getting pissed on. I sleep easy here knowing that if someone tries to rob me, all they'll get is practice.

No longer a student, I've been avoiding the Downtown area for months where the police presence is the heaviest. I only return with a purpose, and today I'm heading back to campus to see if my student account is still active.

I take a seat in the college library and flip through my Inbox when a message jumps out at me. It's an email from Mrs. Rumbough, my godmother and best friend's mom, who I haven't seen in years. And though I'm hesitant to open it, I know it's the least I can do for a woman who's been there for me my entire life. She's never asked for much, and like my mom, has only ever wanted the best for us boys. Once I see the length of the email, I realize how important this is to her.

Do you remember the movie *Hook* with Robin Williams? Jack was Peter Pan's son who had chosen the evil Captain Hook over his own family. Captain Hook did everything to make Jack feel comfortable in the pirate world, even creating a baseball team just for Jack and teaching baseball terminology to the pirates. When Jack stepped up to the plate, he slammed the ball. The pirates all began to yell to support Jack but they had the words scrambled shouting, 'Run home, Jack' repeatedly!

The statement opened a floodgate for Jack, and he suddenly remembered his family! But instead of running home, he mindlessly ran the bases for one meaningless home run after another. Jack was a ten-year-old kid—you aren't! Get out of running the bases and just 'run home' for your sanity.

Run home for your health and your eternal soul. Run home for the sake of your precious mother and the sake of your loving father. Run home for the sake of your brothers and all who are praying for you. We all love you still, even despite yourself. Run home for the little boy with the cutest tiny freckles on his nose, who is so brilliant and could melt ice with his precious smile. In case you forgot, his name is Jordan.

Dear God in Heaven—*run home for him!*

Leaning back in my chair, I breathe toward the ceiling and actively control my anger. Though I am grateful to hear from Mrs. Rumbough, it hurts to learn the obvious, that my actions affect more people than I ever intended. I don't want her involved, but I know there's no choice. I wish my mom wouldn't tell her everything. As a child, I spent so much time at my best friend Damian's house up the street that I became his parents "hānai child" and was loved as a son. I always knew that the only reason they never adopted me was that I had a loving family of my own.

I'm unsure if my mom put her up to writing the letter, but I can tell at the very least my parents have turned to their friends for strength and hope. It's clear that word of my downfall has spread, and my addiction is no longer the secret I had shamefully hoped to keep. The past few months have brought a rash of similar communications that hoped to plug me back into the lives of those who love me, but this one hits home the hardest. It bothers me that my loved ones will never let me forget who I am and what I mean to them. It's a loving message that hurts me more than it helps.

I refuse to respond and let the sound of any feeling resonate. That's the last thing I want to hear, like when a loved one writes to me, *about me*, asking me to forward the message on to my former self. I rarely respond, instead choosing to sever ties with family and friends and anyone else who tries to step in to interfere with my addiction. I have learned that if I write back, it opens a painful dialogue that I am unwilling to engage in. I'd rather be left alone as the ghost I have cunningly become.

I fade away in my seat, recalling—how after being inducted into the heroin lifer club—time had slowed to a crawl even though the downhill ride was immediate. I was head over heels instantaneously but breaking up with life as I knew it took a few months. Shortly after that first hit, nothing else mattered and I was learning the hard way about the finer points of injecting myself. To save money on rent, I moved in with my fiancée Lucy who soon discovered there was a monster under our bed. It was then that she gave me an ultimatum, but not the one I was dreading. If I wanted to keep her, I had to teach her everything I knew.

Lucy was two years older than me, raised in the Pacific Northwest, and harbored annoyance that was always attracted to the appeal of escape. On rainy days, if she looked into the gutter, she could spot her endless reflection being swept away. She was a punky girl with straight auburn hair, tattooed porcelain skin and pain stashed behind her beautiful eyes. I first spotted her in class one day and asked her out as she was gathering her things, but she politely turned me down. The next term, we had another class together and I tried my luck again. Had I been sober, I'm sure I would have been nervous. The stars aligned and Lucy admired my persistence, agreeing to go out for drinks that night. But she soon discovered that on my end, the drinking never stopped.

Like everything else, I did my best to hold it together, but I'm not a functioning alcoholic or addict. It seems that all of my drawn-out years in college instantly became a wasted effort, and I gave up on completing my schooling. Previously, I had finished my Associate Degree and fell short, only two courses shy from my Bachelor's. When Graduation Day rolled around, the college allowed me to walk with my class and the chancellor handed me an empty diploma cover. The plan was to finish my degree the following term, but instead I exploded on the runway, failing to uphold my end of the deal.

Jared walked as well. He was no longer my dealer, as I'd realized he had been overcharging me all along to afford his own fix, profiting off my naiveté. But by the time it dawned on me that I was merely a pawn, it was already checkmate. I didn't blame him. It also didn't take long before I realized smoking wasn't the most effective and economical method of using, and once I hit that turning point, there was no turning back.

Covering my face with my palm, I fumble through the deep storage of my mind, on the hunt for an empty spot to dump this memory where it can be forgotten. I sign out of my account and stare at my faint reflection in the monitor. The silhouette is muddled and featureless—a soulless outline of a man. Standing up to leave with heaviness and nowhere to go, I realize I have shaken the family tree for so long I have finally become rootless.

3

NEEDLE IN THE HAY

It was a realization that changed everything—if a lone wolf doesn't make the kill, he'll starve to death unless scraps are thrown his way. I discovered this reality the hard way once the bad breaks came, then I was constantly reminded of the lesson. Every time the sickness tracked me down, sank in its teeth and took out my feet from under me, I'd regret not having a cushion to break the fall. This went on for far too long before it was beyond containment and something had to give.

I decided to run with the wolves.

Simon is my backup plan. A fellow addict, his glasses are always falling off his beak of a nose, and when not covered by the hood of his sweatshirt, a fluff of unkempt sandy blonde hair adds that bit of height he feels he is missing. Long ago, he acted with a survivor's instinct to form any alliance that would serve him well, and since quitting has never been in my nature, I decided to join forces rather than toss in the flag. It was an easy choice since Simon is likable and we both know that this lifestyle requires sacrificing. He has a way of winding people up and is often harder on himself than he needs to be. I've followed him around long enough to know this burden weighs him down so much he's incapable of walking a straight line.

My foot taps the sidewalk as I wait outside of the store for him, praying he's successful today. When we hedged our bets and teamed up as a criminal team, we decided to take turns shoplifting merchandise to trade to the street dealers for dope. Boosting affords us the quickest and most immediate payout with a risk we find acceptable. Simon and I spend each day the same way, fulfilling wish lists like a wedding registry and tracking down orders like bloodhounds. Over time we've become highly skilled thieves, reducing the odds of coming up empty-handed and knowing that if either one of us gets arrested, we can count on the other to have a hit waiting once we're released from jail.

That confidence goes a long way, especially since we both own substantial habits, far too expensive to maintain by panhandling. I no longer bother with the dream of dealing again, knowing how quickly I'd use up all the product myself. My one failed attempt at dealing was when I partnered with a friend and let him move into my dorm room with me. In exchange, he let me be his runner and paid me half a gram a day to sell dope to his clientele in the Southwest Park Blocks. The arrangement worked wonders for a few months until our bags kept getting smaller and smaller as I secretly pinched off pieces and repackaged them. Eventually, we woke up one day to no customers calling, and he disappeared without a trace.

Life is much harder today, even when I'm observing it from the sidelines. Now that I'm a customer again, I'm a slave to these dealers and despise them for the power they wield over me. Hailing either from Mexico or Honduras, these guys make out like bandits, trading dope that costs them pennies on the dollar for stolen goods at half-off face value. Young, hard-working, reliable and brazen, they are always looking to make quick cash or products to send home to their families before their certain arrest and deportation. And like any infestation left unchecked, they're quickly replaced with similar faces that owe no favors and won't show mercy by fronting dope when I can't pay or trade for it. It's hard doing business where being expendable comes with the territory.

I see Simon exit the mall with a heavy backpack bouncing behind him and praise him from a distance. We'll stop at nothing, stealing anything that we're asked to, including clothes, shoes, Blu-Ray discs, OTC medication—even laundry detergent. Electronics, batteries, diapers and Gillette razor blades are almost worth their weight in dope and fetch a premium. I could use a clean shave myself but I'm in no position to keep any of the merchandise that passes through my hands. Besides, when the heat turns up, I can always shave my face in a last-ditch effort to alter my appearance.

I track Simon as he heads toward the train station. He spots me and I gesture to him, indicating the coast is clear and that I'm the only one following him.

I take a seat beside him and try to guess what's in the bag.

"Two pairs of Converse. Size 9. The checkerboard ones that Armando wants." Simon grows taller in his seat.

My eyes glow bright. Those aren't actually shoes. They're at least a speedball for both of us. "I'll find a phone to call him."

"Hold on for now. Let's meet him in a bit, after we swing by the jail to pick up my stuff." He thinks for a second. "And we should probably hit up Outside In after that."

He's right. We desperately need to get to the needle exchange and trade in our old, bent and barbed needles for new ones.

Arriving at Pioneer Square in the heart of Downtown Portland, I push past an eager crowd trying to board before letting our wave of riders off the train. Staring up 4th Street, it's one foot after the other as we start up the hill toward the jail. As we get closer, Simon hands off his backpack to me, knowing that the guards at the entrance will search him. Killing time while he handles his business, I scrounge the ashtrays for partially smoked cigarette butts and begin to stuff my pockets.

I slowly make my rounds, grateful that the jail is a high-stress environment where even non-smokers feel the need to catch a drag. I'm soaked in cold air, but fortunately the cigarette butts are dry. I twist the burnt cherry off a smoldered cigarette and think it must have been some time before the ashtrays were last raided or cleaned out by maintenance crews.

I work my way over to the other side of the building and I'm distracted by a frustrated woman struggling to squeeze her wheel-chair through the jail's front door. The self-closing action keeps doing its job, and from what I can see, it's not her day to be messed with. She's yelling at the door, beating it with her fist and chal-lenging it to fight back.

Wiping my palms on my sweater, I change course and leave some cigarettes for the next guy. Until this point in my life, I have lost about everything a person could imagine, but held onto my manners, having found that an occasional act of kindness keeps me human. Walking over to help her, I pull back on the frigid handle and prop the door open with my foot so she can proceed. She's not in the mood to be thankful, but that's fine by me. I tell her she's welcome anyway and enjoy the show while she rolls into the security line and continues her act.

Out of nowhere, the sound of my name pierces my ear canals like an ice pick. My mouth drops open. I know that voice and whip around as he repeats himself.

"Jordan? Jordan, *Barnes*?" His voice strains for reassurance as he bends his knees and cranes his neck to see my face. The shock of seeing him tears me open, and in the blinding flash, I swear I see myself standing before me.

"Oh my God—we found you!" Two large hands clutch my shoulders and pull me into a tight embrace.

"Dad?! What the hell are you doing here?" My warm heart pulses against his cheek.

"What are we doing here?" Heavy hands rub my back and he adjusts his grip to squeeze me tighter. "Please don't tell me you've forgotten how much we love you!" He holds me at arm's reach and gently tugs the hood of my sweater off my head. "God, Jordan, I hope not," he begs. "We love you and miss you, and . . . " but that's all he's able to muster, choking on emotion. With a tug on my cuff, he pulls me in, and this time, I embrace him tightly to comfort him. However, my body remains stiff and resistant, even as his hands caress me, seeking a vulnerability in my armor.

When I relax my neck, I drop my chin onto the crown of his head and clear my throat. I want to tell him he shouldn't be here, that I can't survive if my world collapses. That it will only be harder moving forward. That there is no saving grace and never can be.

"I'm so sorry, Dad. For everything."

I wait for a response, but nothing comes. At least, not vocally. At first, I think he must not have heard me, until a light shudder ripples through him, and a glowing warmth radiates from between my arms. Within seconds, I've softened and begin melting. His embrace is all that keeps me from collapsing at his feet.

"I can't believe you're here," I whisper. "I've been dreaming that you and Mom were coming for me, which is crazy because I never dream anymore."

"I promise you this isn't a dream, though it is a dream come true."

I try to pull myself together as we step away from the entrance and walk toward the bench he was keeping warm. We're both guilty of failing to communicate, speaking over one another in a haze of interrupting excitement.

"This is an absolute miracle, Jordan. You have to know that. I can't believe God led us to you, or you to us. I mean, we only started looking for you a few hours ago, and here we are, you and me, standing—"

"*We?* Is Mom here too?"

"Yes, of course she is! She wanted to come more than anything."

"Where is she?" My heart bangs in my chest.

He motions for me to turn around and points past my nose

toward the jail exit. This is as real as it gets, and more than I am prepared for at the moment. I see my mom exiting the building. She shakes her head to correct her vision, beelines toward us and pulls me into her. I'm squeezed so tight that I have to spread my elbows out to breathe. Fingers run down my face and twist my hair before I need to step back. She takes my hands and doesn't let go.

As good as it is to see her, it hurts to be touched.

"Jordan, how are you . . . here?" she asks, welling with tears. She drops her shoulders and wipes her bleary eyes. "Gary . . . I don't believe it."

I'm stunned at how unlikely it must be for this moment to be occurring right now and am trying to process what it means. To be standing here in front of my parents seems both surreal and threatening.

My dad turns to my mom. "Honey, this is divine intervention. We are witnessing years of prayer being answered."

I allow the God influence to fly over my head. I don't have the experience or assurance that God is with me any longer. In fact, I only have faith in the opposite, but I bite my tongue. All that matters is they came looking for me and what that means.

Without warning, I'm hit with a rude awakening as Simon skirts past me, whacks me on my shoulder and keeps going. His gesture is simple—time to go—Armando's waiting. He probably thinks I'm panhandling or bumming a smoke and will be quick to catch up. He can't possibly understand how torn I am until I call out to him and wave him back toward us.

With both hands in his hoodie pockets, Simon approaches us physically, though not mentally. I attempt introductions, and my parents—always polite—are kind and interested, even as Simon avoids eye contact. My mom looks uncomfortable and unsure of what to make of him. She leans in toward me and turns her back toward Simon as if to cut him off.

I see the attitude of the conversation changing, even though my dad is beyond excited to meet a friend of mine. His face says it comforts him to learn that I wasn't as alone in real life as I was in his nightmares. My mom, on the other hand, takes a step back as if trying to draw me to the light, protective and defensive, unsure who is friend or foe. Though Simon and I are both addicts, neither are treated as such, though I sense that behind her friendly smile, she's terrified I may turn on them at any moment. I don't even have to look at Simon to know he's ready to get on with the day.

"Well, we have a beautiful hotel where you can shower, eat and take a break from this miserable cold. It would mean everything to us if we could have a little time together." My mom takes a step closer. "We've missed you, Jordan—we've missed our son." She swipes my oily brown hair back over my ear and sends a shiver down my spine. "We'd love it if you would—"

I stop them dead in their tracks.

"Simon, I'm taking off with my parents for a bit." My words ring out like a cannon, directed toward everyone. For a second, I think of inviting him, but know he wouldn't be interested. "Where are you going to be later?" I ask.

Steam builds behind his eyeglasses, and I know he won't save my half of the dope. He mumbles something, motions for me to hand over the stolen shoes, then takes off. My mom nods with her tearful face and mouths a quiet prayer for him while we all watch him leave. I know that parting ways will make his life more difficult for the time being, and also understand the struggle to reconnect once separated. Without having cell phones, it can take a couple of days to track one another down. But the decision is practically made for me.

I'm an abstract work of art, never a monster. Life has moved past the unbearable, and the stresses and grind of continuing this habit at all times has taken its toll. I've been going nowhere fast for so long I figure it can't hurt to go somewhere safe for once.

The three of us keep bumping shoulders while we walk away from the jail. I can't help but notice how my parents flank me on each side as if their nightmare of losing me overshadows the miracle of finding me. My mom reaches out to hook my elbow with hers, and I wince in pain, dropping my arm to let hers slide off me.

"You guys don't have to worry—I promise I won't run for the hills." I follow up my promise with a nervous laugh.

At least, not yet. I pull my hair back and let it flap on my shoulders. I don't know if they did their research, but I have about six more hours until I'll be pouncing out of my skin, seared from the inside out by waves of hot flashes. After that, it's an overwhelming scramble to score that I'm powerless to fend off. Getting high is no longer a choice or luxury. As we head toward the rental car, I know the clock is ticking and the hands are compressing my heart. I crack my knuckles by squeezing my fists and throw on a fake smile.

Over lunch, I chew through a tough onslaught of failure and despair that must be visible in my smile lines. They keep letting phrases slip that voice their pain. Anger and raw emotion fill in the cracks, and I wish they would hide their hurt better. It sounds like their speech is censored, constrained by delicacy, fear and hypersensitivity. They want to build me up and keep saying they're proud of me, even though we all know I'm undeserving of praise.

In their minds, I'm stronger than I probably know. Whatever they're getting at, it's not us talking honestly. They're trying to protect me from myself and I don't have the heart to fight them. Instead, I face the future and struggle to process the pain I've inflicted on my loved ones. Unless it's cooked up, I don't have coping skills to fall back on.

I've had enough. As I head out the door, my parents squeeze out a step behind me and my mom pins my shadow to the sidewalk with her foot. Taking a sharp breath of the cold Portland air, I look up from the sidewalk and ask the million-dollar question.

"So, where do we go from here?"

"To our hotel," they both say with optimism.

I agree that getting off the streets is the best idea for now. With a full stomach, I dream of a real shower, one not taken out of a public bathroom sink. I follow that spoiled thought even further and look down at my stained hoodie. My head shakes as reality sets in—I'd hate to clean up only to step back into these dirty clothes. Any other day and I would steal a new outfit, wash my body with paper towels over a sink and discard my old threads in the trash like a snake sheds its skin.

I am happy, but not surprised, to learn that my mom didn't make the trip empty-handed. She describes a care package stashed at the hotel, waiting for me on the off chance we crossed paths. It sounds like bait, but I'm no stranger to being hooked. I remember how lucky I am to have such loving parents and how cruel the consequences of my decisions can be toward others.

As I slip into the backseat of their rental car, it finally hits me that I'm really going with them. "This is so crazy," I say, talking it out and trying to make sense of it all. "How the hell did you find me?"

"You'll never believe it," my dad says. He adjusts the rearview mirror to put me in his sights. "But before we get going, I need you to first put on your seatbelt—I'm not going to lose you on my watch."

"We decided a few months ago that we needed an answer and knew that we had to find you to get it. As you can probably imagine, this past year of radio silence has been deafening for both of us. I don't know if you sold or lost your last cell phone, but once you stopped replying to any of our emails, we had no way to reach out to you." His eyes flash up from the road, filling the rearview mirror. "So, we started poking around, which reminds me, what's this deal with 'Near Skidmore Fountain' on your license?"

"Oh, you saw that?" I let out a chuckle.

"Yeah, but I didn't see the humor in it," my dad says.

"Well, that's the best the DMV would do since I didn't have an actual mailing address. I couldn't believe it either, and imagine it would make finding a job that much harder, assuming I was looking for work." Shame washes over me as I hear myself speak and I want to leave it at that. I lean my head against the window and let the rumble of the road rattle my teeth.

"Wait, I thought you were living with Lucy?" Mom asks.

I sit up in my seat, having done everything in my power not to think about her since our engagement imploded. It's been over a year since I've seen my ex-fiancée, when she moved on and I went nowhere. I thought I loved her more than anything, but the dope had something to say about that. "I was living with her for a bit, but she left me for another guy that she met in rehab."

"Wait, what? Was she on drugs too?"

"It doesn't matter."

"I had no idea. I know how much you loved h—"

"Mom, I don't want to talk about it."

"I understand. It's always hard to los—"

"Mom. Stop."

"Jeri." Dad shakes his head, returning to his story. "So, when we were looking at flights, your mom reached out to the Sheriff's office, trying to coordinate our trip around one of your upcoming court dat—"

"What?" I explode. "You guys were talking to the police? Why?!"

My mom flips around in her seat and squeezes her headrest. "Jordan, what would you expect us to do? It's been over a year of sleepless nights, and we had no idea how much longer you would be alive." She regains control of her pale fingers and shakes her head to force the thought out. "How do you think we learned about your court date tomorrow?"

My dad jumps in before I can answer. "Son, it was a crapshoot if we would find you, and we had no idea what shape you would be in if we did." He slowly rolls up to a red light and twists in his seat. "You've been a needle in a haystack, and we came up here hoping you would accept our help, but prepared to say goodbye and hug you one last time if you refused. Do you have any idea how hard that is for a parent?"

I don't want to know. I never intended to hurt them, or myself. We pull away in silence until it becomes unbearable.

"I'm so sorry to have put you both through that, and wish that I could explain why, but I don't have any answers. The truth is probably worse than you think." A heavy exhale allows me to deflate into the backseat before cracking open Pandora's box. "You know what? You both deserve the truth."

I breathe in all the oxygen in the car. "Mom. Dad. I'm not just on drugs—I am hopelessly addicted and strung out. And worse than being unemployed and broke, I believe I am broken. My entire life today, or, I guess what's left of it, revolves around the needle." My eyes glaze over and I feel the need to hug myself in the backseat. "Nothing else. And from where you're sitting, you probably think I'm lucky to be alive, but I don't think there's any life left in me. I wish it wasn't like this and I hate that I have to scramble for something to say to make everything better. I know you're both thanking the heavens you have found me, but deep in my pit, I am still lost."

Neither of them turn around to look at me, which I'm okay with because I've never felt so naked. Instead, they both stare down the long road before us in silence. I'll never quite understand how the truth can sometimes be such a drag, yet so freeing. I drop my arms and clutch my stomach when I imagine how hard the past few years must have been on them. Yet for a child who despises who he's become, I also know I can't imagine any other life for myself. I love the dope too much, more than anything worth fighting for. But if the three of us are to get anywhere together, it won't be with a blurry and filtered honesty that protects them from their worst fears.

I continue what I started. "I still can't get over your leap of faith. It sounds like you've both seen my arrest records, but I'm not sure if you're aware that I'm known for not returning to court after they release me from jail on my own recognizance. That's pretty much always the case after a petty theft or possession arrest because the city is micro-focused on violent crimes.

"But I never intend to miss court, especially since I know what will happen when I don't show up. It's just that if I wake up on the verge of withdrawal, there's no way I can ever stand before the courts. They'd lock me up in a heartbeat. I've seen judges mandate immediate incarceration to force a cold turkey detox for defendants they deem a danger to themselves." I catch my breath. "It's so hard when you're in the thick of it, but maybe I'd be better off in jail? Either way, I learned that the best way to deal with the law is to avoid it altogether."

"Son, no one can run forever." He slaps his blinker. "You know, your mother and I have been doing our best to prepare for the worst, and I thank God that you are alive and here with us, but you need to understand that we're coming from a place where we've been discussing whether we would bring you home in a coffin or an urn." My mom shoots him a glance with a single shake of her head as though he's gone too far. "Can you imagine what a gut-wrenching dilemma that is for any parent to be in? I mean, there were nights when I would lay awake, just so angry with you. No parent should ever bury their child, especially if the cause of death is as avoidable and repairable as an addiction."

"So?" I take a deep breath through my nose and hold it in along with everything else. "What was it?"

My dad's eyes dart into the rearview mirror. "What was w—"

"Coffin? Or urn?"

His eyes drift back toward the road.

"Jordan," my mom says, "we prayed that we would find you, and when we did, we hoped that you would be ready for help, but we also came with no expectation of forcing you into detox or treatment. As much as it kills me, you're not a kid anymore." From the backseat, I catch the corner of her mouth turn upward. "Though you'll always be my baby."

I close my eyes to see light in the darkness.

"Your mother's right. We knew that we would find you because we weren't going to stop looking, and after we flew in last night, we drove around the city in the dark for about an hour before checking into our hotel. This morning, we hit the ground running and kicked off our search at the Sheriff's Department."

My mom takes over. "I've been talking to a sergeant who has been assisting me with regular updates regarding your arrests and court appearances. I wish you could have seen his face when I handed him Hawaiian coffee and chocolates along with a big hug. Then he recommended we start at a nearby homeless transition house."

I try to catch a laugh with my hand before it escapes. "Sorry, I know it's not funny, but I wouldn't be caught dead at any of those places. I'd rather take my chances on the streets, where I can come and go as I please, and I'm not locked inside until morning. I tried those shelters once, but instead of sleeping, I spent the whole night disgusted by the bed bugs, lice, mites, sloppiness and insanity."

"Well, that's comforting to know," my mom drones. "Anyway, when we were outside the shelter, we encountered a homeless man who was so eager to help us. He fired off a cringe-worthy odyssey of soup kitchens and missions that we should explore. Scores of patrons at each establishment offered advice and encouragement on your whereabouts, but it was disheartening as they were all speaking generally.

"No one seemed to know you, even though everyone wanted to help. At the Salvation Army, a young man directed us under a bridge where we found a group of street kids about your age. One of them thought you rang a bell and was kind enough to walk us up to Pioneer Courthouse Square. Your father floated your picture around and at one point, saw a young man whose physique reminded him of you. He approached the man and was struck by the resemblance."

"Honestly, it was devastating. I looked into his eyes, but there was no trace of life left. Meth sores surrounded his deadened gaze. After that encounter, I actually left the plaza thanking God we didn't find you there."

"It was heartbreaking, and after a late breakfast, we held hands, closed our eyes in prayer and asked for help. Your father said,

'God, put us where we need to be and guide us to what needs to be done.' It was a simple prayer. We paid our bill, then headed toward the county courthouse."

My dad digs into his pocket and pulls out a cell phone. "See this? It's a brand-new phone, and I swear I asked it for directions to the courthouse, though it sent us to the jail next door. We had no idea, and when we arrived, we both tried to go in, but security stopped me because I was carrying my pocketknife. As they ushered me to the exit, your mom decided she would look for your courtroom. I took a seat outside in the cold and began to play solitaire, and that's when I heard it. Or felt it, rather. A voice told me to pay attention and put down my phone. Then, through the sea of everyone coming and going, I saw a struggle at the door, and now I realize that woman was an angel that was putting you where you needed to be."

"You really think so," I ask, rubbing my eyelids. "Did you actually hear her? Her voice didn't sound very heavenly."

He stops the car in the middle of the road, turns around and begins to parallel park. "Son, I don't think so—I know so."

Their hotel is ritzier than expected, and for the first time in far too long, I am greeted and welcomed by an establishment with open arms instead of a leery eye. Upstairs the room is clean and comfortable, and I feel as if I dirtied it by stepping foot inside. It doesn't take long before I see my parent's faith is still as unwavering as it always has been—the room has two beds, meaning that all along, they knew they would find me.

I sit down and try to relieve some of the pressure that's been building inside me. Searching for a sense of normalcy is difficult when anticipation and anxiety go hand in hand. A habit is called a habit for a reason, and is a recurring pattern that I have never had the pleasure of taking my mind off of. My skin is sticky and clammy as frustration leaks out my pores. I've got a lot of walls up at the moment since any threat of change can be a shock to my system. It's not lost on me that it's been a couple of hours since my last hit. I sense the shadow of pain creeping around the corner and consider my options.

I mull over how to break the news that my time here is short. I don't like being reminded of how much I hate who I've become, so I block it out like I always do. I will have to leave quickly, letting the shock of my departure rattle their attempts to appeal to my senses. It kills me that I can't even give them a hug goodbye because I know they would never let go of me.

My thought is interrupted as my mom hands me a large brown paper shopping bag. Inside, I see a variety of clothes, shirts, jeans and socks. I can't hide my excitement. Everything is new, including the sales tags and pricing. She apologizes if she has gotten my size wrong, adding that her guess was as good as mine. Reminding her not to be silly, I am beyond grateful.

I take the whole bag into the bathroom and methodically pick out my new outfit, choosing the least valuable items. Setting them aside, I hop into the shower and attempt to clean up as fast as I can. Though the water runoff is a brown tinge, I know there is a certain level of filth attached to negligence that won't wash off so easily.

The skin alongside my fingertips are cracked, and I study the dried and scaled patterns emphasized by dirt. The streets have grown on me, not the other way around. Sitting down in the shower, I close my eyes as water streams down my cheeks. I feel horrible for what I must do next.

4

SCUM

I emerge from the bathroom in new attire, but in no way a new man. My palm rises to my chest and picks at the buttons of my new Aloha shirt, vaguely reminding me of home. A wolf in sheep's clothing, I look up to see awe on both my parent's faces.

"If only getting clean was as simple as taking a shower, right?" My joke aims to make light of the situation, but my attempt at humor falls flat.

"I still can't believe you're here." My mom adjusts herself on the bed and clutches the comforter beneath her. She lets out a heavy sigh of disbelief, brought up by a smile. "Jordan, you have no idea how happy I am to see you." She turns to my dad, who lowers his book to his lap and rejoins us in reality.

"Jeri, I don't think now is the time to—"

"No, Dad, it's okay." I lean back against the wall, crossing my arms over my chest to let my mom take the weight off hers. My fist brushes a tender abscess on the inside of my bicep and I internalize the slicing pain. "Know that I never intended to hurt you." My eyes ricochet between the two of them. "For what it's worth, I'm sorry for what I've put you both through."

"It's worth a lot, thank you." My mom looks around the room.

"I think this is just the start of the healing process for all of us. I want you to know that we've dreamt of this moment for so long." She wipes her eyes, smearing tears across her temple. "You don't know this, but every night, I watched *Intervention*. Religiously." A choked laugh escapes. "As any God-fearing woman would. Every success story gave me hope, and as draining and depressing as the show was, I wanted to learn everything about addiction so I could learn how to help you."

I take a breath so deep it hurts my lungs. "I know I can't change the past, but I promise you, I will never put you both through the same hurt."

My words are hollow, whether or not they know it. I am in no position to honor this promise. Regardless, my gut says it's the right thing to say. If there were an easy way out, so many wouldn't fail trying to break free. The closest thing to any shortcut down this path is a medically supervised detox. I've half-attempted to wean myself off the drugs once or twice before, but I never got very far. The cocaine was a luxury I could do without—it was the heroin that dug in its talons and latched onto me. Even now, the sickness stalks me like prey. I am hunted, and something wants me dead.

"I have to be honest with you both—I wish I could give you a fairy-tale ending, but I'm in no position to hop on a plane and head home. I think that if I tried to fly off into the sunset with you both, I'd be shot down immediately."

"Son, we know." My dad rises from his chair and places his book on the nightstand without saving his page. "Jordan, do you remember Sarah?"

I rack my brain for a second. "Sarah? You mean my former substance abuse counselor from high school?"

"Yes. She wishes you all the best."

"Wait, you met with her? Is she still counseling? She was always so kind to me," I say. I think back to her soft voice, so meek yet stern. I could never manipulate her.

"Believe it or not, she is still working, and she remembers you well. When we were preparing for our trip up here, we had a sit-down with her, and she explained what we already knew—that you'd be highly unstable."

"Come on. I could have told you that."

"No, not really, because you were nowhere to be found! Anyway, Sarah prepped us by saying you would need to detox before leaving the state. She also thinks that you'll get better care up here because of this city's opioid crisis, where most of the facilities back home are geared up to fight the methamphetamine epidemic."

I let out a laugh. Someone needs to make light of the situation. "Isn't that ironic?"

"What?" he asks.

"That I am a vagrant who can't return home." I push off the wall. "Hooper Detox is a clinic located right down the road that specializes in heroin withdrawal. I know it's competitive to get in and it takes a few days of trying. The struggle is always making it back every day on time, because if you're late just once and miss triage, they start you all over again."

My mom shoots my dad a quick smile.

I shiver at the idea of detox and the fear of commitment. I also know that the bigger hurdle I am facing is that I would need to make it to morning without a hit, and it's barely 5 p.m. I understand the time and place for sensitivities, but the light of day also rarely shines this deep down in the rabbit hole. Drugs have depleted any sense of shame and further sucked the oxygen out of the room.

"Mom. Dad. We can go to Hooper in the morning and get my name on the list, but I've got to be honest with you—no one gets in on the first day." There's the give. Now here's the take. "I'm down to try, but what I'm not willing to do is suffer." A sickening silence fills the room.

Faced with the same problem as always, I shake my empty pockets and realize I'm still a broke, poor excuse for a son. I do, however, have a large sack of new clothes that I can trade to any one of my dealers for a couple of bags of heroin. Somewhere outside, darkness is creeping. The sun is ready to set, and with it will go my final window of opportunity. The Hondurans stop working before nightfall and will refuse to meet up with anyone unless they are lured out with good enough bait. With one foot out the door, the time to go has already passed.

I explain my intentions and seek clarity that these clothes are mine to do with what I wish. I expect to see a look of sorrow or hear them begging me to be strong, but I am met with a buy-in of understanding and empathy. There is no objection as if they know that trading these clothes equates to the safest way to get from point A to B. I feel relief that I won't be risking getting arrested and jeopardizing our plan to make it to Hooper in the morning.

With a rumble in my core, deep down I'm aware that I'm technically right but also terribly wrong. Drug use alone hasn't destroyed any semblance of humanity, but it has afforded me the ability to flick my dignity on and off when convenient. This holds true despite my parents having raised me to never be weak-willed, mean-spirited, lazy or inhumane. Since a child, I've always been overly sensitive and compassionate, and as an adult, I can rarely excuse my behavior when my moral compass turns south. My mom is fighting back the tears, crushed under the unnatural weight of helplessness as my reality capsizes her dreams. I can't imagine she was expecting this to be a leisurely walk in the park.

Promising a quick return, I reach for my new bag of clothes and commit the room number to memory. I know I have to find a dealer before they all sell out or call it quits for the evening. I'm about to close the door behind me when my dad speaks up.

"Son, wait up. I'm coming with you, and I'm damn sure bringing you back."

I think about this long enough to realize he's not asking for permission. We have to go, and though there's no way I want him to tag along—if he's willing to drive—I know we can get there much quicker. It's a far cry from the elementary days of bringing your dad to school, but I understand his reasoning. They came thousands of miles to find me, and with the possibility of a way out of this life only a few hours away, there was no way that he was letting me walk down that hallway alone.

As the door clicks shut, I catch a glimpse of my mom sliding off the bed, dropping to her knees in prayer.

Soon I am saying a prayer of my own, but a more ungodly one that Luiz will answer a call from my dad's out-of-state number. My attempts to contact other dealers had all gone unanswered. I expected this though, so I wasn't on the verge of panicking just yet. These guys rarely know who is calling, so it's always hit or miss. Most of their clientele don't even own phones—we either borrow a random cell phone from a stranger or pop into a local business and ask to use their landline. It's always hard to drop fifty cents in a payphone when you're broke.

"Who's this?"

Thank God. "Luiz, it's Jordan. I need to—"

Click.

"Hello? Hello?" The floor drops out from beneath me. "Luiz? Hello?" I stare at the phone in my hand, hoping to see the call timer still running. "Fuck!"

Honestly, it's well-deserved. He's no longer thick-skinned with me since I burned him recently, showing up to meet him under the guise I had new Nike's to trade. Sure, I was a good booster, but we all had our bad days, and addiction never takes a day off. Dope sick and desperate, I lured him to meet me, and once his driver dropped him off, I wouldn't let him walk away until he fronted me some dope. While I hadn't robbed him per se, drawing heat to a dealer until they cave is a surefire way to get blackballed.

I need to make him see I mean business. I can't afford to give up.

I call him again and again—a million times if I have to or until he turns off his phone. He doesn't answer. My mouth is wide open, my fingers dancing across the keypad. This time I block my number.

"Fuckin' puta! What do you wa—?"

"—Don't hang up! I promise to make it worth your time." I desperately plead with him as if talking him off a ledge, with everything I have, but he's still not convinced.

"Worth my time?" he laughs. "You're so full of shit." The call goes silent for a moment. "Text me a photo of what you got."

"Whatever you need! I'll even pay you back for the last time I, well, you know—"

"—Man, that shit was *nothing* to me. Now, hurry the fuck up, 'cuz I'm out in fifteen minutes." A sharp click launches me in motion like a starting pistol.

I encourage my dad to drive faster, still shaking my head in disbelief that we are doing this together. With only a short time to get across the river, it's a mad dash to get to Luiz's favorite bus stop near 42nd Avenue before he changes his mind. I pull some slack on my seatbelt and lean forward in the seat as if that'll somehow make us move quicker.

"Go! Go! Oh, come on! You could have made that!" I slap the dashboard and shoot my dad a glance as we roll to a stop at an intersection.

"You need to settle down. I'm not breaking any laws," he scolds through gritted teeth.

I scoff at his response and bounce in my seat. "Really? What do you think we're doing right now?"

He hesitates for a second as the light turns green. "Saving your life, as hard as you're making it. We need you to make it to Hooper tomorrow, and I refuse to let you out of my sight and walk out of our lives once again." He rolls down both front windows as if the distractions outside will take my attention off of him.

For the rest of the trip, we ride in silence. Since most of the street dealers I know aren't legal citizens who possess a valid driver's license, they rarely drive themselves around. Instead, they turn a lucky addict into a chauffeur and pay them off in dope. Transportation makes them both more efficient and harder to rob, but occasionally a dealer may prefer to stretch his legs and walk his rounds. When they do, they always stick close to the bus line or train tracks to keep the dope flowing through the city.

The public transportation system offers the perfect form of mobility, free to ride in Fareless Square and busy enough to blend in with the other hapless souls. Each dealer carries a mouthful of pre-bagged balloons of heroin or cocaine, color coded to spit out any order desired. When I catch them first thing in the morning, their cheeks are stuffed like chipmunks and I can barely make out a word they say. This allows them to consume the evidence if the police ever get too close. They can vomit up the stash once the coast is clear, unless the officer reaches their throat first with a chokehold to prevent them from swallowing the bust.

We pull over about half a block before the bus stop, and I hop out of the car before it rolls to a complete stop. Walking quickly from the car, I try to suppress the guilt of exposing my dad to such a destructive moment, and hurry to get this over as quickly as possible. Stealing a look back over my shoulder, I can see my dad's intense gaze—a mixture of murderous rage and painful sadness. I would aim to avoid making eye contact with him, but his eyes are intensely locked onto Luiz. If looks could kill, there would be one less street dealer by now.

Wiping the water droplets off the bus stop bench, I sit down next to Luiz and place a crumpled brown bag full of clothes between us. His short black hair is spiked straight up and his popped collar is a year or two out of style.

"So, what you got for me?" Luiz asks. He smells the air and I see my clothes in his mirrored sunglasses.

"Come on, you saw the text, right?" I stick my hand into the bag and flip through the clothes like a deck of cards. As I see a price tag, I emphasize the amount before moving on.

"Don't take them out," he says.

He pretends like he's not interested, but I know that he'd be gone by now if he wasn't.

"All new, right?" Luiz asks.

"What? You don't trust me!" He doesn't return my smile in kind, but I don't take it personally. It hadn't helped that I was so eager to meet up. I can tell by his shuffling feet that he is uncharacteristically on edge. Arriving with an unknown man intensely observing us isn't helping the situation, and I regret not having my dad circle the block. I watch as Luiz calculates the possibility of a setup, but I don't know what to say to help him rule it out. I know it looks bad. My dad, a former Naval Intelligence Officer, can easily pass the part of Detective.

Luiz and I both understand that it's common practice for the police to follow the arrest of an addict with a take it or leave it offer. Immediate release, freedom and sometimes even getting your dope back after facilitating an impromptu sting operation is all it takes for some. Truthfully, it was rarely a hard sell if you didn't know your hustle. The cops provide a choice: give up your dope and money and prepare for a jailhouse detox, or keep your product and walk a free man, just arrange a drug deal. Street dealers were a dime a dozen and loyalty had its place right there with honor amongst thieves.

I scoot over half an inch. "Luiz, look." I drop my voice. "Trust me, this isn't a setup. I wouldn't do that to you. Besides, doesn't he look a lot like me? Would it help if I went and grabbed his license to prove we're related?" I can almost see his wall topple and I make my move before the dust clears. "So, this is it," I promise. "This is the last time we'll be doing business together. I'm off to detox in the morning, and you won't ever see me again." I let out a shallow sigh. "So thank you for all of the times you took pity on me, forgave bad debts, and fronted doses we both knew would forever go unpaid."

Luiz stares back at me with a flat smirk, and for the first time in my life, I accept a trade of lesser value than what my merchandise is worth. Make it to morning is my goal, and with that, Luiz spits out a wet handful of balloons, each filled with a portioned size of dope wrapped in plastic. Plucking a couple from his palm, he snatches a white one and rolls it in his fingers. "Want a bag of cocaine too?"

I do, but I don't, knowing that having my parents around will kill the high. It's not like me to turn down free drugs, but I guess there's a first time for everything.

"Fuck man, not today."

I snatch the two red balloons and instinctively roll them in a small circle against my jeans to wipe off the saliva. Popping them directly into my mouth, I hear the rubber squeak between my molars and cheek.

Our fists bump and what's done is done. Pushing myself off the bench, I take the first step and don't look back.

"Get off this shit, Jordan—" Luiz calls out, as I hear him cram the balloons of dope back into his mouth, "—and go home. While you still can."

I keep walking back toward the car without acknowledging him. I got what I came for and it wasn't hollow gestures.

We drive to the hotel listening to the radio. I change the channel a few times, but nothing tunes out this silence between us. Staring out the window, the skyline is overtaken by dusk as the sunset blends in with the yellowish streetlights. Time always drags in this window between buying dope and using it. As we confront the welcoming curbside appeal of our hotel, I lick my lips and taste the sickness. I can't take it anymore—I'm ready to explode as my dad hunts down a parking spot. I don't think he could take any longer if he wanted to, though I suspect, like me, he also can't wait to get this over with.

Bursting into the room, I notice that our safe return has offered my mom a momentary reprieve from prayer. Her face is drained as if she's been awake all night. I want to console her, but the wheels are in motion to do exactly the opposite. I'm off the rails, a runaway train being chased by a torrent of horses snorting fire.

Where is my dope kit?

I draw a blank for an instant before remembering I left it in my backpack in case we got pulled over for speeding. Scrambling to pull it out, I lunge into the bathroom and lock the door behind me. I don't want them coming in as much as they don't want to see me like this. Utilizing muscle memory, I pluck my cooker out of my kit and flip on the faucet until enough drops of water collect in the small metal cup, barely covering the bottom. I loop a coated twist tie around the cooker, making enough of a handle to prevent me from further burning my blistered fingers. Biting open both balloons, I drop two chunks of black tar into the water and snap a lighter underneath, watching the fluid dance then bubble up and turn from clear to brown to putrid as the drugs dissolve. Never to be shared, this ritual is my own pure and filthy private séance.

A tiny piece of cotton plops into the mixture and is pierced with a needle, serving the purpose of a filter to block out the cut that boils to the surface. Steadying the cooker on the tile floor with one hand, my other grips the rig and uses the back of my thumbnail to extend the plunger and draw the shot. I flick the barrel to get any air bubbles to rise and gently squeeze until the first drip oozes out. Leaning back against the door, I steady myself and tune out the background noise of all life beyond these walls.

I aim to get right one last time, but my eyes flinch as I fail miserably. Again and again, I fail to catch a break and strike gold. My entire world has flipped upside down, and all I want is a final high as good as the first. I refocus and dig in deeper, but no blood squirts back into the barrel. Backing the needle out nearly all the way, I try a new angle and fail again to bottle the magic. My only goal is to see this through and make it to Hooper tomorrow, by any means necessary.

My struggle turns south as I give up on my arms and move down to my feet, slipping and fiddling the needle into the webbing between my toes. The sting is a sacrifice that goes unanswered.

The cold air doesn't help either—my veins tucked themselves in for bed a long time ago. Toilet paper wipes up a few drops of blood off the floor and is discarded into the bowl.

For the life of me, all I want is to make the last hit count, but with vacant eyes, I finally see it's not going to happen. Popping the tourniquet off my ankle, the strip of blue rubber crumbles on the bathroom floor and I'm taunted by the blood that rushes out of my foot.

Though it's easy to miss when I shoot from the hip, I fail to spike a vein so often that missing has become the new routine. I'll resort to muscling my shots and forego the rush if I'm pressured for time or too sick to function. My body has never been receptive to intravenous drug usage, and every extremity tests my patience as I fight an ongoing losing battle. The few veins I once had didn't stick around for long, shrinking away and ducking as if dodging bullets.

I knew I was a real addict the first time I experienced vein envy of someone else.

A frustrated and bloody mess, I pull myself up to my feet using the edge of the countertop and prepare myself to fall on my sword. Arching my back, I drop my pants, then my boxers and plunge the needle deep into my butt cheek. Pressing the plunger in, the shot bubbles under my skin and lingers before dispersing intramuscularly. Scooping a palmful of water from the faucet, I suck up fresh fluid into the needle and squirt it back into the sink, flushing it out. Though I have no plans to use this needle again, it's an old habit that won't die easily.

Cleaning up a second time, I pack up my kit and relax as all the tension I've been harboring is released. I'm not surprised that my parents left me alone the whole time, but as I open the door, I don't know what to make of being ignored. My dad, glued to the TV, has nothing to say to me which speaks volumes. My mom flashes a pristine smile of gratitude that I'm still alive. Without asking, I sit down next to her, swing my legs up onto the couch and sink my head into her lap. Pulling my knees up close to my chest, my breath settles in my lungs as she rakes her fingers through my hair as she often did when I was a child.

Unable to remember the last time I had felt human touch like this, I close my eyes and once again picture a time when life wasn't such a tangled mess, where problems had solutions, and the worst days came and went. I'd be weeping on the inside if the shot hadn't deadened my emotions and suffocated all guilt. My blood turns to tears, and with each passing stroke of her hand, I slip further and further away.

5

HOOPER

DETOXIFICATION STABILIZATION CENTER

The alarm clock rings out early, even though the three of us have been awake for some time. Wiping sleep out of my eyes, I realize that last night could have been far worse—I'm accustomed to twisting through the dark hours with no end in sight. For too long, drug dependency has robbed me of the simple things in life that make it worth living, like deep or uninterrupted sleep.

Now I draw a blank, trying to remember what it takes to spark excitement and think how nice it would be to wake up with the power to choose how the day ought to begin. Those are the choices I've grown to miss and the freedoms I've forgone. My life has been like watching the same show on repeat with no ability to change the channel.

I pack up the few possessions I still cherish with momentum and purpose. Shirts and socks get rolled together as I do a final sweep through the hotel to make sure I don't forget anything. As I move to get out of my own way, my mom watches me reach for a crumpled brown paper bag full of paraphernalia.

"What are you going to do with that?"

"This?" I shrug my shoulders and look down at my kit. "Probably throw it away?"

"I don't know how I feel about that. Someone might hurt themsel—"

"Mom, no one is going to hurt themselves. The needles are all capped, but if it makes you feel better, I can snap off the tips and jam them into the chambers. They're safe. Here . . . look."

Her eyebrows drift together. "No, no, no, no, it's okay. I'd rather, just, not."

"What about Hooper?" my dad asks. "I'm sure they'll have a way to dispose of it safely."

Of course they would, and that way, when I don't get in, I'll still have my kit with me to make it through tomorrow. I expect my mom to object to traveling with the paraphernalia but she surprises me. Leaving the room, I carry everything I own under both arms, and as we head out the door, I imagine we'll be returning to the hotel later this afternoon.

We're not the first to show up this dreadful morning, and I would have gladly gone to the back of the line if it wasn't such a mob mentality outside of the entrance. As the three of us huddle together, a familiar wetness curdles throughout my socks. My jeans are wicking water off the sidewalk as if I'm bringing the streets with me. I shiver in my shoes, terrified of the next twenty-four hours like a death row inmate.

As we wait for the doors to open, I'm pulled into a riptide of addicts, each scratching at the surface of sobriety. I know some of these junkies personally and spot a few I wish I didn't. Most won't make it in, and a handful don't have plans to. Half of them are here to keep working their way up the list, waiting for roll call to come and go, so they can split to cop their morning fix. Others are here as newcomers to the city with no intention of getting clean.

Detox centers and Methadone clinics have always been a good jumping off point if you're looking to get loaded or grow your network. These addicts scramble to link up with fellow users, hoping to gain an introduction to a local dealer, though usually they'll have to settle for handing their money off, hoping the buyer will return with the drugs. It's ironic that some addicts will share needles with one another, but will never offer up their dealer's phone numbers. Some things will always remain sacred, and being a middleman can be profitable. Assuming you don't ditch them, the basic hustle is to take the money, buy the drugs and pinch off a portion for the trouble.

I feel a bubbling beneath the surface—it must be magic hour now. The doors unlock and a desolate lot of antisocial introverts flood inside while a handful linger on the sidewalk to finish their cigarettes. Dousing their ashes in the curbside runoff, they'll stumble in at their own pace. I sidestep through the crowd and slip closer to the front desk. Once I stake my claim and sign my name on the list, I scan the room and spot my dad sitting next to a seat he's reserved for me. I can see a third open chair as my dad points back to the way I came, and I turn to see my mom approaching the reception desk.

"God, Jordan. You don't want to be like this," my dad says as I sit next to him.

The whole spectrum of addiction is on display here, a reckless lot of souls stripped to ribbons and tangled in a mess with no end in sight. A guy next to us looks like a college kid making a last-ditch effort to pull it together and save his semester. A man across the room resembles a misfit who may have toured with a local punk band before giving some drunken tattooist free rein on his face. He looks like he needs all the help he can get. As expected, I don't see many old junkies in the mix. I'm embarrassed to call these my people.

I wonder what my mom is up to as two more staff members approach the desk. They exchange brief words, and as if on cue, all three of them turn to look back at me. Unexpectedly put on the spot, my hand raises as if to wave, but lingers in the air like I'm being called upon. My mom flashes a quick smile and waves back toward me before returning to their discussion.

"Purple? Monkey? Dishwasher?" I mouth, trying to read their lips.

"What was that?" my dad asks.

I tell him not to worry about it and imagine it will all be explained shortly as my mom grabs their hands to thank them both. If it weren't for the desk between them, I know she would prefer to give all three of them a hug. Heading back our way, she has a seat next to me and is fighting to hold back a smile. Leaning over my lap, she whispers to my dad, "Gary, that was Sam!"

"Who?" I ask.

"That was Samajean. She's a counselor I've talked to while trying to coordinate some sort of plan for you. We knew that if we somehow found you, we'd have limited time to get you in."

"You knew about Hooper all along?" I ask, impressed that I'm not the only one trying to stay a step ahead.

"Yes, but Sam couldn't guarantee to get you in," my mom says, sinking into her chair. "However, she did imply that they always take extenuating circumstances into account. Like, if a parole officer or judge orders a patient into detox, that case could jump to the front of the line."

I look down between my feet and force out an exhale. This whole process was supposed to take a few days to play out. I've already figured out our next stop after leaving here, excited to leverage my willingness to enter detox against anyone within arm's reach.

A bellowing female voice rings out, announcing the beginning of triage. She greets the room with instructions delivered emphatically and details the process from memory. The major takeaway is that regardless of what happens today, no one in this room should give up. Room and beds will always become available. Keep trying. Keep coming back. Don't miss roll call and never be late. They are indeed the same thing. I nod in agreement though I know that simple instructions aren't so easy to follow when you're wrestling a gorilla off your back.

Roll call begins in rapid fire, announcing the lucky few who made it in today. When she calls my name, I clench my jaw and drop my head. Name after name rattles the air until her list is complete and the rest of the room filters out. I stay put, but not because I prefer to avoid crowds. I don't understand how my mom pulled it off, and a wave of anger boils in my blood.

I'm not ready.

Looking around, it's clear that there are those who are grateful to have been called upon and others who wished they hadn't been. I know exactly who hoped to get in versus who was served a final ultimatum by a probation officer or Higher Power.

"Son of a bitch," a young kid blurts out. He's sitting across from me, but not speaking directly to me. He punches his sweater into his bag as he packs his things, then flips his hair out of his face. Poking a thumb back over his shoulder toward me, he continues talking out the side of his neck. "White boy, with two rich parents, trumps all and gets in front of the line every time."

He has a point. If I was in his shoes and wanted, or really needed to get sober, I would be annoyed and aggravated about facing another day of grinding, hoping to make it back here tomorrow. What happened isn't fair and I wonder whose spot I had just snaked and question why I deserve this chance over them. But that's not even the worst part to accept—I know that not everyone who was turned away will make it back here tomorrow.

Standing up to say goodbye to my parents, the room is now empty like someone took a hit and sucked the life out of it. My dad embraces the opportunity for a group hug and launches into a quiet impromptu prayer. I'm embarrassed to be praying and wish he'd lower his voice and wrap it up. When he finishes, my mom promises to meet me here a week later and reaches for her purse. I don't resist as she pulls up my arm, takes my hand, flips it over and uncurls my fingers as she carefully sets an object into my palm.

Without looking down, I know and remember what she is giving me.

"Is this what I think it is?" I stare at her with the cold silk bag in my hand and heavy weight in my heart.

"Yes, and it's time for you to take them." She smiles to my dad who wipes a cheek dry. "Every single Sunday, I've taken them with me to Church and prayed over them. I asked that one day, they find their way back to you. Promise me you'll keep them safe."

After submitting a urine specimen, I take a seat in the conference room next to a rat-pack of seven other anti-heroes. We are separated from the waiting room by large glass windows that remind me of a fish tank. The table before us has a simple, free-for-all buffet including fresh fruit and packaged graham crackers. Milk cartons—nestled in a bowl of ice—take me back to grade school. A young kid, barely in his twenties, has made himself at home on the floor near my feet. He's splayed out and shielding his eyes from the bright lights above with his hoodie. A filthy backpack becomes a pillow, breaking the fall of his crash landing.

Tilting my neck back, I roll my head from side to side. All the commotion and excitement from this morning has dissipated. The furniture is stiff and sterile like how we greet each other, and our minds are elsewhere as the countdown begins. Staff begins the long task of processing the days catch, and the ordeal takes longer than I was expecting. Though I have nothing better to do, I struggle to sit still for long periods and my hands search for something to occupy my mind. As my flesh ices over, I breathe warmth into my cupped hands and shake them out. Reaching into my pocket, my fingers land on the silk bag, and as I open it, I welcome the memory that floods out.

I was eight and three quarters, surrounded by a moat of new toys. I propped my small frame up on my knees and held out a present wrapped with Christmas paper that twisted around the gift like a piece of candy. The ends, crinkled and loose, left little doubt—that earlier that day—my young idle hands were hard at work. She often helped me wrap all the Christmas gifts I planned to give away, letting me place the Scotch Tape or hold the ribbon down with my finger while she tied the bow. But as she studied the shape before her, I knew I had kept it a secret.

"Here, Mommy—I made this for you!" I said. My face was adorned with an infectious smile while I gave the gift a jiggle and invited her to take it.

"Oh, sweetie, thank you!" As she reached out, her long, dark brown hair dripped over her shoulder and tickled my wrist. I sat back down on my heels and dropped my hands into my lap.

"I made it for you in art class, when we were making the ornaments and the wreaths, and the Christmas cards and the—"

"Well, someone's been busy this year," my dad said, cutting me off with a smile. He swiped a ball of wrapping paper off the couch and sent it streaming across the room. "We don't save wrapping paper in this family. Life is too short." He plopped down next to my mom, looked into her lap and admired the gift. Both my two older brothers were playing with new presents, sticking grip tape onto an Alien Workshop skateboard deck and digesting instructions for a new salad shooter.

As my mom peeled open the wrapping paper, I split my blonde bangs like a curtain and locked the tufts behind my ears. I didn't want to miss anything. The unwrapping took all but a second and left her staring at a solid round piece of pottery. My dad watched curiously as she twisted the two-inch round gift in her hands, spinning it back and forth between her thumb and pointer finger. The speckled white glaze reflected her curiosity, and I leaned in closer. Around the perimeter of the object was a thin brown border, wrapping the odd-shaped orb like Saturn's rings.

She glanced up to flash me a smile, proud that her baby boy fancied himself an artist, then looked down once more while still trying to figure it out. The unfamiliar warmth of giving a handmade gift washed over me.

"Do you know what it is?" I asked, bouncing excitedly.

"I'm sorry, honey," she said. "No, I don't. Would you like to tell me?"

"Yes, of course! It's my Good Thoughts."

My brother looked up from his skateboard and chuckled.

She cocked her head slightly as if she didn't hear me correctly. "Your Good Thoughts? What do you mean by that?"

"All of my Good Thoughts are inside!" I said. "I sealed them in there when I made it for you, and I want you to have them."

Her shoulders dropped. "Oh, honey, that's so sweet. Come here." She reached out to grab me and pulled me up onto her lap. She ran her fingers through my hair and whispered into my ear, "You know, you didn't have to do this, but since you did, I promise to take very, very good care of them."

Someone knocks on the door even though it's open and I look up from my Good Thoughts to see a team of acupuncture students disturbing the monotony of the room. As they filter in alongside their instructor and surround us, I safely put my Good Thoughts away and maintain the smile the memory painted across my face. I'm compliant while they introduce themselves and inform our group that they will begin a session on us. Before they start, an energetic, short-haired female student asks to inspect each one of our tongues and works her way around the table, stepping over the kid on the floor. Exciting my curiosity, she explains that she's looking for cracking, discoloration and swelling that may be indicative of chronic illness.

Once their session kicks off, a movie is started more for background noise than entertainment and to help inject a semblance of normalcy into the air. The kid on the ground rocks irritably as one of the acupuncture students takes it as a challenge and tries to rouse him. This continues for too long until the instructor steps in to intervene, directing the students' focus elsewhere. As the kid wriggles back to sleep, the student mumbles something selfish about needing the practice and spins in circles to discover that the rest of us are already being tended to. He ends up settling for a repeat session on the girl next to me who gets more attention than she bargained for.

Once the acupuncture team reclaims every last needle, I try to escape the boredom and muster small talk with those inclined, interested or awake. But as soon as I make a new friend, they're removed from the room until there is no one left to talk to and I'm left alone with my thoughts. The isolation is manageable until it's interrupted by a middle-aged Black man who raps his knuckles loudly on the door jamb. He motions for me to follow him with a curled finger and scratches the air.

Down the hall, we step into a full bathroom with a desk that doubles as his office. I'm instructed to take a seat in a soft, cushioned chair that lets out a whistle of air. Directly across from me, the man mumbles to himself and shuffles some papers. I can't distinguish whether he has lost the passion for his job or is merely burned out. He takes my vital signs and cracks open a new medical chart while I verify the information on my hospital wristband for the hundredth time.

The conversion drags along, made slower as my excitement for the process crumbles. I realize that nothing of value is coming with me the moment that all of my worldly belongings are tossed into a clear trash bag. After stepping into the stall, I strip down and go through the motions of taking a shower. When I cut the stale water off, I pass my clothes around the curtain and swap them out for scrubs with the facility name printed on the back.

Tossing a pink paper with my last name into the bag along with a gentle pat, the staffer finally emits a sense of enthusiasm and brings me up to speed.

"I've been doing this for many, many years," he says as he opens the door to see me out. "And need to thank you. Working with addicts like yourself reminds me why I need to stay sober."

He allows me to exit the room first, but doesn't point me in the right direction. When I realize the decision of which way to go from here is mine alone, I twist my wrists and never look back.

Entering the male dormitory, I am surprised to see how many of the beds appear unoccupied. I've heard rumors that budget cuts have prevented the center from maximizing their full occupancy, but this is worse than I would have thought. I'm curious if it's the same story in the female dormitory, but I'll never know for sure since the only shared space in here between the two genders is the nurse's station. Even there, staff screens both sexes separately on alternating schedules to keep our eye on the prize.

Before I can get settled, the nurses check my vitals, noting the levels of my withdrawal symptoms before escorting me back to my bed. All around me, the attitude of the other patients throughout the dorm is somehow energetic, though not quite infectious. I try to tune them out and avoid contact, focusing instead on the tingling sensation coursing through my veins. It started from the soles of my feet and by the time it spewed its way up my legs, I knew there was no hope in stopping it without a tourniquet.

Forced to sink before I can swim, I'm churning toward a head-on collision with full-blown withdrawal and am unable to receive the first dose to alleviate my distress. Hooper follows the preferred method for detox, administering Suboxone, a drug that massages the opioid receptors inside of a strung-out brain. The week-long regimen should be a smooth ride once on board, but it's a painful hill to climb to get there, especially if the timing isn't right. Some clients shoot up in the bathroom on the days of triage, only to discover they have the longest wait once inside. Of the seven of us processed today, only the young kid scraped off the floor was considered sick enough to be medicated and now he's out like a baby.

The nurses will monitor my vitals and require me to exhibit painful and visible symptoms before forking over any medication —vomiting, aches, nausea, anxiety and turmoil. These symptoms are required to prevent initiating precipitated withdrawal, which is caused by taking Suboxone too soon. When used correctly, the drug can provide a tolerable, predictable and perhaps even comfortable detox. But if administered prematurely, the active ingredient works as an opiate blocker that will unleash a torrent of hellfire on the opioid receptors in the brain, and no one in their right mind wants to see that happen.

Legend has it that nothing will pry the wings off an angel like a precipitated withdrawal. I've heard it described as if a brain was a tree full of opiates, and someone came by and violently shook the trunk until all the leaves fell off at once. It's instant withdrawal in the worst possible way and can only be reversed with time. The blocker casts an addict into limbo, suffocating their opiate receptors and prohibiting any chance of getting high in the near future. Many patients have found this out the hard way when they've faked or over-exaggerated their symptoms to get dosed prematurely, hoping to skip the withdrawal altogether. Others learned the definition of helplessness after they walked out of detox only to realize getting high is futile for a day or two.

Laying back on my bed, I stare up at the ceiling and struggle with the inevitable. I'm terrified to face my biggest fear, having always expected to die a junkie and to go out without a fight. I had long been accustomed to running away from the slightest inkling of dope sickness, scrambling to postpone the wretched clock of dependency when unable to satiate its hunger. Sickness can creep on in many forms, like a moist breath on your neck or a scratching under your skin, but once it comes knocking, it won't be turned away. Struggling with the body aches, I want nothing more than to relax, but the restlessness has already spread far and wide. Twisting from one side to the other and back again, I claw at my thighs and bury myself alive under the thin white sheet.

Bouncing my heels on my mattress, I pray to be put out of my misery. I can barely breathe. I don't know how long I was out, but the warmth of my breath trapped beneath the sheet has ignited an internal fire raging inside my head. The heat and sweats linger, even after I peel back the sheets to let the A.C. shock me alive like a defibrillator. There is a warm stone glowing deep in my belly and a chalky dryness in my throat. Even in this frigid dormitory, this radiating warmth is encompassing, and I fling off the blanket I was curled under. Having been in this position before, I know the most comfortable way out and am tempted to take it. Struggling to sit up, I notice a fellow patient peacefully sleeping on his bed next to me and envy his calmness.

Opiate withdrawal is an ominous experience I wouldn't wish on my worst enemy. If left unchecked, vomiting and defecating will come as tremors tear through the body while the soul caves in. The inability to sit still will tire your eyes just from witnessing it. Opiates are notoriously difficult to detox from since users physically adapt to the exposure of the drug on the brain. Many who detox unassisted have been to hell and back and will do everything in their power to prevent being sent back, which explains why most cold turkey detoxes take place during some period of incarceration.

I head over toward the nurse's station and request to be assessed with my blanket around me like a cape. I wait my turn until I am called inside and the nurse checks my wristband against my file.

She looks me up and down. "It's Jordan, right? Let's see where we're at." Her hand pats my knee to comfort me. I don't recall the last time anyone outside of a family member has treated me with such humanity. But all I want is my dose to help stop the onslaught of withdrawal. I pay attention as she completes her assessment of me and rates my symptoms on a multitude of observations. She measures my resting heart rate, restlessness, pupil size, runny nose and irritability.

"Trust me, I feel your pain," she says.

I stare her down, knowing she is likely speaking the truth since most of the staff here are addicts in recovery. As she works down the list—rating my symptoms—I follow along and do the math and realize that I'll pass the Clinical Opiate Withdrawal Scale metric with a score high enough to initiate dosing. I'd give her a hug if I was allowed to.

I am led to a bench that borders the nursing station, take a seat and hear my knees knock against one another. Placing an orange pill under my tongue, the nurse monitors me out of the corner of her eye, making sure I don't cheek or pocket the pill. They're aware that some patients enter detox with the sole purpose of stockpiling a week's worth of Suboxone, taking only the first few doses to make it over the hill. If they're ever caught, they'll be kicked to the curb and blacklisted from the program. Suboxone can be abused as a street drug and is hard to come by, carrying high street value for two distinct reasons: it can be sold as a last resort backup to avoid becoming dope sick, or can be crushed, injected and abused like any other drug.

Holding the pill under my tongue, I'm reminded not to talk or swallow my spit for the next fifteen minutes. Taking the medicine effectively means allowing it to absorb into the mucous membranes in my mouth. Closing my eyes, I realize that I have reached a turning point, and it's a scary milestone. I'm torn between fear and relief as I consider life without getting high. I've been driving myself toward a useless and lonely death for so long that it started to seem like fate. This tiny pill has the power to change everything and it blows me away.

After my fifteen minutes come and go, I continue to let the medicine work its wonders. Flopping back on my bunk, a salivated bitterness of medicine lingers in my throat like Drāno. Since I am now committed, I expect to be feeling better already, though I no longer remember the feeling. As I lay down to rest, I realize the difficulty in lying on my back with a mouth full of spit. I switch to my side, but any comfort eludes me. For the first time in years, I can close my eyes knowing time is no longer working against me.

. . .

I wake up unsure of what to do with myself. My eyes bulge as the overhead light casts doubt all around me. I instinctively flip over onto my stomach and retreat into the shadows. Though finally in a safe place, there is a disturbing sense of pressure and urgency to rejoin the battle outside and combat the clock. I have a weak hollowness in my bones which makes me watch my steps. Pulling at my cheek to stretch my jaw, there is a rattling in my brain as I prepare for uncharted territories.

Life has always been go-go-go, but today is the day I grab the wheel, pump the brakes and coast to a controlled stop. I'm used to navigating life with no bearing or wind in my sails and about as much hope as a captain of a sinking ship. With no rush, sense of urgency or impending doom defining my next steps, I rise to float around the dormitory shadowless and mild-mannered. I have no issues cooperating with every request asked of me because for once I have no worries.

The dinner bell rings out and startles my belly. Patients scurry to line up in the mess hall next to the sleeping quarters and I follow suit, waiting in line for the servers to roll up the gate and open the buffet line. The guys I'm sandwiched between introduce themselves with a mixture of humor and positivity, contrary to what I was expecting from the bowels of a detox facility.

The frenzy kicks off with steaming lasagna piled sky high on my tray and I can't wait to dive in. I'll take this food any day of the week, enticed by greasy, monstrous portions and the lure of second servings. Coming from a lifestyle where every piece of currency went toward feeding my habit, the food I'm accustomed to was always scavenged or shoplifted. Nothing in my diet was close to healthy or nutritious—my food pyramid plateaued where candy collided with coffee.

I look around and can almost see that a spell has been broken. Once irritated zombies, most of the guys are laughing and joking, united with a common purpose. Even when talking with food in their mouths, they do a better job of explaining the schedule to me than the staffers ever did. I hear that the days fly, and if I ever come across time to kill, movies are the weapon of choice. A couple of Narcotics Anonymous meetings here and there are no big deal. Mandatory weekday acupuncture clinics are a fan favorite. There is always enough food to go around, with no distinction made between the quick and the hungry.

Though a lifelong lover of chess, I pass on the board games after dinner and opt for a movie. I swing by my bunk to grab my blanket and enjoy the comfort of no longer needing to spin my wheels. A conference room is converted to a makeshift theater, and with the lights off, some of us talk, annoying the others who would rather follow the movie plot. Genuinely interested in others for once, I shut my brain down with no plans to update and restart.

Ever rooting for us, the nurse's snap us out of our trance once the movie is over and administer a subsequent dose of detox meds. After sitting in silence, I float back to my bunk and sink into the sheets, realizing I can do this as long as I don't get in my own way. Finding distraction in a book, I know that I'll be safe when I'm asleep. But I struggle to focus as the patient across the way is painfully detoxing from methadone. He flops in his bunk like a desperate fish in a net, gasping for life. His agony reminds me that I have it bad, but it could be worse.

A laundry cart delivers clean sheets to my bedside and I look around, struggling to find something to complain about. My breathing feels irregular and I long to get high. Anywhere else at this hour, I'd be hunting down my dealers or psyching myself up to barge into a store. Perhaps this mental obsession is the hardest habit to kick.

There is struggle all around me. Nearby, a staff member pleads with a patient not to walk out of the program. With experience and the friendliest demeanor, he guides the young man through a carefully constructed thought experiment. Their conversation reminds me I couldn't get high if I wanted to.

The nurses executed a shift change last night while most of us slept, and I find the new team to be equally as kind and supportive as the previous group. They call me into the hot seat, so I bounce from bunk to bench and am greeted with a professional courtesy I am undeserving of.

"You hanging in there?" the nurse asks while glancing at my chart.

It's obvious to me that she cares about her job when she treats me as her purpose instead of a paycheck. And I have every reason to trust her, but when she reaches out to strap a blood pressure arm cuff on me, I kick my rolling chair backward and offer her my other arm instead. She smiles my way, then demands an answer.

"My left arm is injured—it can't be compressed." My explanation is clearly not up to her satisfaction. Before I can say no, she rolls up my sleeve until I wave her hand off and take over. As I pull back my hand to expose my arm, she launches into rapid response mode.

I'm startled by how she reacts to my casualness. I suppose I've been living a life where one can't afford a crisis, either literally or figuratively. This abscess on the inside of my arm, hot to the touch and bulging, has been unchanged for months. It's the result of finding a good vein, falling in love and not knowing when to move on. I half expected the problem to cure itself as similar complications have in the past, but I also didn't care much either way.

The golf-ball sized infection is a painful protrusion of soft tissue, squishy, angry, throbbing and stubborn. Deep down, I know it's rotten, and it scares the nurse to death.

"Jordan, do you understand how serious this is? What's wrong with you? Why didn't you bring this to our attention?"

I mutter a response that doesn't include an answer.

"An infection like this isn't just limb threatening. It's serious. A dislodged blood clot could make its way through your bloodstream toward your heart, and if that happens, you don't need to have a cell phone for your number to be called." She shuffles through her desk for a business card. "God, I can't believe you somehow slipped this past my colleagues during triage. Here, take this right now."

She gives me a Suboxone and calls the number on the business card. As she spins around on her rolling stool to draft a quick letter on an official letterhead, I watch the pieces of her plan fall into place. Part of me wants to burst out the doors. The other half is grateful for her compassion to know that I can't be sick where she is about to send me.

6

FIRE IN THE HOLE

While being escorted out to the main lobby, I appreciate that the staff required me to sign up for the Oregon Health Plan during triage yesterday. The nurse seems convinced that my new insurance will cover this emergency surgery, and I have no option but to believe her. We both know I can't afford an ambulance expense, so she phones me a taxi. I learn my fare is taken care of and suspect the nurse paid for it out of her own pocket.

A stack of paperwork is slapped into my hand with instructions to pass it off to the ER receptionist. Draped over my forearm is a puffy loaner coat I'm expected to return. The nurse scratches out a phone number onto a small piece of paper and stuffs it into my pocket. When I am ready to return, this will be my ticket back.

Cut loose at the curbside of Oregon Health and Science University, I apologize to the driver for not having a tip, but he laughs off my gesture and it becomes obvious he's done this before.

The moment I slam the door shut, a gust of panic fills my lungs and my self-worth takes a hit. As the driver pulls off, I catch myself in the reflection and realize that I don't stand a chance. I haven't trusted anyone for so long it's no wonder I don't trust myself. I see a payphone on the corner and walk straight to it.

When my mom picks up, she can't believe that I am not where she last left me. "Stay there, honey," she begs. "Or better yet, stay on the phone until we get there. Your father and I are on our way now." Her voice drips urgency as she whispers to my dad, concerned that I am an unescorted flight risk.

Their flight back to Hawai'i doesn't leave for another six hours, so I stay on the line and guide them in like air traffic control. As soon as they arrive, they both reach out to inspect my arm. Sliding up my sleeve, my mom holds her breath and gently twists my elbow, absorbing some of my pain.

"Thank God that nurse had the wisdom to send you here as quickly as she had. She may have just saved your life," my mom says in disbelief. "Though I wish they hadn't sent you alone."

"Normally they wouldn't, but it's after hours and they're on a skeleton staff."

"I knew it—I knew something was wrong," my mom says, kicking herself for not pressing me earlier on my injury. "You know, when we were walking away from the jail, you pulled away as I grabbed your arm, and I knew that wasn't normal." She clicks her tongue. "But I wanted to focus on the bright side of being with you."

My dad isn't as hung up on it. Having had some medical training in college, he prepares me for what I should expect, and actually thinks he's doing me a favor. At a certain point, I have to cut him off. I roll my sleeve down and slowly lead the way, drained of every last ounce of self-respect.

Checking in is quick and uneventful thanks to the paperwork I brought with me, and after showing off my arm like a tattoo, the nurse doesn't doubt that I require immediate attention.

"Do you want your parents to come back with you?" she asks over her shoulder as I follow her toward a room in the back.

I stop cold in my tracks. I don't know how much more pain a son could inflict on his helpless parents. Yet more than ever, I could use their support and don't want to go through this alone. I invite them to follow suit.

"Very well, right in here please," the nurse instructs us. My blood pressure levels are non-remarkable, and as a forehead thermometer is swiped across my brow, I cherish feeling attended to. My parents enter the room shortly after I change into my hospital gown.

"You doing okay?" my mom asks.

"Yeah, I think so, thanks." I look down toward my chest. "What bothers me though is that I can't remember the last time I've felt any pain. I mean real, physical pain that I couldn't numb or turn off. Honestly, I'm terrified of it. I don't know if I'm making a smart decision."

"I don't think you really have a choice. And besides, you knew there had to be consequences at some point to your decisions," my dad says. "But you're going to get through it. It'll be quick and over before you know it, then you'll never have to live through this pain again." My dad is talking to me yet studying the charts on the wall.

"Knock, knock. Coming in!"

In walks a doctor with a medical student in training. They're both smiling, friendly and kind, first greeting my parents and saving the worst for last. The doctor forces me to smile by smiling so much herself. I know from being seen here before that this is a teaching hospital, so it's not uncommon for special procedures to be shared as hands-on training exercises. When I was last seen here, my nurse discovered a heart murmur and returned moments later with a doctor followed by a long line of medical students. They all filed in, one at a time, while I introduced myself like we were speed dating.

"So, looks like we're having a party!" The doctor is still smiling and untroubled. The student laughs along and scrunches her shoulders. "You're so kind to let us crash it. Now, I hear we have an abscess—which arm is it?"

I raise my forearm over my head and show the doctor my

discolored bulge as she leans in close. She bends forward and compresses it with her thumb, causing me to wince in pain. "Perfect. Thank you. You can lower your arm now." Turning to her student, the doctor raises an eyebrow while drawing a small circle in the air with her index finger. The student understands the directive and startles me as she rolls up on me with her stool.

"Jordan, after we make the incision, we'll need to drain and pack the wound. First, we'll prep the area, then anesthetize the site with Lidocaine and Epinephrine. Then, we'll make a small, linear incision to explore the recesses and expunge the . . . "

Her words fall off as I am distracted by the tinkering student. I turn to watch the prep work and twist my hand to expose the underside of my bicep, showing off a long progression of track marks. Using a red Sharpie, the student traces the perimeter of the infection where the red discoloration meets my pale flesh. The visible infection site is extensive, so the border will help to monitor the reduction of the swelling over the next few days. The baseball-sized outline resembles the shoreline of Africa.

Catching the tail end of the procedure, I realize my dad was correct. Once the abscess is lanced, it's critical to force the pus, dead tissue, white blood cells and bacteria to escape. Looking down at my arm, I can't ignore that there's a lot of pressure that has been building up for weeks.

"You ready?" the student asks. She's too sweet for what I'm about to put her through. I shake my head a few times and take deep breaths. "Try to relax."

The student has me lean back on the treatment table and holds my arm out to the side. My mom supports my hand, taking the stress off of my shoulder. Behind the student's face shield is a spark of excitement in her eyes. The doctor micro-manages from a distance as the procedure begins. A quick shot intended to numb the pain does the exact opposite. As the needle burrows in, a flash of white light blinds me and I can see through the ceiling. My eyes water and I crush them shut. I bite my lip to offset the pain and thrust my free palm into my eye socket.

"Breathe, Jordan. Breathe." My mom jumps into Lamaze breathing that fades into the background.

I hear the student exhale through her surgical mask as she closes in on the abscess. Holding out her gloved hand to prevent spraying, her scalpel sparkles as she reaches out to lance the bulbous tissue, bursting the abscess on contact. A creamy mixture of blood and pus sprays out like a pinhole leak in a garden hose, finding its way onto the doctor's sleeve and full-face shield. Neither of them flinches, though my mom jumps back. The student could have easily stopped but doesn't. Poison seeps out of me like a reversed spell, and a blanket of relief swoops down.

The feeling of relief is short-lived. As the student works her way around the incision, her gloved fingers move with purpose, squeezing the deflated abscess to drain the fluid into a pan. My eyes tear up as I pray for the oozing to slow down. Since I was born without a sense of smell, I can only picture the stench of death wafting through the air as I see my mom cover her nose. Looking down at the collection pan under my arm, I can't believe it's filled. Once the flow subsides from a stream to a drip, I relax my neck while the student cleans my inner bicep and commends me for my bravery.

"You both are doing very well," the doctor observes. The student and I exchange glances like war buddies who have the shared experience of returning from hell.

The final step is a painful packing of the wound, stuffing me right back into the woods I thought I was almost out of. Tweezers shove an endless strip of gauze into the incision to prevent the cavity from sealing prematurely, which would allow the infection to return and fester. With a tail of gauze hanging out of the wound like the wick of a candle, the student carefully wraps my sensitive arm. I can finally breathe again. I take all the time I need getting up. The doctor hands me a prescription for antibiotics but nothing to numb the pain. All three of us thank the doctor and student for their superior care, and as we walk out of the ward, I look back and witness another mess of my own creation that I'm so keen to leave in my wake.

Outside the hospital, a jarring breeze tears through the corridor and I fall in line behind my dad to let him bear the brunt of the attack. I shake it off, jam my hands into my pockets, then feel the paper note with the number I have to call for my ride back to Hooper.

I roll the paper between my fingers and mindlessly crush it into a ball, figuring that since I'm already here with my parents, I might as well catch a ride back with them. I can pay the nurse back by saving her a couple of bucks, and while we're at it, make a pit stop for a quick bite to eat.

In the back of my mind, I know I'm not following directions, but with what I've just been through, I deserve the creature comfort. A drive-thru menu and a quick trip through memory lane will hit the spot.

"Thanks for dinner," I say, reaching for my door handle. I feel the car lurch into park.

"Not so fast! I need my hug," Mom says, flinging off her seatbelt. She hops out of the passenger seat and motions for my dad to follow suit.

I step onto the sidewalk and wait for him to walk around the bumper to join us on the curb. Across the street, Hooper's front entrance is illuminated by yellow streetlights. I rub my bloated belly as I size up the pearly gates.

"That was some operation, huh?" Dad asks. "How you holding up?"

I shrug my shoulders. "It's starting to sting a little, but I like to think I've been through worse."

"I can only imagine," he says, looking toward my mom for direction.

"Come on, Jordan, let's get you out of this cold." Mom steps off the curb and into the street to lead the way.

I don't blame her for wanting to see this through. I wouldn't leave the fate of my future in my hands either.

We stop short in front of the entrance. Despite my arm, in many ways, it feels good to be back.

"Mom. Dad. We're going to be okay." My hand drops to the door handle and I tug, but it doesn't budge. I yank once more and wince in pain when my bicep flexes against the resistance.

"It's locked?" My dad brushes my hand away to give it a go.

"What the—" I put my nose to the tinted glass and see the reception desk is dark and unoccupied. I wait for motion, and when a staff member finally cuts through the lobby, I rap my knuckles on the door to attract her attention. She looks our way but seems hesitant to respond. I wave my hand to call her toward me.

"Sorry, we're closed," she mouths, then waves me off with a shrug of her shoulder.

She doesn't understand. I am a patient. I have a bed inside.

My parents lean in and crowd me, breathing down my neck.

"Quick! Where's my paperwork?" I ask.

My father instinctively taps his pocket. "I don't have it!"

"Check your pants, Jordan," my mother fires off.

Pulling out my discharge papers, I unfold and slap them against the glass to show the staffer before she disappears. I point to it like a warrant, not wanting to kick the door down. She pauses for a moment, then changes her mind and approaches the door, but stops just shy of opening it.

I press my lips to the cold metal door and speak through the cracks. "My name is Jordan Barnes. I am a client here. I'm coming back from the hospital where you guys sent me to have an operation." I point to my arm, but her eyes don't follow.

Immediately, I realize it's not me that she's worried about—she's more concerned about who I am with than who I am.

"Who are they?" she asks, pointing back and forth at my parents through the glass. "And where is your driver?"

I finally understand. I am supposed to be with my ride and no one else. I've violated a protocol much more stringent than I'd expected.

The woman slowly turns to walk away. My mother, on the verge of panic, struggles to stay silent. I know that she could fix this if only the woman would hear her out. I begin to string words together and realize why it's such a big deal that I deviated from the plan.

"*Fuck!* I'm such an idiot. She has no idea who you guys are or where else I have been. And for all she knows, I could have gotten loaded, or maybe I'm packing contraband to smuggle back inside. I'm sure she has to assume the worst, right?"

Neither of them respond.

"It's my fault," I continue. "Of course they have to play it safe. It's just fucked because I'm stressed out and about to be in a lot of pain. I don't need this right now."

Dad sighs and slips his phone out of his pocket. "It's okay. I just need to reach someone here of authority."

"No, Gary, I don't think so," Mom interrupts. "She's coming back!"

The three of us watch as the nurse magically reappears with two male employees at her side. This time, she unlocks the door and the three of them step out to meet us. If I had any question as to the severity of my decision, it was immediately confirmed.

I would swallow my pride if I had any. "Before you start, I know that I fucked up," I admit, stumbling through the logic that landed me here. "I didn't think it through, and am sorry."

I apologize to the nurse, and then to my parents.

Besides the physical pain from the surgery, the Suboxone is wearing off, and I feel the rumblings of an old familiar friend knocking to be let in. I only know two ways out of this dilemma. I want to take the higher road, but beggars can't be choosers. If I am sent away, there's no doubt I will use, especially in this pain.

"Please help me," I beg. "I have nowhere else to go."

. . .

Hugging my parents goodbye, I breathe a sigh of relief and follow two Hooper staffers back into the men's dormitory. After I empty my pockets and submit to a quick search, I fork over my antibiotics and I'm released back into the collective conscious of the program. I imagine I'll be able to maintain a good attitude and intend to take part in every required function while suffering through the healing process.

Of course, not everyone's heart is in the right place. Occasionally other patients skip out on activities like the Narcotic Anonymous meetings, lying flat beneath their bed sheets, hoping to go unnoticed by staff.

Another breed of clients are so ill they can't even summon the will to get out of bed. For these cases, their vitals, evaluations and feeding all take place at the edge of their bunk. Most of these patients, who are rotting away on their bunks, tend to be alcoholics suffering through some of the harshest and most severe detoxes. At their worst, they are inconsolable and insane. I find solace knowing I don't drink like I used to because I remember those thrashing nights without the benefit of Librium to settle the tremors.

Hands down, heroin users make up the lion's share of patients here on any given day. Although medically speaking, opiate withdrawal isn't considered deadly or life-threatening, it still feels like death knocking on a straw door. But when compared to alcohol detox, which can end a life after dragging it through a terrifying episode of delirium tremens, I know it could be worse. Much worse. And having been down that path before, I don't want to be reminded how graphic the scenic route can be.

Male patients circulate in the dining area that's used as a multi-function space between mealtimes. We try to arrange the plastic chairs in a circle, but we end up settling for our egg-shaped arrangement. I watch as everyone takes a seat and I can't help but smile. Most patients, including myself, have gathered here today wrapped in a blue comfort blankie. I guess what happens in Hooper stays in Hooper.

"Hurry, hurry, gentlemen, you're wasting valuable time," the acupuncture instructor says, ushering us into our seat like children.

Two more patients join us, stragglers discovered by staff and reminded that participation is not optional. They each grab a seat and squeeze into the circle, forcing us to adjust our chairs to accommodate them. Hooper requires attendance at group acupuncture for every patient that can make it out of bed without collapsing or vomiting. Though it was news to me that many addicts claim to be terrified of needles, I was not surprised to learn there's no exemption granted from those who suffer from trypanophobia. And for those who try to weasel their way out of the activity, the staff likes to remind them they knew what they had signed up for.

The session begins. "Everyone, please slow your breathing, and follow my count. In . . . Two . . . Three . . . Four. Out . . . Two . . . Three . . . Four. In . . . Two—"

I close my eyes and listen to the background music playing from a portable CD player. Sounds of Nepal reverberate off the concrete walls. The handful of acupuncture students that came here to practice their craft and log hours begin to work on our group. They make their rounds behind us like we're playing duck, duck, goose, silently moving from one patient to the next. Outnumbered, yet not threatened, the students are eager to use an ancient practice to combat a modern epidemic.

They start off by connecting with us through touch. A feather of a hand lands on my shoulder and a fingertip pulls back my long hair and tucks it behind my ear. In the same breath, the first needle is placed, spiking the slightest release of dopamine. Their primary focus is to target the ear or scalp, and the students have been instructed to keep all needle points above the shoulders. Now and then, when the instructor isn't looking, a student who can't resist the repetitiveness will sneak a needle into the meridians around my hands or neck, hoping to unleash a geyser of clogged-up chakras. Because I always keep my eyes shut, I can never pinpoint the lone cowboy gunslinger with good intentions, keen on breaking their own rules and wanting to be of further help.

While I appreciate the therapy, I can't help but feel these students are playing a dumbed-down version of Russian roulette that could end in a drawn-out death. Sticking intravenous drug users with needles while still perfecting their practice seems unnecessarily risky, especially since none of them are wearing gloves. I assume the intent is to assure us we are all people, not specimens.

After the session, I return to my bunk where time marches on. The local anesthetic is past its useful life and I'm no longer oblivious to the pain in my arm, having not been prescribed narcotics for obvious reasons. The lancing and packing of the wound was a brutal invasion and I'm reminded of the pain every time my elbow drops to my side. My arm throbs, amplified by the gauze wrapped around it like a tourniquet. I feel like it's wrapped too tightly and don't know if I should re-wrap the dressing myself or have a nurse do it. I would love to remove it entirely, but know I need to keep the wound protected, especially in here where staph infections can spread from bed to bed like chlamydia.

I feared finding myself in this position, coming from a world where all physical pain is deadened. It's going to take more than a positive attitude to keep my head in the game. Slipping my finger under the thin wrap to help ease the constriction, I touch a moist ring of sweat and breathe in through my nose. The tingling in my chest reminds me I don't have the heart for this. I was willing to give detox a shot, but this isn't what I signed up for.

The nurse looks up, but otherwise doesn't acknowledge my presence.

"Did you hear me? I said, *'I'd like to leave.'* How do I get my shit and get out of here?"

She pushes back from her desk, straightens some papers and takes her time approaching the threshold of the nursing station.

"Jordan, I heard what you said, but I think you need to understand what you're asking. Being discharged against medical advice, especially with that—" she points at my arm, "—doesn't sound like a smart, *or mature*, decision. It will also make it harder for you to get back in here down the road. Besides, aren't you only two days away from finishing? Let's talk about—"

"I'm not doing it." I wave the back of my right hand over my other arm. "I can't do this!" My voice is louder than expected. "I can't sleep and you guys won't give me anything. It's only getting worse, like someone dropped a red-hot lump of coal into my arm and wrapped it up."

"I know it hurts, but I also know you're tough. Let's just talk about what you leaving means, before you shoot yourself in the foot."

I laugh as I stare at my arm and see that my options are limited. I know what she's doing, having seen this process play out earlier in the week when another client tossed in the towel. The entire nursing team went out of their way to make it a painful experience. They dragged out the process to buy him more time to think, hoping he might change his mind. Instead, it just irritated him that they treated him like a dunce in a corner, separated from the other patients and not allowed to speak with anyone while he waited for his property to be fetched.

"You know that you can't even get high, right?" the nurse asks.

"Yeah, but I'm sure I can find something else to help. I don't see why I should suffer through the pain. It's inhumane."

She shakes her head like I've got it all wrong. "There's nothing 'inhumane' about it." She reaches for my file. "Let's stick to the facts. Since you've been with us, we've put you on Ibuprofen and Acetaminophen for pain, Phenergran for nausea, Immodium and Lomotil for diarrhea, Levsin for stomach cramps, Visatril for anxiety, Trazodone for insomnia and even Nicotine patches and gum. So I don't think you can say we're not doing our part here. We're committed to you, but are *you* committed to *yourself*? Besides, don't you think that if you walk out of here, you'll break your mother's heart?"

"That's a low blow and not fair. At least I tried."

"You only have two days left."

"Too many to endure," I say. I look away to cut her off. "How can you ask me to keep going when you have no idea what I'm going through?"

"You can do this. I know you can. And what about your father? Isn't he flying up to meet you? And taking you back to Hawai'i? I mean, Hawai'i! Who wouldn't want that?"

I smack the desk in a flash of fury. "That's his plan, not mine! Look, I didn't ask to be found, and I don't owe you, or anyone for that matter, a fucking explanation!"

Her silence says it all. I clear my throat, preparing to repeat myself, even though I know she heard me.

"Wait, wait, wait. Stop. That doesn't make any sense, Jordan. What do you mean 'you're outside?' How is that possible?"

"Come on, Mom. We don't need to do this." I aim to deflect her anxiety. "You know what it means."

"No, this isn't right. I need you to get back inside. Jordan? I need you to open the door and go back inside."

"Mom, just stop, okay? They're not going to let me back in. The doors are locked, and there's no one around to open them." The man who loaned me his phone has offered up a few feet for privacy, but is keeping me within arm's reach in case I'm feeling froggy. Hearing my conversation, his hands drum on his thighs as he closes the gap between us. I turn my back toward him.

"What do you mean the doors are locked, Jordan? Bang on them if you have to. I know someone is there—someone will answer! Tell them you made a mistake. Tell them you need to get back inside!" She catches her breath. "Jordan, I need you to find someone who works there and hand them the phone! I need to talk to them. Hold on—" I hear her in the background ask my dad to get Hooper on the line.

"Mom, please, stop. It's not going to happen. Listen to me." I pinch the bridge of my nose. "I'm not ready. I asked to leave and was discharged against medical advice. The only way I'm getting back inside is if I start the process all over again, and with my fucking arm killing me, it's not going to happen anytime soon. I'm sorry, but I can't talk any longer. I'll be in touch."

A long silence fills the void.

"Oh, my God. You are going to die," she whispers.

"No, I won't! Stop being so dramatic! I'll be okay. I promise. Look, this isn't my phone. I have to go. I love you, and I'm sorry," I say vacantly. "Please tell Dad not to fly up." I hang up and hit the end button as she tries to call back.

"Thanks for letting me make that." I hand the phone back to the passerby who plucks it from my hand like it's cursed. I consider bumming a cigarette but he's done enough already. My arm stings as I beeline toward the train station. I should have known better, and hate myself for pretending I could walk away unscathed.

7

ROCK BOTTOM'S BASEMENT

My time in detox has done little to disrupt my old routine, and every new low in this moral wasteland reminds me that suffering is my deserved destiny. Faced with this inevitable fate, I realize I was inept and naïve to believe I could walk away without a trace after setting foot into a pile of tar. My penance for this failure was stretched over the course of a few days as the opiate binders in my brain slowly fell to the wayside. It took forever to get high again and finally feel normal.

I see him in the distance, then glance up toward the heavens, certain that it's not normal for a black cloud to follow you everywhere you go. But this is the perpetual forecast for us addicts—cloudy with a chance of anvils and passing showers of raining knives.

When he spots me shambling toward him, a smirk from Luiz says he knew I'd be back again. It's business. Bad business, but still business. We have a love-hate relationship that makes me resent the power he and every other dealer will forever reign over me. I allow his arrogance to roll off my shoulders since I am already dragged down by the hurt of turning my back on my parents. I struggle to imagine the pain they must be enduring back home. I slip into a public restroom at Fred Meyers for a fix that allows me to forget.

I'm a failure but I don't want to think about it, which makes me appreciate that I have a way out, a hole to crawl into when I can no longer face myself. Mom and Dad don't have the same escape. Because their hurt is real, I don't want to be a part of it and can't muster the backbone to pick up the phone. I try to forget ever seeing their faces at the end of the tunnel and hate myself for how I let them down. They deserve better, and it was a cruel trick on my part to offer up false hope, only to spit in the face of their miracle. It bothers me to no end, so I pack my kit and keep running.

Leaving Fred Meyers, I cross the parking lot to Kohl's to wash, rinse and repeat. Switching on auto-pilot, I work my way to the back of the store and swiftly stuff a pair of Converse shoes into my waistband. Bottled emotions flare up as my lazy eyes dart around the racks of clothes, but no faces fall into focus.

My childish grin turns callous, having tasted the warm comfort of a day off in detox. I can't help but resent this life, and my movements are careless and sloppy. I rarely check twice for loss prevention—my modus operandi of small thefts throughout the day have been replaced with larger, brasher heists that pay for the whole days' worth of using in one shot. These shoes are an exception, an impromptu snatch on my way back to the 82nd Transit Center. Sputtering toward the exit, I care less and less about the endgame.

Knowing that it didn't have to be this way is the hardest part. The cycle of fear, then relief, then resentment for having to repeat it all again has taken its toll on my sanity, leading to mild paranoia that the police are hot on my heels. Crime is nothing more than a numbers game, and most junkies understand that being apprehended comes with the territory. So while I could say I am caught off-guard when it happens again, I'm not surprised when a gloved hand grips my shoulder.

"Whatever you do, don't make this a felony, bro." My knuckles turn white and my lungs empty. The loss prevention officer looks younger than me and takes his job far too seriously. "Cops are already on their way—they're just around the corner."

My pulse pumps before I'm able to accept that there is no way out. The exit is locked and I am trapped. Realizing I have my kit on me ignites the urge to fight for survival. My instinct to weasel my way out of the situation is subdued only by his biting words of caution. He's right, and perhaps I'll thank him later for reminding me of it—any physical altercation during the event of a petty theft can up the ante and modify the charge into a robbery. This includes pushing someone back or even tearing away from their grip.

I succumb to the promise of another long night and coopera- tively walk back to his office to begin the wait for my free ride Downtown. Plopped onto a hard bench, I allow myself to be hand- cuffed to a ring embedded in the backrest. I'm face to face with a large console of video surveillance monitors that wouldn't be out of place in a casino.

Before loss prevention can finish burning a DVD with my crime on it, a cop knocks on the door. The leather holsters on his belt squeak as he steps into the small, windowless room. His eyes bounce off me as the loss prevention officer describes how cooper- ative I was. As the officer takes the disc, he seems disappointed I didn't fight back.

"Is this his property?" the officer asks.

"There's nothing else in there," I swear. "You can review the footage." I nod toward the screen.

The police officer ignores me and reaches for my backpack.

"You don't have permission to search my shit!" I stomp my foot, my long hair shaking in protest. It's rare, but occasionally criminals can get their rights violated as well.

He looks up at me with eyes that detest my very existence. "You see this?" He points to a section of the zipper, open just wide enough to stick a finger inside. "I just took you into custody. Your bag is open. I have reasonable suspicion to believe there may be other stolen merchandise in here."

I laugh once in defiance. "It's not *open*, it's just not fully zip—"

"Save it for the judge."

As the officer removes a hard-shell sunglasses case from my bag, I stretch the handcuffs against my wrist. With an audible snap, the case opens to reveal a dope kit crammed with needles, cookers, twist ties, a blue tourniquet and some brownish stained cotton balls. Licking his lips, the discovery appears pleasurable for him.

"Let's see this get thrown out of court."

Somehow the booking and processing areas are as deep into the bowels of the jail as I ever seem to get, having never been taken upstairs to wait in a cell for my day in court. With a written promise to show face at my court date, I am released on my own recognizance and am shocked that they still take my word after all of my previous Failure to Appear charges. Cut loose from jail, I return to the crux of my worldly ills feeling none the wiser.

The night and darkness are one and the same. Since standard protocol to prevent suicide is for jailers to confiscate shoelaces during booking, the cold air washes over my socks and seeps out of holes in my weathered soles. The small plastic sheaths on my shoelaces have fallen off long ago, so I throw them away when I steal a new pair, knowing I'll never get the frayed ends back through the eyelets.

I turn my back toward the biting wind and realize I have nowhere to go as the breeze nudges me down the sidewalk. Something is trying to clear me from the city. I lurch along with frozen joints—the sickness has taken over and is eating me alive from the inside out. With no kit, money or momentum, I'm at a loss unless I beg, borrow or steal. Racking my brain, I'm committed to doing whatever it takes to get loaded. The dreaded anxiety of a lone wolf lifestyle is barely manageable at best and not for the faint-hearted. Having a partner in crime has almost always been beneficial unless the choice of a cohort is a lazy thief or parasite. Fortunately, there's a large enough opioid epidemic in this city that picking a competent sidekick shouldn't be rocket science.

I need to track down Simon.

Not only do I have no other choice, I don't have a choice at all. I have to ride the horse until it bucks me off or I'm forced to put it out of its misery. I weave like a rat in a cabinet toward a forgotten corner of the city, hoping to find him camped out and well off. I start arranging the right words in my head to get what I so desperately need once I find him.

Simon religiously saves a wake-up hit, and I'll promise him anything in this world to get him to break me off a piece. A time-management specialist, it's remarkable how he'll intentionally go to bed dope sick if holding out means he'll have a shot locked and loaded for the morning. That's what has always worked for him, and tonight, I pray it works out in my favor.

Though my life is a broken record, I don't skip a beat and track down Simon like a drug sniffing dog. We usually take turns boosting to keep the hits coming, but a deal is a deal. For the past two days, he's stood on the sidelines cheering me on while I ran in and out of stores, keeping a steady stream of product coming to trade to the closest available dealer.

I can't wait for him to get back to work and know it will be good for him. His style is reminiscent of how I used to operate, more conniving and calculating than blunt and brash. With his short stature and plain face forever hidden behind a pair of prescription glasses, he has learned the benefit of blending in with the herd of casual shoppers.

He makes it a goal to always try to change into a clean outfit before going inside a store. Removing a crisp button-down shirt from his backpack, he can pull a Clark Kent behind a dumpster, bus stop or bush. Whenever I see him head into a store, I can barely tell that he's been homeless for longer than I've known him. Donning clean clothes likely reminds him of better times, but they are also like his own private key to the city. Dressing to impress has gained him entrance to higher-end establishments and stores, places that turn me away at the door.

Working our way across the city and back, Simon and I have worn a rut in the roads less traveled. The spots where we get high vary greatly. If neither of us feel sick, we take our time to find a clandestine alcove or dark corner. Making use of anything from a public restroom to a corner in a park, we shoot up with leisure as if it's ordinary and commonplace. Both of us have perfected our process and can finish within a manner of minutes, if I skip finding a vein and muscle my shot.

Now and then, we encounter a situation where the two of us can't both enter a facility at the same time to cook up. Our dilemma then is that neither one of us trusts the other to cook up both shots. I'd water down his hit if given a chance and he's no different. Honest enough to admit we're crooked, we've learned to split the baby and crack the dope in half. Even then we cheat one another, trying to squish our half to make it look smaller to argue for more. We both stopped carrying scales long ago to avoid intent to distribute charges when arrested.

Whenever either of us gets sick, we become significantly less picky about when and where we get high. I remember times where we've each fixed up on the back of the bus, covering for one another and running the part of a blocker, so the driver can't see what's going on. Riding on a train, I've even unzipped my backpack and cooked up a shot inside it while rumbling along. Whatever it takes, addiction affords lesser and lesser luxuries. Anyone who slams into rock bottom hard enough soon learns it has a basement.

Even though neither of us trusts the other, our friendship has still grown over time, and I have long considered Simon to be less of an acquaintance and more of a brother. He's had many opportunities to think of himself first, but he has also proven to be invaluable in the darkest hours. He has been forthcoming over a bonus or two that dealers gave him when I would have never known. For us, the standard for each drug deal is that whoever stole the merchandise meets the dealer and negotiates the deal. Dealers typically only want to meet with one person at a time as a precaution against being jumped and robbed, especially in a vehicle. Simon has traded items on a handful of occasions and returned with much more product than expected, sharing the extra dope instead of pocketing it for himself. He's taught me that not all addicts are selfish, at least not all of the time.

Simon has caught wind of a dealer pushing a higher quality product and tries to convince me to travel with him to the ends of the earth to meet up with Mario. I'm less inclined to travel the long distances for superb quality alone, placing a higher value on quantity because of my struggle to fire off clean hits. I don't see his point of seeking the best dope if it's just going to be wasted. My veins are shot and my last hope, my inner bicep, is no longer an option after the surgery.

After I tore out the stuffing, I let it heal under wraps and scar over. Now I'm restricted to muscling most shots, rarely able to capture the pure rush. Simon, on the other hand, is a purist and will never stop seeking out the greener grass. I've known him to hold out, even through sickness, if he knows he can locate cleaner and purer dope than what's right in front of him.

Because of this difference, we occasionally split up. In my mind, black tar is black tar, and though I would always pick the better of two evils when given a choice, I had long become accustomed to the mantra that beggars can't be choosers. It doesn't take much to take the sickness away, but it always takes something.

Simon recently chased down a dealer with quality brown powder all the way to the neighboring city of Gresham. I hung back in Northeast Portland, shaking my head over the past few days when it became obvious he wasn't returning any time soon. My fears are confirmed by a newspaper that prints mugshot photos and reports that they have hauled him in for a litany of charges.

From the list of crimes, it sounds like he was snatched up on the train, most likely caught by the rail police for catching a free ride and not having valid fare. They booked him for interfering with a public transit officer, Trespass and Trespass II, providing false information to an officer and possession of a controlled substance.

To make matters worse, Simon is being held on a county hold that will transfer him back to Gresham County, which has a much lower tolerance than Portland for drug offenses and criminal activity. Their police and judicial departments have been pursuing stricter sentencing guidelines across the board, fighting the widespread crimes directly resulting from the opioid crisis. It will be at least a month before they will release him.

I feel his suffering. He is undoubtedly facing a painful detox in jail. The only realistic direction for me is to switch into self-preservation mode, and over the next few weeks, I keep my head above water while missing Simon's company. Simon has always kept our spirits high and it's tough to hold it together when I feel ready to burst at the seams.

When Simon is finally released from his month-long stint in jail, it's back to business as usual without skipping a beat. Simon seems hungrier than before—as if playing catch-up—he doesn't sleep well and harnesses an insatiable appetite for both dope and food. He's put on a couple of pounds and throws his weight around as if time is of the essence.

Stealing dinner each night from Fred Meyer, we return to stalking the Northwest quadrant of the city. For the past few days, we have made ourselves at home outside of Beth Israel Congregation. As I wind down for the night and struggle to make myself as comfortable as possible, I say good night to Simon and slip into sleep, ready to end the day.

8

LOST ONES

I drag my shoes across the wet sidewalk, lacking energy and motivation beneath each step. It's now been a month since Simon's passing, and I still have to remind myself not to think about it. His death has introduced a lingering depression that reminds me all junkies are worthless pawns in a game with clear dangers and no do-overs. I assume the time will come to grieve, but I've been unable to shed a tear.

I can't help it—the drugs block all emotion. I'm deadened to pain. Nonetheless, hearing stories of overdoses, close calls and tragic endings is one thing, but living the experience is much different. I wish the impact of Simon's overdose was life changing for me because I don't want his death to be a waste. I want something good to come of it as if flipping his body over will somehow help me turn over a new leaf myself.

As word of Simon's passing spreads, dealers begin turning me away. They are concerned over associating with me or being accused of distributing the dose that ended Simon's life. By default, I am presumed to be working with the police, and it takes too long to prove that I'm not a liability.

My hand is forced and I put Northwest Portland behind me. I

can feel the heat turning up, eyes glowing in the thicket on the lookout for my false steps.

It started on the morning of Simon's passing when I had too much interaction with police officers to ever blend back into the fray as just another statistic. Now, I am a face to a name, and the cops on patrol send a clear message: I am no longer welcome to waffle about in their section of the city. Just yesterday, they gave me fair warning as an officer pulled his patrol car up beside me. I'm now well aware that they will search me on the spot every time they see me walking down the sidewalk if I am stupid enough to hang around.

They don't have to tell me twice.

Across the river, I make the 42nd Avenue Transit Center my new haunt, giving up boosting for a new hustle I created that I should have thought of much earlier. This train stop is the first stop outside of Fareless Square, the area encompassing Downtown Portland where you can ride public transportation for free. With this stop being a popular hub, a lot of riders coming from Downtown will buy a two-hour train ticket before boarding, ride the train for just a few minutes and then depart.

Sitting at the top of the steps, I start the day off by asking for partially used tickets from every rider getting off the train. People don't seem to mind handing out tickets as much as they do money, though they're practically one and the same. Stuffing their transfers in my pocket, I am thankful the mentality of recycling is so ingrained in this city. Almost nobody wants to see a good train ticket go to waste. I keep a close eye out for new riders who step up to purchase their tickets from the machines and if they're paying with cash, I offer to resell them my passes for half price.

Most people will pay me a discounted price, and some even cough up full face value. I make off like a bandit, and if it's a good day, I can pull in a hundred dollars before lunch. I tell myself that my hustle is a gray area that's looked down upon by Metro, but not technically illegal. All-Day passes fetch about four dollars each, and if someone is headed home, it's useless to them, but it's a gold-mine for me. I'm surprised by how many riders will hand me their tickets without me even asking, but at least I'm not boosting anymore, not in the classical sense. As a result, my anxiety levels each day are remarkably manageable.

I am still taking money from the city, but TriMet authorities will be slow to catch on. The Transit Center is a great location to post up because I have three ways out if I need to jam. From up high on the overpass, I have a view of the steps and landing that leads to the train tracks below. I can see the police coming from the street to my right if they roll up in patrol cars, and if they debark the train, I can flip over my skateboard and ride down the ramp into the neighborhood across the freeway. While unlikely, if I ever get swarmed from both sides, I can always hope to hop on any train that pulls through the station every couple of minutes.

Like all good things, my hustle—as great and profitable as it has proven—doesn't stay a secret for long and out come the copy-cats. I pay them no mind, not worrying over things I cannot control. But when my regulars seem to realize they're contributing to my habit, I turn the gears on my next play. There's a pressure to wrap this hustle up, which is easier said than done.

I want a normal life, but know that addicts such as myself rarely make it out alive. I can think of a few addicts who have managed to get sober for a bit, but I don't know anyone who's successfully quit. I'm also unsure if abstinence is the same as sobri-ety. The court has a way of stepping in and interfering with the natural rhythm of users, but not having and not wanting must be two different things. Either way, everyone seems to return to the dark side in time.

I need to see the light for myself and get out of this gray city. I want off this wave and I'm tired of fighting to stay afloat. Having never lost the love for my family and friends, I am tired of facing my biggest fear—that some tragedy will occur back home and I'll miss a funeral or lose a family member without them ever seeing my redemption. That fear has long settled in the back of my mind. There are certain things in life that I am terrified of missing out on, and the longer I play the game, the more the odds are stacked against me.

Something has changed inside of me over the past few weeks, and I can't move past the idea that most decisions in life are irreversible. It is a tough thought, trying to imagine the pain and loss that Simon's family must have experienced when they received the phone call in Florida. I imagine my own parents have constantly feared a similar call, reeling from a shock of terror each time their phone rings out before their alarm does.

Walking down the sidewalk today, my stride feels different, almost sped up. The ground beneath each step is solid. Sure-footed, it's as if two hands are pushing me from behind, urging me to move along.

My miserable steps lead me to the local library, one of the few locations that will grant me free Internet access. Logging in to an old email account, I reach out to my mom to explain that I've taken to frequenting an eatery where something unusual has taken place. It seems appropriate to let her know where she can reach me if she ever needs to. I want to open the door, if only a crack. A little light can do no harm.

Near the fledgling public transportation hub of buses and trains, and next door to Trader Joe's, Panera has become a happening community space full of hipsters, artists, soccer moms and street kids. Junkies brush elbows with lawyers over bagels and coffee. Perfectly Portland-esque, the national bakery chain opened a new location and swapped the register behind the counter for a social experiment. The concept seems simple enough—order what your heart desires and pay what you wish into an unattended wooden honor box on the counter. If I have the money to eat, I can drop it in the slot, but if not, I'm still allowed to order and eat a meal in peace with dignity. Some will overpay if they feel generous and can afford it, while others slip in a single dollar or a handful of change.

I can't help but foresee the opportunities for abuse. The people running the show must either be crazy or have deep pockets. The concept is noble, but like other patrons lacking in respectable character traits, I move with a crooked smile and allow others to pick up the tab behind me. My priorities haven't been straight in a long time. I rarely have disposable income, and when I do, I would never consider wasting it on something as unnecessary as food.

The staff seems well-trained in being non-judgmental and accommodating. They joined a mission to be of service to the public in addition to brewing coffee, serving muffins and sweeping floors. Every employee is eager to check on how my day is going, especially the full-time greeter stationed at the door who explains how it works to newbies. It feels good to be welcomed somewhere.

Still, I can never stomach the guilt of how I'm taking advantage of their system. It wears on me. I don't want to be a freeloader, until I weigh eating here for free over stealing a meal and realize it's one less risk of being sent to jail. The collection box up front serves as a constant reminder that I am worthless. And there's an opportunity cost of taking the time out of my day to sit for a free meal. How much money could I be hustling during the time it takes to stop to eat? I may not be paying for my meals, but I am forking over what little choice in life I have left.

I have no problem taking whatever I want, whenever I want to feed my habit—the irony is that charity is hard to accept. Taking anything with nothing to offer is no different than attending a beggar's banquet, and I struggle to stoop that low publicly. I work hard to never let it get that far, always hustling, conniving and thieving to avoid panhandling. My mom raised me better. The only way I can stomach charity here is by pretending to be paying my own way. It's not lost on me when the manager notices a patron overindulging in the charity structure and puts them to work pushing a broom or cleaning windows.

The greeter at Panera meets me with a smile and opens the door to allow me inside. Heated air rushes my lungs and warms my hands. Sliding my palms together to take advantage of the newfound feelings in my fingertips, I line up next to the wall of windows that looks out on the sparsely occupied outdoor seating. I inch forward as the guests before me place their orders. A step here, another there, slipping my thumbs behind the straps of my backpack.

Then I see it, out of the corner of my eye. A yellow Post-it note with a simple message: "Jordan B. from Hawai'i—Call Home." Below is my mom's phone number in case I forgot. An employee's simple directive among a litany of job postings begs me to reach out.

I tear the sticky note off the bulletin board and feel my rib cage tightening as I shuffle forward to order a Caffe Mocha and an Everything bagel with cream cheese on the side. Palming a folded-up dollar, doubling it back on itself to give the appearance of multiple bills, I jam it in the slot. I doubt I fool anyone, but at least I don't look as blatantly entitled as others who never bother contributing a cent.

I ask to use their phone, knowing that my request violates their policy. They've been burned more than once, and it only takes a few callbacks from dealers before everyone catches on. But I show the cashier the yellow note, and he sees the chance for their business phone to be used for a valuable purpose for once, a higher calling.

Ring. Ring. Rin—

"Jordan?"

"Hi Mom."

"Oh, thank God you called. It's so good to hear your voice."

I twist her message in my hand. "I was surprised to see your note—I've been thinking about you guys a lot."

"And we've been thinking about you every day. Your father will be so happy to hear that you called."

"Happy? He probably hates me."

"No. Don't say that. He loves you more than you'll ever know.

One day, you'll understand—when you have children of your own, you'll do anything for them."

I clutch my cheek, not knowing what to say. I want to hurt myself for the pain I've caused them. "I can't wait to see you guys again."

"Good," she says, her smile shining through her voice. "Which is fortuitous, because you won't have to wait too long. We're coming back in two weeks and want to see you. Your father bought our tickets last night."

I pull the phone away from my ear so I can think without distraction and start to count the days, but stop the instant I realize it's not about the math adding up. Her faith is contagious and inspires me to consider offering myself a second chance.

"Mom, it's going to be tight, but I guess that if play my cards right, I can be freshly detoxed when you guys arrive. The only problem is there are a lot more junkies out there who need help and haven't fucked themselves over like I have." I hiss through my teeth. "Sorry, I don't mean to swear, but remember, I left against medical advice. I don't think I can get back in."

"Oh, of course you can," she promises. "Besides, I don't think you can afford not to."

I realize that my last run may be coming to a close. From this point forward, the thought of sobriety and taking back control of a boun-tiful future sounds so great, yet still seems so impossible. If I can't make it a day without a hit, or even a few hours, how can I ever muster a lifetime? The thought poisons my mind. A lot of users get onto a methadone regiment to kick the habit, but that seems just as hopeless. I've gone to methadone clinics before, looking for dope connections because it seems like only a small percentage of them stop their heroin usage once they dose. And from the looks of it, the majority double down on both addictions and dig their own grave, one sip of the synthetic opioid syrup at a time.

I know that detox is just around the corner, but I want to take the scenic route to get there. Everything I know, hate and love sprouts out of the cracks of this city. Leaving this world behind will be a struggle even though there's not a lot of hope here. What excites me most, though, is this one last week of using. If I play my cards right, I can stay high from now until the day I'm readmitted back into Hooper.

Starting tomorrow, I'll be knocking down Hooper's doors like everyone else and hoping to avoid jail throughout the triage process. They'll turn me away at least four or five times, and as long as I don't miss a day, I can make this work. Portland is famously known as the city of bridges, and I intend to burn every last one of them on my way out.

With two outstanding felony warrants, I've already proved that I'm incapable of showing up to a court date. Since my parents are planning to come back and meet me, I imagine that my choices are to either leave detox and the city, fly home under their escort, or go directly from detox to jail and then back home to Hawai'i. Jail seems substantially more enticing once detoxed, but I'm not convinced yet that I'll only be locked up overnight. My outstanding warrants are both for drug-related offenses, but because they were non-violent, I think I can exchange jail time for some form of court-ordered rehabilitation effort. I also have a Failure to Appear charge, which means I am a proven flight risk in the eyes of the court.

Kicking the thought around in my head over the next few days, I push my personal limits further than normal. With a new batch of clean and sharp needles from the exchange, I take my time to make sure every hit counts. Figuring the direction I am headed to is honorable, I've got to take advantage of every situation I can and avoid apprehension. As I march forward to the looming count-down of my mom's arrival, for once, time is on my side.

I make sure to check in with her every couple of days and make a point about not being a stranger. By now, she knows that I only call her when I'm high since that's the only time I can seem to catch a break. That's also when I'm most open and honest, contrary to the classic example of a street junkie. I am rarely wasted away on some sidewalk, unable to support the weight of my head. That isn't my style or how my body reacts to the narcotics. I'm not the one to be caught performing some ungodly balancing act on my feet, wobbling around like an infant gazelle.

Taking advantage of riding high, I find a pay phone and call my mom, hoping she'll accept the charges. At first, the pleasantries are nice, but what I'm really after is her unwavering support.

I cut to the chase, lowering my voice. "Mom, even though this ride is coming to an end, it's bumpier than ever. And I can see the light at the end of the tunnel, but it's closing in on me. If you could help me see it through and just wire me a little cash, I think I could make it—"

"I'm so proud of you Jordan," she says, cutting me off, "but that well has run dry long ago. I can't send you any money, and you know why."

I crush the receiver in my hand. "Look, I don't think I'm asking for a lot. I'm just trying to make it to the finish line in one piece."

"And you will. I know you will, but this time, you need to make it on your own."

"Do you know what will happen if I get arrested again?"

"No one is forcing you to steal."

"Are you serious? What don't you understand about me not having a choice?!"

"You *always* have a choice. You just have to hang in there," she coaches. "I promise you it will all be over soon. We can pull through this together."

I want to believe her. It's hard to imagine attempting to pull this off without her support, but impossible for me to see it any other way.

"All you have to do is make it through the next twelve days," she says, "and we'll get through this together."

I hear her talking, but don't believe her. "No, Mom. You're wrong."

"What do you mea—"

"I can't believe you. It's *eleven days*, not twelve. You guys will be here in eleven days."

"You're counting the days?"

I wish she could see my face. "I'm not counting the days—I'm counting the hours! What did you expect?"

She goes silent for a moment.

"You there?" I ask. "Hello?"

"Sorry, Jordan." She sniffs. "I'm still here."

"Are you crying?"

"No, I'm not. I'm thanking God."

"What? Why?"

"Because I finally know that you are going to make it."

9

VIBRATO

AUGUST 19TH, 2011

I f I'm honest with myself, I know there is a false sense of freedom in addiction that is hard to quantify. It's easy to confuse not having a job, relationship or responsibilities to be the same as a life of free will. In most cases of severe addiction, I imagine this couldn't be further from the truth—the game stopped being fun the moment it forced me to play. Sometimes I run into people who have only dipped their toes in the muddy waters of this life. They think they can relate, but I'm not the one to change their mind. Time will do that for them if they have the makings of an addict.

The very nature of my addiction is a self-imposed imprisonment, one that requires me to return to my dealers like an animal to a watering hole. I have no control or independence regardless of how tough I act. No matter how I cut it, there is no free will here. Dependence has taken away any illusion of choice.

It is what it is. Long ago, I had to accept the hard truth as a once prosperous future slipped through my fingers like dry sand. Everything that had once mattered, if it possessed any value at all, got traded or sold for pennies on the dollar. My koa Kamaka

'Ukulele, a one-of-a-kind graduation gift, followed many other belongings into the pawnshop, a loan to be defaulted upon and a mistake that can never be undone. Though it hurts, by now I am used to this feeling. Things fall apart and things slip away. Selling off my possessions became a new low, especially since I've always been sentimental, clinging onto memories through belongings.

The grind takes its toll. I'm at the point where I want to be over it and move on with my life. Sometimes I hope to quit being a junkie, but I don't see how I can break the chokehold. Sobriety seems so impossible. I love getting high, but the drugs aren't loving me back like I need them to. I remember how I used to hover and float around the city when my tolerance was low, but the current wave of dope flooding the city is trash. I'm burned out from spinning my wheels and reality is wearing thin. Change. I need it. Something has to give.

With my mom and dad ready to fly back up here, I know I have to hold up my end of the bargain. I am sore from head to toe, have aches and pains that throb off-rhythm, the syncopation preventing any sense of relief. A walking pincushion, I must stab, poke, skewer and prod myself no less than a hundred times daily, searching to spike a vein where there are none. My body hates me, and in this endless cycle, I can't help but hate it back.

With over a week until my parents fly in, my addiction has evolved to a preference for mixing cocaine with heroin, the speed-balls frying my wits. Sometimes I can't find a vein and miss the target, wasting the hit, or at least the coke. Not that I'm keeping score, but I miss more than I hit, which makes me appreciate the times when I can fire off a clean shot and the rush pounds my brain like a freight train. I can feel it coming, screaming toward me as if the operator is getting his kicks off by leaning heavily on his horn. The headlights engulf my vision while the rails tremble beneath my feet. I'll cook up in a public bathroom and brace myself for the onslaught, holding on for dear life. Throwing both palms against the walls of the stall until the locomotive has roared by, the heroin takes over and I coast to a complete stop.

Today is no different, except the shot rings out before I hear a sound. For an instant, a bolt of fear tears through me, thundering through my veins. I wait it out and force a grin, knowing the cloud of dope will puff out of the smokestack and the train will disappear from view. It's a brutal rush followed by a mellow crash that seems to make life much more exciting and colorful. The added accelerant is another addiction to feed and one that keeps me on edge. It's a fine line to walk, only manageable until I'm sent over it.

The fallout is disturbing. Anxieties upon anxieties have made me scared to cross the street, questioning my surroundings and the surety of each footstep. I look over my shoulder so often I think I should walk around backward and start to suspect that the people inhabiting my world are all against me. Some don't seem real.

I find the confusion entertaining until its ever-constant presence brings concerns of borderline paranoia. Ridiculous and graphic vignettes infest my mind, and I wonder what would happen if I could reconstruct reality, always for the worse. If I step out in front of this fast-approaching train, how long will it take to clean me up off the tracks, and will they find all of me? How could I operate in this world missing both legs? Would I get more sympathy?

Crossing a bridge, I wonder how much force it will take to push this passing cyclist off the bike path and into the water below? Perhaps this car heading my way will skip the curb and smear me across the dampened sidewalk, mixing flesh and blood with the moss on the cobblestones. My mind is playing tricks on me and I get a kick out of playing along.

Realizing I am sick in the head, I know I'm vibrating on a different wavelength as I take the first step to re-enter the Hooper intake building. More than ever, I need to be here. Adding my name to the list, I steal a seat and wait until I don't make it in. Every day I'm not admitted is both a blessing and a curse—I leave the center feeling relief that I can get high just one more time. At least I am trying to do the right thing. I no longer trust myself and need help, whether it's today, tomorrow, or just around the corner.

. . .

Washing down some salt and vinegar chips with flat, luke-warm root beer seems like a good enough start to the day. I suck between my gums and spit out the sticky saliva and feel a tingle on my chapped lips. I have given up brushing my teeth long ago, along with most other rudimentary hygiene habits.

I burp out the last rumblings from my disagreeing stomach and drop the empty plastic bag on the floor of the bleachers, letting the wind carry it away for me. It feels somewhere around 6 a.m. and I have already been awake for an hour. I rise with the traffic, garbage trucks and buses as if we are all one entity starting our early morning routines.

Tucking my sleeping bag underneath the bleachers, I give the roll a quick smack to shake off the icy dew. I always have high hopes it will still be here waiting for my return, yet I've lost a few nights of sleep when I had found it stolen or removed. I've learned to fear the pain of freezing nights, and that hell on earth is walking throughout an endless night, dope sick while I try to keep the blood flowing. Grabbing hold of the shaky fence near the backside of the dugout at Erv Lind Baseball Stadium, I grunt and struggle to flip myself over. I head toward the NE 60th Street train station a few blocks away and enjoy a short walk through a neighborhood that appreciates its small outside baseball diamond. I wait for the Max Train and board with no ticket.

The ride to the Rose Garden is short, merely a hop, skip and a jump away. I take a seat near an exit, in case TriMet Transit Police come looking to write tickets for riders without a fare. I have given them the slip more times than I can remember, but I can't afford to encounter them today. Nothing and no one will get in between me and Hooper's morning triage.

With undeniable certainty, I know that to escape this city, detox is both critical and mandatory. As the train rolls up to the Rose Garden, I ready myself near the exit door, making sure that the coast is clear. The cold, biting morning snaps at my face as I step off the train. The rain is light and fluffy, dusting my shoulders as I move out from under the overpass. The tips of my ears lose feeling, which is enough to encourage me to pick up my pace and make my walk brisk. Chasing my visible breath up the low-grade hill, I find myself panting by the time I tug on the freezing door handle. Out of shape and excuses, I slump into a chair and hang my head.

Before the roll call process even begins, I sense that today is the day. I look around the room and wonder who else is coming with me. There is a pregnant couple across the way holding hands as the woman dabs her tearful eyes with a tissue. She looks miserable, but not in the way a typical addict does. No, by the ring on her finger and face heavily emphasized with makeup, I imagine she is vying for her husband to get in, paving the way for the fleeting possibility of a happy life together.

An old man to my left snores with his mouth wide open and something tells me he won't make it, either in here or out there. Just past him, three young street kids wearing blackened matching rags have folded up cardboard signs poking out of their backpacks. This life isn't that cool after all, huh? The beggar's signs often take a stab at humor, but there is nothing funny about this life if one can be honest with themselves. "Bet you can't hit me with a quarter" may earn a laugh, dime or a buck, but the joke is always on us users. This lifestyle, often glorified through Pop Culture, Grunge, Punk and Rock, is truly no life at all.

The nurse steps forward with her trusty clipboard and doesn't bother repeating herself. A buddy of mine from the streets is the last name called. I watch as he uncomfortably raises his hand to announce his presence. His other hand squeezes his forehead as he hesitates to scramble his belongings together. I remember that feeling of not being ready and I can't blame him for it. Holding onto my seat, I pan the surrounding room and unwavering sea of addicts as they slowly clear out. I needed my name to be called.

As quickly as he heads to the bathroom to submit his urine sample, he returns. I overhear him advise the nurses that the metal specimen pass-thru cabinet for his drug test canister will be empty. He says he's having trouble urinating, having just emptied his bladder only minutes before they called his name. I look down and smile.

I know exactly what he is doing. The nurses encourage him to drink fluids, but he insists that he knows his body and drinking won't speed up the flow anymore. Without a baseline sample, the nurses advise him they can't admit him and finally cave, settling on having him return to try again tomorrow. They'll save his spot in the meantime, though they shouldn't. I watch as the door hits him on the way out to complete whatever unfinished business he has left in this world. As the alternate, I'm next in line and claim his vacant spot.

It all happens so quickly, the thought doesn't even cross my mind to borrow a phone to call home and alert my parents that I have made it back in. I'm overwhelmed by my first actual step, taken on my own accord, to disassociate myself from the lifestyle I have long struggled to endure. Rising to the occasion is more than just empowering—it's authentic. Having lived utterly out of control for so long, the act of standing up to claim my spot has me feeling like a civilian volunteering to go off to war. It's heroic in my own eyes, and that's all that counts.

My second stint at detox kicks off surprisingly much more enjoyable than the first. It is a thought unlikely uttered too often—I half expected this go-around to be much worse than my last time. But this time I know what to expect and don't have to deal with the horrid pain from the unexpected abscess lancing. That sharp pain, that *constant throbbing*, ultimately proved to be the nail in my coffin.

How I had previously walked out has caused me to struggle, then settle with the thought of how selfish I have become. It was never lost on me. Since leaving, self-pity, shame and worthlessness have become identifiable characteristics emanating out of the dope cooker, reflecting off the burnt-brown liquid every time I prepped a shot. Recalling how the nurses had pleaded, and in one case practically begged for me to reconsider my self-imposed discharge, I am loathed to see their faces again. I expect some of them will lecture me for not getting it right the first time.

Much like everything else of late, I am dead wrong. Every staffer, without fail, couldn't seem to be more pleased to see me back in the facility. They are all vocally supportive and encourage me to be proud about my decision to return. Over the next few hours, I slowly readjust to the detox regimen and see how clear it is that each employee at Hooper wants us patients to succeed. The staff, more so than the nurses, know firsthand that this game isn't a game at all. They're in the trenches and are well aware of the statistics. Both staff and nurses also know firsthand that not every man or woman who leaves through that door is provided a second or third chance to make it back.

Sticking out the Post-Acute Withdrawal Symptoms, I keep my spirits high as I flop in my bunk. My focus has switched from obsession to embracing the detox regimen and settling into a consistent routine to manage the week. Having figured out that my parents could call to confirm that I've cleared triage and made it safely inside, I avoid looking at the wall clock behind my bunk to count down the days, hours, minutes and seconds. Thankful for the dry socks that let me sleep like a baby, I turn on my side and close my eyes.

"Hi, Jordan?" her voice is raspy yet calming. "Do you have a second?"

I slowly open my eyes and focus on Sam's knees. I turn on my back and scoot myself up toward my pillow. "Hey, Sam. What's up?"

She flashes a rolled-up piece of paper. "Your aftercare plan. We need to talk in my office, but take your time getting up."

"I'll be right there."

Moments later, I enter her home away from home. Sam asks me to pull up a chair at her desk. I like her as a counselor and even more as a person. In a stale environment, her wardrobe is always bright and illuminating, complimenting her bronze skin which is draped in colorful tattoos and dangling red hair. Sam's job primarily focuses on arranging post-detox action plans, varying from transfer to treatment to housing allocation to mental health referrals. In my case, she knows the best way to be of help is to have me sign the HIPAA Release Form she unrolls in front of me, so she can speak freely on my behalf to my mom.

"Did you let anyone know you were coming here?" Sam asks.

"Yeah, my parents know I've been trying to get in. Why, what's going on?"

"Well, your mom has been calling the front desk, and she sounds panicky. She's trying really hard to find you."

I grab the back of my neck. "Sam, why didn't you just pass the word on for me?"

"I can't, not with the Health Insurance Portability and Account-ability Act. Your status as a patient is confidential until you release me to speak on your behalf. Until then, legally, I can neither confirm nor deny your enrollment in the program. Not to employ-ers, wives, girlfriends, mothers—you name it—we need to keep the center a safe place where you can focus on healing. Anonymity will forever be essential, but if you're okay with me talking to her, I just need you to—"

My pen carves a signature into the paper and I slide the form back to her. "Of course I am."

"Good, because damn is she persistent." She spins her phone around and places the receiver on her desk. "You can dial her number."

I make the call, remembering the Post-it note.

"Hello, it's Jeri."

"Mom! Guess what?"

She pauses, hoping to get this guess right. "Please tell me you're in Hooper?"

"Can you believe they let me back in? I'm actually sitting across from Sam right now." I feel my mom's breath creep out the handset and down my neck.

"Jordan, you are doing the right thing. We were praying you were there. I had no idea they took the privacy laws so seriously! I mean, I'm your mother!"

"It's my fault. I'm so sorry I forgot to reach out to you. It surprised me to get in and I figured you knew where to reach me. Anyway, I'm here with Sam and she needs to talk to you."

I turn the phone over and listen in to the faint voice of my mom as Sam picks up where I left off. I can make out some words here and there, notably a sense of relief and concern for my well-being. I rub at my chest and wonder how much worse this process could be as I drag them along for the ride. Looking forward to my chance to hear her voice again, I wait while the two of them cook up a transition plan for me. Leaning back in my chair, I pick up what new information I can.

I am a mess, a rudderless ship with no bearing or heading that will land me safely on the shores of the Promised Land. All the resources available to Sam are centrally located to the very city I've been physically dissolving in. I hear Sam working with what she has and know that none of it will work for me.

Central City Concern can add my name to a list for housing, but that would put me right across the street from an infamous corner my dope dealers love. And her list of shelters won't help me weather the storm when the cold wind blows. Outpatient services are readily available, but I can't hide out in meetings forever. This city is a trigger-happy dope mine and I have to leave it to stand a chance.

Sam hands me the phone, and with it, a relief which takes over as my mom fills me in on the plan.

"Jordan, Sam and I both agree that the best way forward is to bring you home."

"Right, but what about my warrants?"

"Turn yourself in. We'll pick you up from jail and go from there. In the meantime, I'll contact treatment centers back here and see what I can arrange."

I hear my dad disagreeing in the background, fearful that I might get tangled in a legal web. I hand the phone back to Sam, trading the receiver for a handful of candy that she stores in a dish on her desk.

I can tell the nurses are proud of me when my time comes to check out. This is my chance—I am reminded—to decide which path I wish to follow. From this point, I can only go one of two ways, and it is up to me to play or fold the cards I'm dealt. With seven days of detox behind me to clear my mind, I still feel weak, exhausted and drained, but I've had enough glimpses of sanity to find my backbone. For years, I had struggled to stand up for the right thing, and today is my chance to take a step toward an uncomfortable responsibility. It's a strange feeling to know what I need to do. Mom's right—I have to turn myself in.

Walking out of Hooper with my plastic bag full of belongings, I hit the streets running. My parents are flying in this evening and I don't want to mess up the plan. When the desire to use instinctively crosses my mind, I have to remind myself that I'll ruin a good thing if I'm allowed to. But it helps to know that my opiate receptors are still on strike from the Buprenorphine I have been taking all week. I don't have to look at my hands to know that they're tied. Getting high isn't possible—the choice has been made for me.

The only choice is to head to the Rose Quarter Transit Center, ride the rail into town and go straight to jail. I've spent enough time in court to know that judges almost always reflect some appreciation during sentencing for those who turned themselves in over those who were apprehended. "Do Not Pass Go" is my mantra as the bright sun warms the concrete under my feet. The walk to the train isn't far and the momentum behind my steps gain traction while I move with a purpose.

Reaching the Rose Quarter, I intend to board the next train heading for Downtown. Red, green, yellow—any line will do. A rail car is pulling out of the station as I approach, but I know another will be hot on its heels. Popping up to have a seat on the handrail, I stabilize myself with a foot against the steel post and stare down the tracks.

Intending to see a train, I am taken aback by a friend of mine who is fast approaching. A former high school wrestling star and the son of an All-American coach bears cauliflower ears born from a childhood of aggressive training. Zane wrestled every day, a bright star burned out from being pushed past his enjoyment and love for the sport. Today, he is a far cry from his collegiate aspirations, where he once competed with the best wrestlers in the country. Somewhere along the line, injuries, pain or sheer curiosity got the best of him, and his downward crash started from the all too common infatuation with Oxycontin. It's no surprise that the source of prescription pills will always dry up or become too expensive. Zane is like most street kids his age, strung out on and enslaved to heroin, the cheaper and more accessible alternative to pills. Still, he is always somehow in a good mood, wearing a champion's smile like he's only visiting this world for the time being.

Our fists bump, typical in a world where you don't shake hands unless you're passing contraband. Glad to see me, I realize he's not going to let me get the first word in.

"I wasn't expecting to see you around man—the cops are looking everywhere for you." There's a sense of urgency behind his pinpoint pupils.

"For me? What the—" My heart sinks, immediately dragged down by two thoughts: either they have built a damning shoplifting case on me, or they want to find me for further questioning or charges related to Simon's overdose. I am confident that my two warrants alone, though serious, wouldn't justify anyone working to track me down.

Portland's justice system is up to its ears with non-violent drug offenses, unless something has changed over the past week. I can't make sense of it, but either way, don't plan on getting to the bottom of it. I've been chased out of malls, through neighborhoods and even off of a train, but never heard of anyone looking for me afterward.

I want Zane to give me more information than what he's got. The detectives didn't say why they were looking for me, which troubles me further. Spooking me into hiding would only work against them.

"Damn, Zane," I say, taking a step back. "Thanks for letting me know."

Now I don't know what to do. I'm scared at the possibility of being sought for anything in connection with Simon's passing. Learning that my mugshot is being flashed around the city makes matters worse—I keep thinking there must be some mistake. I did the right thing by calling the police. I am sure of it.

Did I miss something?

I reflect on what had happened and see myself walking away from the synagogue and turning back to face the bitter morning. This is what I feared. As I called for help and the help called the police, I waited for them to arrive against every instinct to run. But I knew I couldn't leave. I answered every question honestly and hid nothing but my dope kit. Simon and I were both caught up in this life, living by the sword.

I know that it could have just as easily been me.

Being a wanted man changes everything. I thought I was ready to ride a train straight to jail to turn myself in, but my fears get the best of me and throw a wrench into the spokes. "Something is wrong," I think out loud, as the headlight of the next train crests over the hill in the distance. Why am I wanted now and not after his passing?

Nothing feels good about this.

The train doors close, and the Max rail car speeds away, which leaves me motionless on the platform. There's no way in hell I'm going that way. Untying my plastic bag full of clothes, I pull out a hooded sweater, put it on, flip the hood up and give my best to Zane. Looking both ways, I step off the curb and cross the train tracks. Boarding the platform on the opposite side, I wait for the next train to pull up and get me as far away from the city as humanly possible.

10

LAY LOW

Once again, I'm at a loss. All I can think of is that any trail I may have paved must have gone cold over the past week I spent cooped up in Hooper. Since no one, as far as I know—cops included—can pursue a patient undergoing detox or even be made aware of their location, I know I have the jump on them.

Turning myself in isn't entirely out of the question, but it's no longer as simple as I need it to be. I don't know if they'll want to keep me for questioning or for how long. The thought of the police trying to pin Simon's overdose on me stirs up a throbbing migraine. Boarding the next train headed to the 42nd Train Station, I cross my fingers that the Transit police won't be checking for fares at the next stop.

The coast is clear. I bound up the all too familiar concrete steps and blend in with the crowd. Rounding the elevator, I watch my feet skim across the overpass and walk shoulder to shoulder with a sea of working hipster types. Passing 24 Hour Fitness, I hook right and make my way to the corner at Halsey Street. I'm betting Kat and Jay have staked their claim earlier this morning.

Long married, Kat and Jay are a semi-homeless staple in this area. A talented artist, Kat likes to spend her days posted up by the

I-84 off-ramp intersection, where cars line up at a streetlight when heading into the 42nd Hollywood District. With a captive audience, Kat can paint all day long, making fanciful scenes of colorful fairies to brighten up her otherwise dreary surroundings. Her canvas of choice is cardboard squares, so she skips the gesso, creating real street art that she sells or sometimes gives away to motorists. I imagine people appreciate her effort to offer something of value compared to flying a sign and begging for change.

Whenever she needs to rest her feet, Jay will take over, hawking her art through driver-side windows and chatting them up in ninety-second intervals. Together they've amassed a lot of regulars over the years and are highly territorial of their corner. From time to time, they may secure a temporary roof over their head, hence their semi-homelessness, but are often on the corner as early as two or three in the morning to beat out the competition and get the worm.

About thirty years my senior, they are both not only my friends, but also the eyes and ears of the streets around here. They know everybody, including most of the police that patrol this area, and play a pivotal role in keeping the peace. While uncommon, I have seen Jay drive a bad seed out of this area on more than one occasion with threats of a beat down if they crossed paths again. Within reason, the streets can be a somewhat tight-knit community, as long as it's understood that anyone will screw you over the moment they have a chance.

Kat and Jay are different, coming from different times and different rules. If they accept you into their world, you can always count that they will step up to take care of their own. Jay has gotten me right more times than I can remember, often letting me work his corner for a half hour to put ten or twenty bucks in my pocket. That camaraderie goes both ways—if asked I'll hold down their corner while they take off to handle business, whatever it may be. What goes around comes around.

Walking up to their corner, I lean in to give Kat a hug and it surprises Jay to see me. He jumps up to greet me, knocking over the five-gallon bucket he was sitting on. He comes in for a hug, and as he pulls away, flips the hood of my sweater over my head.

"Let's walk," he insists.

Drawing me away from his location, I can tell I'm dealing with serious Jay, rather than just my familiar easy-going friend.

"Welcome back from detox. How you feeling?" His tongue flicks between his missing front teeth.

"Been better, honestly." I pull out a half-smoked cigarette I picked up from off the ground on my way over and twist off the filter. I snap a match, inhale a deep drag and let the smoke curl from my lips. "Jay, what's going on?"

"Too much to have you around." He hooks my neck with his arm. "Detectives rolled by yesterday and flashed your mugshot. Told 'em we haven't seen you around here for a bit. They're out for you but wouldn't say why. Look kid, I saw it in their eyes—they're gonna' find you."

I exhale a mixture of smoke and confusion. There is obviously some mistake—something doesn't sit well about this whole situation. I could turn myself in and clear my name, but with no idea of what I am wanted for, it's too much to process. I don't feel right about this.

I turn to Jay, asking for one last favor.

"I know it's a lot to ask, but can I borrow a couple of bucks?"

"Borrow? Or have?" he asks. We both know they are two very different things, but I'm sure he's only giving me a hard time.

"Either or?"

"'*Either or*' my ass." A wad of cash pops out of his pocket and he peels off a five-dollar bill, dangling it in the air before me. "You know I always got your back."

I snatch the cash before the wind takes it for a ride. "That means a lot, man. Now, you know what's coming, right?" I hold out my arms.

"Back off! Don't make me change me mi—"

"Too late!" I wrap my arms around him and give a hug. "And

promise me you'll pass this on to Kat. Thank you both, for everything."

He breaks the hold and pushes me back. "Tell you what. I promise to pass it on, if you'll promise to pay me back in person."

I look him dead in the eyes and smile.

Back at the 42nd Avenue Transit Center, I straighten out my five dollars and slide it in the ticket machine. Snatching my change, I pocket the fare somewhere I won't lose it and wait for the next train heading away from town. Riding around aimlessly wasn't in the cards today, but I need to settle down somewhere I can safely stay put, unquestioned. With Mom and Dad flying in later this evening, it makes sense to wait for their arrival at the airport and go from there. A red line train screeches up with "Airport" emblazoned in yellow LEDs.

I cherish and appreciate the brief stint of freedom that allows me to lower my heart rate and enjoy the vacation I am setting out on. While using, one of my favorite ways to enjoy a day off was to acquire an all-day train ticket and ride the rail line from bitter end to bitter end. Hillsboro to Gresham will always be a beautiful experience no matter the weather. The Oregon countryside is sometimes all it takes to brighten my day, assuming I'm able to prop my eyes open wide enough to see it. Trains are also a nice, dry respite from rain for the comfortably numb. I can nod out to the dull rhythm of the tracks beneath me and feel untouchable, going nowhere fast.

Arriving at the airport, the rest of today will be a wash, as it rightfully should be. After checking the flight schedule, I head to the baggage claim and settle deep into a seat, waiting for the evening to fall. I read the *Willamette Week* and bury my face in the paper. My skin feels stale and thin like rice paper, chalky as the Suboxone is painstakingly processing itself out of my system. Both my knees enact a haunted restlessness that aches with abandon. Grateful for Hooper and the avoidance of withdrawal at full bore, I reassure myself that this could be much, much worse. I also know this action is a step in the right direction, then debate, prod and torment that idea until the sun sets outside.

A young Polynesian girl in University of Hawai'i sweatpants passes by and I spring up from my seat, hoping to find myself in the right place at the right moment for once. It's easy to spot the arrival of a plane from Hawai'i—there's always at least one passenger carrying packaged Macadamia nuts or a 'Ukulele case lazily strung over a shoulder. And there he is. I see my dad arriving with the crowd, wearing a thick sweater, well prepped for the contrasting Portland weather. My mom follows suit.

Wasting no time, I cut them off with an apprehensive smile and open arms, welcoming them back to the city.

"Aloha!" I greet them privately, with toned-down excitement that dissipates among the commotion. Dad smiles while Mom shakes her head. Visibly angry, her eyes stretch wide open and she explodes like a volcano.

"Jordan! Why aren't you in jail?!" she says, upset that I'm not where I am supposed to be. "You said you would be in jail." She looks as though I have manipulated her, confused as to why I'm not upholding my end of the bargain.

Dad's head slowly shakes back and forth, his eyes elated to see me.

"Jordan! Why aren't you in—"

"Mom, shh! Please keep it down. Look, there's cops all around here and some of them may be looking for me. I'm not sure why. I think it must be a mistake and hope it has nothing to do with Simon. I don't know—it could be lots of things." I grab my neck, releasing the tension pent up over the day. My shoulders settle down from the scrunched-up ruffling.

"Look, I went to detox," I say, "*and* stayed the whole time. I was on my way to turn myself in like we talked about, but a friend intervened and said the police are looking for me. It was suggested I get out of Downtown—so I did. I didn't know what else to do, so I came here."

Nothing. No response, at least not verbally.

"For what it's worth, I didn't get high," I say. I slowly nod my head in agreement with my own statement, awaiting some response, which unexpectedly comes first from Dad.

"Well," he begins, "if what you say is true, it sounds like they're not only looking for you but perhaps for answers. Either way, it's so good to see you!"

I flip my palms upwards—I have no idea. "I don't have any answers. I told them the truth and left nothing out. I've got nothing to hide."

His gaze seems to trail off. Turning to look at Mom, he speaks toward her but at me. "Son, I have no idea what's going on, but we are here for one reason and one reason alone—we are here to save your life."

Her head nods in agreement, reading between the lines.

Helping out with the luggage seems like the least I can do while the three of us board a shuttle and head to the rental car facility. Sandwiched between the two of them, I can't believe I am doing it, that I am making my way out of this mess. Neither of them would have expected me to greet them at the airport, so there's no way they planned for anything other than a single queen bed at their boutique hotel. Finding street parking outside of the inspiring architecture, Dad and I unload the luggage with a purpose. As we head inside to the River Place Hotel, the sun sets lazily, painting the Willamette a rich, muted gold. We can't hide that three people are checking in instead of two, so we don't even bother. My mom has an honest flair about her that reassures the receptionist that there is a bigger picture unfolding. Failing to disappear into the background, the receptionist calls me forward and hands me a hotel key card tucked inside a white paper card holder. A gentle bellman steps forward and insists on seeing us to our room. My mom insists he try out a box of chocolate Macadamia nuts.

"A gift of Aloha, from us to you," she says with a relaxed smile.

The bellman's look of confusion quickly switches to gratitude. The small box of chocolates stretches much further than any monetary tip, especially as he shares how he has always dreamed of a trip to Paradise with his wife. Talk of beaches, lava, Hula and everything else touristy fills the elevator. I remove myself from the conversation and fall inward to my rippled mind, envisioning how nothing sounds better than a hot shower and a warm shot. The aches are returning, building inside like a sneeze you can feel coming and just can't hold back.

A hotel has long been a luxury not afforded in my current lifestyle. Now in the room, I head straight for the shower, making sure no one else needs to use the toilet first. The water steams the mirrors as I undress and step out of a pile of clothes. The water burns my back, a painful reminder that I've forgotten one of the simplest, most basic human functions—check the water temperature first before regretting it. Once the water is tolerable, I let it build back up as my skin morphs from pink to red. Scrubbing as hard as one can with a soft washcloth, I can't exfoliate the heavy dirt rooted in the cracks of my bare flesh. Instead, I'll try to burn it out with heat, expunging toxins as I inhale the heavy steam.

Exiting the shower, I dress my damp body and step into a conversation between my parents about our changed plans. None of us feel good about the situation—we're all concerned over the worst-case scenario. Without knowing what I am up against, I resign to the only method I understand to get through trying times —to move forward and never look back.

Looking around the small room, I decide to sleep on the couch and in response to my parent's protest, remind them both that it is a considerable improvement from a sidewalk. Pushing down on the sofa cushions with both hands, I look toward the closet hoping to find an extra blanket, when a sharp knock raps on the door.

Our heads snap in unison like Ghidorah. My mom, the first to her feet, instinctively puts herself between me and the threat of whoever is out there. Room service wasn't announced, which seems odd, and she closes in on the peephole to see who in their right mind could be knocking at this hour.

Twisting her head back toward us, her shoulders drop in relief. "It's Tim, the bellman," she says.

Dad shoots me a smile, but I am still expecting the worst. Besides having nowhere to go and no way out, I don't trust Tim, having seen sting operations play out before. I know the hallway could be lined with officers. At a certain point, when you've seen and lived through so much, and watched COPS enough, it's hard to startle your senses. Knowing that no one can put me through worse situations than I have put myself through has dulled my trepidation, which helps me brace for the worst.

I watch her open the door. My heart bumps. I wait for Tim to step aside and let an army of officers rush our room. Instead, the bellman stands at the doorway, informing my mom that the hotel staff insists on upgrading our rooms for us.

"Upgrade our room?" she asks, surprised and confused.

"Yes, Ma'am. It is our wish to move the three of you into a much more comfortable room, furnished with two beds instead of just, well—one. And it just so happens that a suite is vacant and we can accommodate your . . .'*Ohana.*" There's the smile. "At no additional charge, of course."

"Wow. That is a very gracious offer," she says, "but we couldn't. We've already dirtied the room, used the shower and made ourselves at home. That would mean double the work for the cleaners, and that's n—"

"Do not worry about such small things," he says. Tim hands over two new key cards pinched in his grip. Not wanting to be rude, Mom takes the keys and opens up for a hug.

11

PAPER TRAIL

Settling into our new suite, Dad unpacks his clothes once again and transfers them methodically into his dresser drawers. It is a funny habit of his, at least in my eyes, and one that wasn't passed down to me. I've always been able to live out of a suitcase or a backpack, even on the rare occasions I found lodging that would take me in. Either way, I never put forth too much effort to make a roadhouse my home.

Watching my dad bumble around and arrange his clothing with sincerity is reassuring. I have missed him for so long and I can't believe we are together again. Sinking myself into the edge of my queen bed, I pull up my legs and cross them beneath me. I need to control and quiet my mind—I am unsure of what to do with myself.

As he continues to unpack, I notice a new package of Hawaiian Host Maui Caramacs in his luggage, the corner of the box rising from his ocean of socks like an atoll island. My mouth waters at the taste of home. I lean over, swallow my saliva and silently pluck the box from his suitcase. Holding them up for my mom to see, I take her smile as permission to separate the box from the package wrapper. Leaning back in my bed, fourteen chocolates dwindle to none as my offer to share what's not mine is politely declined.

My stomach hurts as I nuzzle the lamp to the side with the edge of my hand and set the empty box on top of the nightstand. I suppose I could have gotten up and pitched it in the trash, but I can clean up this mess later.

A soft thud resonates throughout the room as I lean back against my pillow, smashing into the headboard and interrupting the Pundit on TV. Mom twists her head toward me to catch a glance, but we are all burned out, and small talk doesn't seem necessary. She keeps stealing looks as if my frail frame could vanish at any moment. Besides, though barely 6 p.m., Dad is already snoring, having fallen asleep amid a world of lights and background noise. Neither of us intend on interrupting him.

It doesn't take long before I lose interest in politics, violence and voting. Nothing I'm watching fits into the pinhole of my worldview or the problems I am facing. All that troubles me now is the recurring thought that it's time to stretch my legs. The muscles within feel so taut and rigid that the inability to relax is overwhelming. The challenge to sit still for longer than a moment's notice drives me to prop myself up and launch off the bed. Unsettled, I step into the space between the two beds in the room and quietly speak over Dad.

"Mom, we need to feed the meter, or they'll probably ticket your car. If you have a couple of bucks, I'll run downstairs and take care of it for you."

She pauses for a moment, then motions to her black purse on the chair wrapped up in her light blue windbreaker. Reaching into her bag, I withdraw her wallet, and as a known thief, keep it in full view of her. My fingers flip through the twenties until I spot a five. I see that she still carries extra cash when she travels—there's maybe a couple hundred dollars here, more cash than I've seen in years. I slip the cash into my pocket, grab the room key and kiss her on the cheek. Stepping into my shoes without tying them, I walk out of the room as a sharp click behind me echoes down the hallway.

"Mom, what's wrong?" I put the key card down on the desk and sit next to her on the bed. "Are you okay?" She's staring straight ahead at the door, her light smile and tired eyes make her seem as peaceful as a saint.

Her silence drags on for a moment. "You know," she whispers, "after you walked out the door, I got hit with such an immediate sense of failure. I lunged toward the peephole and watched you disappear into a darkened blur." She puffs her cheeks and combs her fingers through her hair. "I'm sorry. I shouldn't be telling you this. I don't mean to—"

"Mom, it's okay." My hand curls over her shoulder. "I know I'm not the only one going through this."

"No, you're not," she groans. "You're absolutely not. It's just, I glanced through the peephole, watched you slink out of sight and suddenly you were gone again. I realized I had let you slip away and I was so angry with myself that I didn't run after you. I ran to the window but couldn't see our car, then wanted to chase after you, but realized I couldn't force you to choose life.

"It was an unsettling, almost sobering comfort. So much of this is out of my hands, and as much as I want the best for you, I know that ultimately, it's about what you want for yourself." Her eyes lock onto mine. "Of course your father was still snoring. I didn't dare wake him up. I felt a familiar helplessness and turned to prayer. Then I went to check my wallet."

I feel so worthless, ashamed and insensitive as she relates my own personal demons as her worst fears.

"Mom, I would never steal from you, though I did take a box of chocolates to deliver to the front desk. They gave us these as a thank you." I hold out some vouchers for a complimentary breakfast in the morning and rub my eyes with my palms. "I also grabbed some earplugs."

Smiling down on Dad while he adjusts to the time difference, I reach for the remote, lay back on my bed and flip through the channels. I try tuning out my apprehensions, but my mind is on my life and what matters most. What have I become? I want to be excited about where I am going tomorrow but I can't stop obsessing about where I have been. As night comes, we decide to stay put, catch up on much needed rest and order room service.

Early morning rolls into the toasty room where the air is set to a temperature worthy of soft throw blankets and sleeping with socks. Staring at the ceiling, I've failed at navigating through the future of leaving this world behind. The pillow is cold against my cheek, exactly how I like it, yet I am still wide awake, my mind rambling while my body begs to rest.

While I had slept outside for the better part of last year, I never got used to the cardboard mattress where the biting cold radiates up from the concrete below. The thought had often occurred that somewhere along Dante's many levels of Hell is a pit stop where you can shiver from cold yet sweat bullets from withdrawal.

Across the room, I sense Mom is also awake, though I have noticed no movement in the dim lighting. She lies in bed, next to my dad, barely breathing.

I wonder if she is thinking of the day she brought me into this world. Or how she pulled me to her chest and saw a light in my eyes that was so fascinated and interested in the unknown. Her love for me is more than enough to lift my spirits up and carry me until I learn to love myself. If that's not enough, there is a support system back home I can lean on until I learn to walk on my own accord.

That was how they raised me, to help others and care more for them than myself. Wherever I went wrong, it was only a bad turn. I can still correct the course.

I wonder if she is curious about how long it will take until I learn to laugh authentically again, and not just the nervous chuckle spewed with a mixture of burned-out confidence. The sound of my laugh—if she remembers—has always been uniquely identifiable, projected from the depths of my belly with a rapid-fire onslaught and no care in the world.

I wonder if she remembers.

The waitress tops off my coffee cup, leaving room for cream and even more for sugar. Hunkering down to eat like a linebacker, I take sips of orange juice between bites of crumbly croissants. My manners seem to still come naturally. Across the table, my parents savor this nearly forgotten sense of normalcy.

"You know, I always admired that about you."

I wipe my mouth with a napkin and stretch my jaw. "What's that?" I ask.

"How you eat. Slow, methodical, purposeful. The way you rest a hand in your lap when you're not using it."

I take a sip of my full coffee, careful not to slurp. "Don't be weird, Mom."

She smiles back. "Your brothers were never like that! I have no idea where you get it from."

Dad reaches around her for a roll. "Not from me," he jokes.

I crack a smile, which splits me down the middle. We shouldn't linger in this city any longer than necessary, and with the detectives searching for me, the sooner we skip town, the more likely we are to make it.

Finishing my plate, I push back from the table and watch Dad leave a sizable tip sticking out from under his plate. It's his way of showing his appreciation for what was so freely shared with us. Looking at the money, I consider how hard I have to work to thumb through that much cash and shake my head.

Because our plans have changed, Dad heads back upstairs to see what he can do about changing our flights to get us home earlier. Mom and I continue through the lobby and walk outside. The hotel is near a lazy hill and harbor that overlooks a glassy

Willamette River. An unoccupied bench near the bike path calls our names.

I sit down and rub the small of my back with my fist. My chest feels tight. A quick shiver runs down my spine. Scooting closer to Mom, I rest my head on her shoulder without asking if she minds. She has always been here for me, I realize, whether or not I wanted it. The scene surrounding us is beautiful. Cars in the distance rumble over a bridge as the wildlife makes do with Mother Nature below. Hawks are flying overhead, so free and unrestricted.

Looking up toward the heavens, my eyes lock onto an Osprey circling high above the river's surface. The bird swoops again and again until out of nowhere it falls from the sky, plunging into the frigid water below.

I pop forward, transferring the weight of my head off of my mom's shoulders and lurch to my feet. I don't know what's wrong with the bird, only that it crashed and needs help. Desperate, I turn towards Mom.

A palm lands on my shoulder, a smile on her face. "It's okay, it's okay," she says. She's both trying to reassure me and hold back her laughter. "The bird is just fishing, Jordan. It's completely natural."

A second later, the hawk pops up with a fish in its mouth.

"You know, despite my biggest fears, you haven't changed much," she says. "Here we are, in the fight for your life, and among all the chaos, fear and anxiety you must be feeling, you still exhibit the same childhood tendencies to care about other living things."

Dad welcomes us back into the suite with his palms lifted, celebrating that he had bumped up our flights. Our new itinerary is now slated to fly us out tomorrow, instead of later in the week. I welcome this news with relief, but my heart also sinks. Something is holding me back—my foot is nailed to the floor. Running my hand through my hair, I feel as though I can't catch a break. I hate to say it because I know what it means.

"Hey, Mom, Dad. I can't get on that plane," I say. I know exactly what this means. Dad's smile tumbles into oblivion. "I can't get on the plane because I don't have any identification." My arms drop and slap my thighs, the sound resonating through the silence. "I wouldn't make it past check in."

Time slows as the reality settles. I am right, and we all know it. There is only one way out and with time against us, whatever I need to do to get a license or some form of identification has to happen quickly. A leisure day in the suite soon flies out the door as we pack up everything and head to the car. Stressed and defiant, I bum a cigarette from a hotel guest smoking outside and shake off the cold. My parents continue on and enter the rental car while I hold up our caravan and puff the smoke down.

Off to the DMV, Mom looks out the window and agrees that we're in a bad spot. Back in the heart of Downtown, I think she fears that I am once again among a world of routines and triggers. As much as I love this town, I know that there is no love in the heart of the city.

Everywhere I look, I remember spilling blood from a needle tip at some point. From the riverside to these bathrooms, under that bridge and behind those bushes. I see it on her face. She is concerned to no end, yet remains calm as a rock. None of us have any idea who or what has the power to reach out and snatch me from our mission, but there is no other choice. Parking the car as close to the entrance as possible, we step out together and walk toward the DMV on eggshells.

I don't even know where to start. With no paperwork, bills or mail to prove my identity, I don't know how far down this road I'll get. I'm banking that my picture on file will suffice as proof of person, but time will tell if that will be enough. There's also the paperwork from detox, which has my name and date of birth on it, though I don't know if that will help or hurt my case. Before entering the office, my mom calls a quick huddle and slips me a fifty-dollar bill along with her cell phone. Taking the money, I realize that while my habit was at least twice this amount a day, I can't remember a time when this much cash was handed to me at once. Closing my other hand around her phone, she instructs me to place it in my pocket.

"Just in case we get separated," she says.

I get it. As I head inside, my parents distance themselves a bit and hang a few steps behind me. Approaching the desk, I can see the two of them take a seat away from the entrance. There is no line or need to pull a number. I walk up to the desk without apprehension, knowing I have no other choice. Giving the man my name and a quick explanation for my visit, he rattles on his keyboard while I scribble out some paperwork. While I pay my fee, I steal a glance behind me and see Mom turn to Dad and whisper in his ear.

I imagine she is saying something to the tune of, "Gary, pay attention. He's going to run, and if he does, let him go. Once they pull his name up, the police will be called and he'll bolt. We can reach him on my phone, just be ready to let him go and we will find him again."

I am on high alert. The tension is thick. The wall clock is playing with me.

The man behind the computer is nice enough, but I can't get a clear reading. I focus on his eyes, searching for a telltale sign that he's alerted to something on his computer screen, but I see only his mundane eye movement. I must be gazing too intently.

He looks up from his computer with an awkward smile, my cue to focus my nervousness elsewhere. Outside the window, buses roll down 6th Avenue, their bypass safety valves hissing as they brake downhill. Once the clerk is ready, he asks for my application, which I fork over along with my payment. A quick glance over and he confirms it looks good with no further questioning. I try to sneak in one last read but to no avail—his glasses barely reflect the blue light of the monitor.

He plucks at the keyboard and coughs into his fist. I take my change and he motions for me to have a seat while they process my temporary paper license. Heading back toward my parents, my mom flicks a finger to usher me past them, reminding me to wait in the vacant seat closest to the entrance.

What a spot to put them in as I wait for my license or the police, whichever comes first. Perhaps it would be better to go outside for a cigarette or in for questioning. I can clear my name and move on. Answering their questions could put it to rest. I remind myself that I had been open and honest about Simon's overdose, forthright with each question posed by the police, detectives and medical examiner.

"Mr. Barnes."

I look up and see the temporary paper license hot off the press. To me, that paper looks like the golden ticket out of a chocolate bar. I don't believe it. We are good to go, and together, the three of us breathe a unified sigh of relief. Grabbing the paper, I look at the ID. I can't help but laugh at the address line. "Near Skidmore Fountain" is still my state-sponsored address.

In the car, I sit in the back seat and take one last look out of the rear window to make sure we're not being ambushed. Then I stare at the paper license in my hands while my eyes trace the edge of the ID onto my swollen forearm. Any distinction of knuckles has been rounded out and consumed by a pudgy mass—my fist and arm, filled with cellulitis, are the size of a man three times my body weight. Tracks run up and down my arm, riddled with tiny black and blue tattoos where contaminants in the dope have left their mark. Injecting between my fingers and into my knuckles, I had sought out every vein until they had all withered away. Warm to the touch and radiating heat, the swelling in my arm hasn't increased or decreased in recent weeks, lingering without a chance to heal. I feel and look like Hellboy, straight out of the Dark Horse comic universe.

"Eiji can help you with that," Mom promises. She looks back between the two seats at me while I study my hands.

"Who's that?"

Back home in Hawai'i, I am told of a miracle worker and family friend who operates a licensed acupuncture business from his beautiful home in Hawai'i Kai. As we head back to the hotel, Mom gets him on the line, explaining and describing what we are working with. I vaguely hear his voice, but it sounds as though he agrees. Somehow, he understands where I am coming from and says he is more than willing to help. Alerting him I was an IV drug user, she cautions him that none of us know what diseases I may be packing. I hear Eiji politely dismiss her concerns and advise her to bring me straight to him.

I stroke my right palm up and down my forearm, squeezing the solid bumps beneath the skin, finding a large, solid mass near my elbow. It's hard yet malleable. The skin above my knuckles are dry and cracked, the flesh is a muddled and crinkled canvas with underlying hues of blue. Nothing more than a human pincushion, I am dotted with pinpoint scabs. The entire length of my arm is spotted and bruised, like an archer who let off a whole quiver without a protective arm guard, the bowstring destroying the flesh with each progressive twang.

Sensing my restlessness, Mom decides that a sit-down dinner will beat room service, but we soon discover that The Old Spaghetti Factory is shut down for renovations. Disappointed, Dad circles the block on the hunt for other options. Reading my mind, he makes an executive decision and parks outside a sushi parlor.

The waitress seats us and dishes out utensils and menus.

"Excuse me, can we have chopsticks instead please?" I smile her way, knowing that back home I wouldn't have to ask.

"Everyone okay if we eat family style?" Dad flips his menu over.

Mom smiles and pulls out her phone. "I would love that. Why don't you two order and I'll call up the treatment center and see what we need to do. They're a few hours behind and should still be open."

"Awesome. I have a couple of questions for them as well, if you don't mind." I still know less than I would like about the program and their website left more questions than answers. It's as if every time I try to dig deeper, I keep hitting rock. I don't want to believe that I'm being kept in the dark on purpose.

"I don't know much either," Dad admits, "but I did visit their property a few years ago. I met with the Director to discuss a new canopy, but we ended up spending most of the sales call talking about you. After telling him I could only dream of seeing you in a treatment facility, he assured me that if I ever managed to bring you home, he would allow you to be admitted. His only caveat was that you needed to be ready to change, and I thank God you finally are."

I look down at the menu, knowing that it matters very little what I want. "Dad, you know that people like me almost nev—"

"Hi, this is Jeri Barnes, and I am sitting here with my husband and my son Jordan. We are in Portland right now and I can't believe that we found him. We'll be heading back to Hawai'i tomorrow. I'm wondering who I can talk to about getting him checked in as a new client?"

I lean in toward her phone call while Dad orders by pointing out items on the menu.

"Okay." Mom glances toward me. "Uh huh. Yes. Yes. Heroi—"

"And cocaine," I whisper.

"And cocaine. Correct." Mom scratches her cheek. "No, I don't believe he's on probation"—she looks for answers and I shake my head—"and he's not under any court orders." She pauses for a second. "Oh, really?" She goes silent for a minute and runs her fingers through her hair. "Wow, that's a lot." She pinches the bridge of her nose. "Yvonne, I can't even imagine how many people need help and I hope they all get it, but for what it's worth, my husband met with the Director a while ago and was told that if we could find Jordan and bring him to the program, we could get him in."

"Ask her how long the program is?" I whisper.

She holds up a finger to cut me off. "You can call me anyti—"

"Mom, ask her how lo—"

"We'll be looking forward to your call. Mahalo Yvonne." Mom hangs up her phone and takes a deep breath.

I stare at the exit. I know she heard me. "Why didn't you ask her how long the program is?"

She deflects my question. "I would think that if I were in your shoes, I would take any help I could get. Besides, I'm not even sure I can get you in. We'll know more after Yvonne makes some calls."

"They'll let you in," Dad promises. "I know a man of character when I see one and the Director is a man of his word."

"I don't doubt that, but Yvonne just told me they have a significant wait-list and are operating at full capacity. There is more demand for beds than space available. Priority goes first and foremost to pregnant women, then active IV drug users."

"Jeri, he'll get in. Let's just wait for their call and enjoy dinner."

Back at the hotel, I am surprised by how drained I feel from the stresses of the day. Mom seems to be right there with me, mentally run through the wringer. She looks like she needs to catch up on sleep. I realize we're both worried sick about each other.

Dad flips through the hotel brochure. "Honey, look. It says here that the spa is equipped with a Japanese Hotsi bath and steam room. Doesn't that remind you of our time stationed in Japan?"

"Let me see." She bends down the corner of the brochure. "That looks amazing. I say we do it!"

I can't decide if a steam bath sounds appealing. I'm burning up as it is, sitting in an air-conditioned room.

"Why don't you guys go ahead—my body is already on fire."

"Are you sure?" Dad asks.

"Yeah, go on without me. I'll try and get some rest."

I can tell Mom's not happy with the idea when she decides for the two of them not to go. I realize there's no way we're ever splitting up. If I stay, they stay, but they deserve a break and some stress relief after all I've put them through. Selfishly, I also don't want to be left alone. Admittedly, I don't trust myself.

The sauna and Hotsi bath shake me to the core. I had introduced foreign contaminants into my body for so long that sweating brings me back to the fold, back to where I belong. I am here and the time is now. My breath is heavy as I taste the wet steam filling my scratched lungs. I exhale with the rattle of a loose exhaust pipe and continue dripping sweat onto the bench. I feel clogged yet purified. It's a fleeting feeling, but for the first time, I entertain the self-talk that perhaps I have the wherewithal to change my stars. In fact, if I can drop this ball and chain and actually pull it off, maybe I can go on to realize great things.

For once, my muscles unwind and my shoulders drop. I feel relaxation encompass me while I let out an unholy yawn. Exhausted, my long hair slips into my face, but I don't brush it away since I'm still compulsively anxiety ridden.

Once I've had enough, I step into the refreshing shower. I feel like I'm getting clean, but I still can't wash the dirt out of the cracks in my skin. Earlier, Mom had commented on how a rancid stench seemed to be emanating from my pores. As I reach for my clothes, I know that getting clean is going to be a long, drawn-out process.

12

BROKEN WINGS

I wake up to hasty preparations to depart the city. Luggage is crammed with belongings—dirty clothes are mixed with clean. I split what little clothing I own between my parent's luggage as I attempt to gauge the weight of each suitcase with miserable bicep curls. I haven't worked out in years, so anyone's guess is better than mine.

Mom wants to arrive at the airport at least three hours before our departure, which seems excessive, but I am merely along for the ride. We grab coffees to go, check out with the front desk and drop off the rental car near the airport. Checking under my seat for valuables, I pause briefly and remember that I have lost everything worth keeping long ago. Though Hooper was a gift that set me straighter than expected, I still feel like a rat stuck to a glue trap who can't peel my foot away. That first step—it's all I need to gain some desperately needed traction.

I'm happy to be going home for many reasons, but the biggest one is this guttural reckoning to escape the rat race. Rubbing my palms over my eyelids, I strain my tunnel vision and mentally dissect all the garbage I'm leaving behind as we approach the TSA checkpoint.

Earlier in the day, Mom had voiced her concern about the possibility that security could flag and arrest me, but her apprehensions didn't quite resonate with me. If my warrants would trip me up, so be it. I figured when everything else in life is so out of control, acceptance should come naturally.

My lungs expand as I take a deep breath. Here I am, face to face with a TSA officer whose demeanor is perfectly traditional and conservative. I am judging him by the clean-cut hairstyle and how he seems to treat today no different from his first day on the job.

Still flanked by both my parents, the agent calls my dad forward first, but gets the three of us as a total package—my mom makes sure of it. From here on out, there is no way that my parents will leave me behind like unattended baggage.

I hold my temporary driver's license in my hand and have no idea if this paper ID will fly. I watch as Dad withdraws his military ID and hands it over, his name cross-checked to his boarding pass and initialed by the agent. A polite discussion about his service occurs that doesn't make much sense to surrounding civilians. He's free to go.

I'm next and I avoid eye contact while purposefully distracting myself. Uneventfully, we pass through like cattle. As my mom brings up the rear, we are ushered through the last section of security when a loud "Sir!" catches us off guard.

We all look back, but the agent only appears interested in addressing my dad.

"The best years of my life was being stationed in Hawai'i," he says. "Have a safe flight, sir."

I can't believe it.

We are home free.

As my parents quietly thank God for our passage, I thank Dad for his service.

Clearing security, my hunger gets the best of me and I suggest killing time in a restaurant. Taking a seat, we place our carry-ons on the floor and kick them under the table. My appetite is barking and I want to eat everything.

Growing up in Hawai'i, I have always loved seafood, and while the clams looked good, the oyster special sounds interesting. I've never had them before and figure turning over a new leaf means a willingness to try new things.

"Do you guys mind if I get the oysters?" I ask.

"Oysters? No, I don't mind, though the last thing you need right now is food poisoning." My mom is the realist, while my dad throws caution to the wind.

"Son, order whatever you want."

A smile breaches my mom's face and she just has to share. "How do you go from homeless . . . to oysters?"

I hold my hands up. "Hey! I prefer residentially challenged!"

All jokes aside, I can't finish the plate—the texture isn't up my alley.

As Pualani Gold Members, my parents are allowed to board early, and naturally I follow, taking my seat directly in front of them. Before we boarded, I bought a magazine on a borrowed dime with no means of being able to pay it back. I have been selfish for so long, old habits die hard. Behind me, my dad, an avid reader, tries to flip on his overhead light but notices it's burned out. Thinking it odd, he tries to use my mom's, but quickly drops his hand to his lap when hers doesn't work either.

"That's odd," he says, tapping my shoulder from between the seats. "Does your light work?"

I reach up, clicking the button a few times before giving up, twisting my hand back and forth. "Nope."

"Honey, I hate to say it, but I don't think we're going anywhere." His positive outlook crumbles.

Mom and I both know that he knows what he's talking about. Having retired as a Naval Commander, Dad had followed his childhood aspirations of being a fighter pilot. Graduating at the top of his class from the Navy's Officer Candidate School, the only thing that stood between him and his dream was his eyesight, closing that chapter before it even opened. When the Military Vision Standards wouldn't allow exceptions or the use of glasses, they offered him the option to be a fighter pilot's navigator, a painful alternative. He couldn't do it and opted instead for Naval Intelligence. In short, he knows planes and a problem when he sees one.

My poor mom, bless her soul, is stressing out behind me, probably thinking I am being arrested and the airline is faking an electrical issue just to stall the plane. She could be spot on or not—I have no idea.

The flight attendant comes across the loudspeaker, clearing the air. "Ladies and gentlemen, I apologize for the inconvenience, but it looks as though we are having a minor technical issue on board today. If you can bear with us for a few more minutes, we will provide an update shortly. Thank you."

I turn around in my seat and see Mom's face drained of color, blending in with the rest of the pale vacation-goers hoping to see some sun. Outside on the tarmac, aircraft maintenance technicians buzz around the fuselage. They come and go, retreating from sight under the bowels of our plane.

"Mom, I think we will be okay," I whisper. "There's nobody coming for me." Closing my eyes, I click the button on my armrest, lean back as far as possible and try everything in my power to lie still.

"Ladies and gentlemen, thank you for your patience while we assessed the situation."

I open my eyes. I've been awake the whole time.

"We were hoping to find the broken part locally, but just learned that the nearest replacement electrical component is at Seattle–Tacoma International Airport. So, our two options would be to either disembark the entire plane and wait three hours for the part to be brought to Portland, or take off now and fly the half hour up to Seattle, then continue onward to Hawai'i. The captain has decided to fly up to Seattle."

Murmurs in the cabin echo confusion about how a broken part

that prohibits us from flying to Hawai'i somehow isn't necessary to fly to Seattle. The logic is lost on me, but that concern is above my pay grade.

Landing in Seattle, the flight staff makes up for our inconvenience with free meal coupons and offers of hotel vouchers if the repair takes longer than necessary. As a bonus, every passenger is given a one-way flight voucher and called up by name to receive their travel coupon. After grabbing mine, I look at the date and see it's slated to expire while I'll still be in treatment. I jam the ticket into my back pocket for safekeeping, just in case.

Everything, it seems, has finally fallen into place, from the acupuncturist back home on standby to the three of us being able to leave Portland. My stomach grumbles again and we leave the gate in search of the closest open table at a restaurant.

The signs say to seat ourselves, so we take the least sticky table available. I dive into the menu while Mom apologizes in advance, then passes on the food and orders a beer. I know she feels guilty about having a drink in front of me even though it wouldn't bother me. She looks spent and the last thing in the world I am craving is alcohol.

I remind her that I am the one with the problem, not her, and she caves and orders the largest beer on tap. I'm disappointed that she drinks cautiously in my presence, taking her time along with small sips. I know she doesn't drink often and doubt something has changed over the past few years, unless I drove her to drink. I ask Dad, who confirms that isn't the case.

"Dad, if you want a drink, go for it. Not that it's my place, but I have no problem with it. I'm surprised you guys held out this long."

He dismisses my provocation. Dinner comes and goes, and with it is an opportunity to catch up with my parents in our first real conversation in years. Looking towards Mom, Dad describes all the relief she must be feeling following all those nights of sleepless worry. On one hand, it feels great to know she won't be suffering on my behalf anymore. Yet on the other, it feels horrible to see the pain I knew I must have been causing confirmed.

"That doesn't really help, Dad."

"You're right, you're right. I'm sorry."

Poking at my plate, I let the dust settle for a moment. It is hard to connect with Dad but through no fault of his own. I realize that every discussion moving forward will probably be masked with a protective filter to keep me in a good place. I wonder if everyone will always be on edge with me.

As Dad changes the subject, I am surprised to learn just how large of a support system exists for me back home, where friends, family and parishioners from my parent's church have been praying for my freedom from addiction.

This is the first time I realize how widespread the knowledge of my addiction has become, and though initially embarrassed and ashamed, I knew it was out of my control. It's understandable that my parents needed support for what I've put them through. It takes a moment to sink in that close friends have been praying for me daily, with one couple even hanging my name in their hallway to remind them to pray for me every time they pass it.

I'm not quite sure how to feel about it all. In my dad's eyes, I need to be grateful for the miracle of us all being reunited, because he knows that without God, there's no way we'd be sitting here today. In my eyes, I can only picture Simon's death and how life can end so abruptly.

Face to face with his body, my openness to consider any continuation beyond death crumbled, and with it went an already challenged faith. The moments after death, I discovered, were a lot of photos and a single body bag, and little else. I wanted to feel a sense that he went somewhere better, but was left wanting. I couldn't see how any soul escaped that tragedy. Besides, I've always felt that if I believed in God, I'd surely be destined for Hell, so the stance of a disbeliever is actually one of crippling convenience.

Another door closed to save me from walking through. I am a far cry from the young blonde altar boy and student at Our Lady of Sorrows Catholic School who was once so sweet to his teacher. Dad and I flank the entire spectrum—because of my addiction, his faith is stronger than ever, while mine is all but a memory.

I cast the thought away, knowing that I'll cross that bridge if I ever get to it. For now, I am happy to be heading home with my flight voucher, knowing that I have a way back if I change my mind.

A pixilated voice on the intercom announces that our chariot is waiting. On board, every passenger is excited about the long flight. The only exception is the poor man seated in front of me who must wonder why a grown man is kicking the back of his seat. Regardless of how hard I focus, I can't help it—the spasms, cramps and restlessness won't allow me to sit still long enough to act my age.

13

EIJI

(PRON. EH-JEE)

The sweltering island air slaps me in my face and my core temperature rises rampantly under the hot Hawaiian sun. Strangers bless me as I sneeze until I lose count, taking me back to a childhood stuffed with allergies and vindictiveness. Wiping my hands on my jeans, I know that whether or not it feels good to be here, I am home.

A quick tug at the neck of my long sleeve shirt vents the stickiness but does little to cool me off. It's easy enough to conceal track marks in a cooler climate like the Pacific Northwest, where junkies burrow under hoodies and heavy coats to go about their business and hide in plain sight among the living. It's different back here on the islands, where I'm either overdressed or wearing my heart on my sleeve.

Once we grab our bags, Mom learns through a voicemail that a bed will be available for me come Monday morning. Treatment is there for the taking, and for the first time I consider where this path will lead. Until now, with no confirmation or acceptance, I considered where I would go if I wasn't welcome anywhere. Now, moving with a purpose, we head across the island to the windward side where my parents live among a lush landscape, both vibrant and reviving.

I'm the last one out of the car, slow to move and slow to think. My middle brother Jonathan welcomes us home and inspects me up and down. He reaches up to hug me like a python, unaware of my frailty. His curly hair flaps in a Kona wind as he slaps my back.

Offloading is a workout and I need a moment to catch my breath. Jonathan's dog Sierra, a spry Labrador mix, is off leash, zipping from me to the water's edge and back again, panting in excitement.

The property is affectionately dubbed "Serenity Pointe." Mom and Dad live in a small, two-bedroom home, with less than nine-hundred square feet under their aging roof. It's packed with memories, salt air and every keepsake us boys have left behind.

My brother Jonathan and his dog rent the second home on the long rectangular lot. Behind him in the backyard is my parents' home, but that depends on who you ask. Mom considers the ocean her front yard and often asks people if they agree.

When friends come to visit, a narrow, long driveway leads them past the front house and onto their lot. Barely large enough to turn a truck around in, most people have to back their way out when it's time to go, though nobody ever really wants to leave.

The label "backyard" is debatable because it's easy to get turned around after stepping foot on their property and ringing their pull-string nautical bell. When it's high tide, the water splashes a rock wall littered with crabs holding on for dear life. The backyard is surrounded on three sides by Kāne'ohe Bay, the largest sheltered body of water in the main Hawaiian Islands.

The view always puts my troubles into perspective. Violating every set-back law known to man, this property couldn't be built today or rebuilt after destruction by fire or hurricane.

Grandfathered in from long ago, their backyard is a peninsula, jutting out into the bay like a grounded barge. On the port side, you can plant a palm on the kitchen wall and scoop saltwater in the other, the water level just inches below their seawall. On the starboard side, beyond a channel thirty feet wide, is an ancient Hawaiian fishpond that's been feverishly preserved through the ages.

This property is, and forever will be, a healing place—the sound of the ocean has always settled my soul. My favorite place on the lot has always been their "guest room," a private, free-standing fabric "Tentalow" that was the original prototype from when Dad first won the job at Molokai Ranch years and years ago.

Both I and the family business were still young back then, the company teetering the fine line between success and bankruptcy. Struggling to operate a small company with Mom after retirement, this single project paved the way for a future that drove them to become the largest awning company in the state. Touching the fabric walls, I feel the ocean breathe outside as I sink into the queen bed. The salt air tickles my skin. Below the ceiling fan, I rub my fingers through my hair and close my eyes.

Kalaniana'ole Highway is more than breathtaking. The two-lane road wraps the easternmost point of our island and is always the preferred route when headed to Hawai'i Kai from the windward side. The highlight of the snaking drive carved through the cliff is the view of the Pacific Ocean as the rock sinks into the vast blue expanse.

Outside of my window I see coves, lookouts and finally the world-famous Hālona blowhole. A forceful spray of sea mist blasts off thirty or more feet into the air, surfing the trade winds like ancestral spirits at a jumping off point. This is a powerful route to head down for any purpose.

I think back to my childhood road trips as we pass the parked tour buses and know that today's not the day to play tourist. The worst place to be on the whole trip is in the driver's seat where Dad is, focusing on the hairpin turns while we're entranced, spotting whales on the horizon.

I'm having trouble sitting still and I can't wait to get out of the car to stretch my legs. We pull up to a nondescript two-story home in this manicured Hawai'i Kai neighborhood. With better-than-average pronunciation I sound out the street name—Kuliouou Road. A looming valley dominates the background and my eyes settle on Eiji's front gate. A walkway on the left draws us further into his property, and as we follow it, I realize we've entered a lush garden oasis, reminiscent of Eden. Emerald green Monstera leaves flow around the home and geckos launch off long blades of grass.

"Everything here just . . . *thrives*," Mom whispers. Her voice has taken on a soothing tone interrupted only by the chirping of baby chickens. A small dog yips twice and hobbles out onto the back patio, warming up to us immediately, begging for attention. A tiny bell around his neck dings as he spins in circles, smiling from ear to floppy ear.

"Hello!" a voice calls out from inside the house. "I am coming out now!"

Shuffling down the steps, Eiji steps out to greet us, approaching Mom with open arms. I am struck by how closely he resembles the man I pictured in my mind, noting that I presumed he was Chinese and not Japanese. He is neither short nor tall, and his hair would be black if it weren't shaved off. Simple round glasses obscure the faintest smile lines from his ever-present grin. I try but I can't pinpoint his age.

"Jeri, it is so nice to see you!" he says, while he withdraws from their embrace and transfers his hug to Dad. "And Gary, it's so nice to see you too! How is your back?"

"So far, so good, Eiji. Thank you. I'm hoping the treatment may postpone the surgery for a bit." Eiji plants a hand on his shoulder, just as Dad reaches for his spine as if his back has gone out again. "Nah, I'm kidding!"

They laugh and I can't help but jump in. It's good to see Dad laughing.

"Ah, and you are Jordan!" Eiji grabs my shoulders and pulls me in for a hug. "Thank you so much for coming!"

"You're welcome," I say, before catching myself. "I'm sorry. I mean, thank you for fitting me in."

"No, no, no, no, no," he assures me. "It is no trouble. I am here to help. Now, may I please see your arm?"

I nod and let my gaze fall from his trusting smile, down to the back of my hand. Lifting up my arm, it's a struggle to pull up my sleeve. I have to stretch out the cuff of my shirt to fit it over my swollen forearm. Eiji reaches in to assist me, sliding my cuff up with both of his thumbs. He grabs and squeezes my wrist with both hands clasped and works his way up my arm, stopping just shy of my elbow.

"Your arm is hot," he says. His free hand rubs his head. "Please, this way."

As I follow him into the acupuncture studio, my parents wait outside in his open-air patio on the couch.

In the middle of the studio is a massage table. The walls are adorned with ancient tapestries mapping out the human body and acupuncture points. Eiji hands me a new patient chart and as I dive into the questions, he excuses himself and slips out of the room. The inquiry kicks off as one would expect in any medical setting, pressing me about drug allergies and medical history. One by one, the questions become more introspective, until I can no longer foresee their relevance, but assume they must serve some purpose.

Eiji returns to the room and hands me home-made herbal tea along with a cautionary warning on the taste. The taste is sharp and bitter, which clings to the inside of my throat.

"Jordan, can you say 'ahh' for me?" Eiji opens his own mouth to demonstrate.

I mimic him and stick out my tongue as far as I can for him to inspect it. After he makes an odd sound or two, he moves on and asks me to dress down to my underwear while he lights a stick of incense.

"Please, lie down on your back."

He immediately sets to work and sneaks in a few needles

before I work up the courage to caution him. I crank my neck and lift my head up. "Hey, Eiji. Just so you know—I don't know if I'm . . . dirty."

He smiles down on me. "Please, just relax," he instructs, while he continues to orbit the table.

I tuck my chin into my chest and look down the length of my body, struggling to keep up with the pace and the area he is covering.

Needles fly everywhere, guided by skilled hands that under-stand the rhyme and reason for each point. Within the first handful of pricks, I learn the cadence of his rhythm. He presses into my body with his thumb right before the needle placement, feeling for the exact spot he needs to address. Once in place, the needle is set with a few light taps from his finger before he pulls it away, twanging the needle in place.

Some points hurt much more than others, but they are not always intuitive. I thought the one between my eyes would be excruciating, but I barely notice. Numerous needles in my face may have me looking like the guy from Hellraiser, but they aren't nearly as uncomfortable as the handful that were set in my stomach area. A surprising metal taste invades my mouth while he puts one into the side of my belly.

I wince in pain. Eiji's head floats over mine. "Hmm. That last one is your liver," he says.

Finally, his attention turns to my left arm and for the next hour, nothing else matters in this world. Every so often he disappears for a few minutes, leaving me alone on the table. I drift away with the relaxing music in the background until he returns and removes the needles, then replaces them with a whole new set in a different area of my arm.

Every now and then he shifts his focus and massages my muscles, compressing them while being focused on the troubled areas. When all the needles are in place, he covers me with a light cotton blanket to connect the dots, then exits the room.

Falling asleep, I settle into a slumber so deep that my mind seems carried off with the force of an undertow. Since leaving detox, there hasn't been a single moment where I didn't want to physically lurch out of my own skin. Loathing my body and the damage I had caused, the aches that attended my waking life were an ever-present reminder that a fix was just around the corner. Obsession haunted me. Sleeping on the table, I'm finally able to let my guard down.

Eiji returns sometime later and peacefully brings me back to the present. One by one, the needles are removed and discarded into a sharps disposal container. If a point bleeds lightly, he dabs it with a napkin and a bit of light pressure for a quick second. As the pins are removed, he gently runs his fingers through my hair and slightly shakes his hand to make sure none fall out. Eiji tugs on my shoulders to assist me in sitting up, and just when I thought I was done, he lets out a small laugh and instructs me to flip over.

As he begins the process all over again on my back, he uses a butane lighter to ignite herbs placed on the top of the needles. He doesn't bother explaining the technique and wouldn't need to—I trust him instantly. As the moxa burns away and drips down the needles, burrowing into my back, the warmth emitted from within is replaced with a fire that encompasses my body.

The heat is no longer isolated at each needle site, but ravages over my whole body like a forest fire. Eiji monitors the burning and breaks his silence to humbly tell me it is an honor to have been asked to be of help. He begins to pluck the needles out and applies pressure to a few runaway droplets of blood.

I stumble out of his studio in a trance-like state. My arm no longer feels like I am holding it over an open flame. It's been troublesome for so long that I had forgotten how bad it was. My elbow that once creaked and groaned now operates smoothly. Eiji, apparently an herbalist as well, comes over and hands me small packets of powdered brown medicine to drink with water over the week.

My parents had both fallen asleep, cuddled on the couch, and while there's no pressure to leave, I know we can't stay here forever. Mom, wrapped in Dad's arms, glows like a saint and it would be a sin to disturb her. Not wanting to wake her, I look to Eiji for a way out, but he only smiles and takes pleasure in my dilemma. I laugh it off before reaching down to shake my dad's foot, then take a step back as his jostling rouses them both.

Slowly getting to their feet, they check the time and question if the clocks are accurate. Turning to Eiji, I thank him for all that he has done for me. Ready for the best sleep of my life, we head home the same route we came, though something feels . . . different.

"In the land of the blind, the one-eyed man is king."

DESIDERIUS ERASMUS

14

GATEWAY

AUGUST 29TH, 2011

Today is both the day of my admittance and the first time I am hearing that Sand Island Treatment Center is a two-year inpatient drug and alcohol rehab. Such sticker shock should be a tough pill to swallow, but I have to be honest with myself—I don't have any other options where I stand a chance. I tried, in vain, to learn more about the facility, but my parents could only repeat what little information they knew.

I haven't heard of any treatment center on Sand Island before. Formerly known as Quarantine Island, the small island lies near the entrance of Honolulu Harbor. It is partially a man-made island, born from a combination of trash and tailings from when the harbor was first dredged. My parents had operated their umbrella company out of an old industrial complex on the island for the past seventeen years. Besides the Coast Guard, shipping conglomerates and various commercial facilities, the only other inhabitants are the outlandish feral cat colonies and the homeless populations that come and go at will. Like everyone else on this island, I had always considered Sand Island one of those places where you need a good reason to visit.

Today is an over-exposed August morning that's hard on the

eyes. Riding in the backseat of my parent's car, we head over a metal bridge that rumbles beneath us. I look down at my arm and still can't believe that overnight, the swelling has reduced by half and the radiating heat has dissipated. I'm convinced that Eiji is a miracle worker.

As we cross over onto Sand Island, Mom reminds us to keep an eye out for the entrance, in case we may forget our final destination. I'm the first to spot and call out the sign, confused that the building looks much more like an actual commercial treatment center than a rehabilitation facility. The building exterior is equipped with a maze of pipes and massive holding tanks. A giant steel orb dominates the background, standing many stories high, blocking out the early morning sun as we blow past the parking lot.

"No, that's not it," Dad says. "That complex is actually the Sand Island Wastewater Treatment Facility."

Before he could finish his sentence, he flips on his blinker and pulls into the very next driveway. We roll to a stop in front of a six-foot-high, galvanized chain-link fence where most of the facility in the background is hidden behind tall brush. The fence surrounds the whole property—the only visible break is a large rolling gate that closes off the outside world. I wonder if they're keeping the world out or the addicts in.

A small white guard shack on the facility side of the fence houses a man who steps out to meet us as soon as our tires touch the asphalt driveway. I can tell that no one comes and goes from this place unnoticed or uninvited. The guard is wearing a white shirt and carries a walkie-talkie, and though he approaches the gate, he stops short of opening it. He sticks his face close to the chain-link fence to ask how he can help us.

Dad's left shoulder bounces while he cranks down his window. Half-sticking his head outside, he speaks on behalf of the three of us. "Good morning. We're here to check him in for treatment," he says, sticking his thumb back over his shoulder toward me.

"Checking in?" the guard asks.

All three of us nod in unison.

"Oh, okay. Then, if you don't mind, can you please pull your car over to this side of the driveway? We can't block the gate." His hand motions for us to scoot over as he speaks into his walkie-talkie. He turns his back on us and retreats to the safety of his cracked plastic chair. As Dad parks the car, Mom looks confused as to why we're not allowed inside.

"About time, huh?" Dad says, trying to hide his irritation after baking in the morning sun for longer than expected.

I peer over his shoulder and through the windshield to see a trio of staff members approach the gate. The guard hops back to his feet to let them out. Ty and Deborah introduce themselves to us while the third man lingers in the background. Ty looks to be one of those people who can't stop smiling if he wanted to, a positive energy radiating from somewhere within. I usually assess people who smile nonstop as fake, but that doesn't seem to be the case here. All three of them appear healthy, fit and strong. Deborah looks like a surfer, her arms toned and tan.

Cordial greetings aside, Ty turns to me. "It is so nice to meet you. Are you ready to save your life?" He is manicured and clean-cut, taking a break between workouts to save lives.

I open my mouth, but before the words come out, Deborah steps in to takeover. Her thick, familiar Hawaiian Pidgin slang solidifies the reality that I'm finally home.

"Braddah, you betta be ready fo' dis!" She nods while she speaks, glances to her right, then presses down on the corner of Ty's clipboard to remind herself of my name. I'm taken aback and think that's the point. Deborah points to my parents. "Eh! Look, Jordan. You see your parents. You see da hell you puttin' dem t'rew?"

My head follows her finger and my gaze falls on Mom's face first.

"Howz you? You stay all buss and tink you can do whateva

you like, and Mommy and Daddy goin' just bail you out. Wassamattah you? Dey wen and pay a lot of hard-earned kālā just to get you in hea. How dat make you feel? I bet not too good, yeah? I bet, you no mo' one dollah to your name, yea? At least, not one you went earn. Braddah, try pull out your pockets, guaranz you stay broke!" She tugs on my sleeve. "Dey probably paid fo' everyt'ing you get on."

She's already under my skin. It's irritating how spot on she is.

Her voice drops to a low level as she talks as if it's just me and her. "You need to appreciate dis opportunity. Ev'ry day, our phones ring off da fuckin' hook with people hopin' fo' get inside. We no mo' time fo' waste hea. Get choke clients inside fighting fo' save their lives. So if you like come in, if you like what we get, I need to hear a commitment, right hea, right now. So! Watchu' you goin' do?"

I pause for a second, wondering what the hell I've gotten myself into. I try to play through the alternatives and realize there are none. For once in my life, I may just be right where I need to be. I go to clear my throat, but I let out a weak cough instead and exhale.

"Come on *aurrready!*" she says. "It's hot out hea! Now, watchu like do?"

"Anything?" I say, surprising myself. "I'll do anything."

"Aurite, bumbai we'll see bout dat," she says. The rigidness in her face falls away into a somewhat welcoming smile. Then she turns toward my mom, the one most taken aback from our exchange. "No worries momma—we goin' take good care of him. He goin' on Blackout for the first month, so no phone calls or messages, keh? Visits, if approved, start afta t'ree months. If we get one emergency, we goin' contact you. If you get one emergency, you can call our office anytime."

Ty steps forward and takes a down-and-dirty inventory, doing a quick run through of the list of banned items. I watch the third staffer begin to bag my belongings in a large, clear plastic bag. During the transfer, he stops for a moment when he comes across my Good Thoughts and starts to give it a shake, likely checking for contraband.

"Oh, let me have that." I reach out and snatch it from his hand, then pass it on to my mom for safe keeping.

"I promise to keep it safe," she musters.

He shakes his head and writes my name on the outside of the bag, then heads back toward the office while I say goodbye to my parents.

Mom is on the verge of crying and thanking God that this moment came to fruition. All she seems to want is to remind me how much they love me and to ask that I make the most of this opportunity. As we embrace for a hug, her hand drops to the small of my back, applying pressure to my spine. She whispers into my ear, "This is your backbone. Stand up for yourself and use it."

I promise her I will and kiss her on the cheek.

Dad hugs me next. "You're heading in the right direction, son, and I can't wait to see where it takes you. I love you."

I take a few steps back, wave goodbye and turn my back on them. The guard behind us opens the gate, and with Deborah and Ty in tow, I step into the light.

15

CHRONOLOGICAL

W alking by my side, I feel more guided than led while Ty escorts me into the facility. As the gate closes behind us, I steal one last look over my shoulder and wave goodbye to my tearful parents.

Ty smiles as I drop my hand. "You know, you're very fortunate," he says. "I've been doing this a long time and don't see that sort of love every day. I'm impressed."

I hear him speaking but I don't respond. I'm much too focused on taking in this new place I'll call home for the next two years, though from the looks of it, there's not a whole lot to take in.

This facility is a ghost town. Someone in the distance slips between two buildings and disappears from sight like an unsettled spirit. I am surprised and wonder where everybody is. I expected to see a bunch of clients going about their day, doing whatever it is people do in treatment. Instead, there's only two plump feral cats and countless chickens that mosey around, paying no mind to my shuffling feet.

I hear a voice talking passionately, growing louder as we approach what appears to be a Rec Hall. Following Ty, we stay on a path that continues down a sidewalk that leads us even closer to the room. We walk past the side of the building and I steal a glimpse through the screened window. The room is packed with seated men and women, at least a hundred and fifty lost souls who can finally rest. It appears to be a class, and suddenly the voice that is speaking yells "save yourself," followed up by a maniacal laugh. The whole room bursts out in laughter. That building must be the heart of the property.

Ty and I round the corner. He ushers me through an entryway that leads into the lobby of the Rec Hall. Just beyond the entrance is a small administration office with glass windows, and directly in front of us is the sea of clients in white shirts staring us down. Between them and me sits a head table where the counselor leading the class has his back toward us. He continues with his story as I pick up blurbs of "rock bottom" and "eating Friskies." He has the attention of the whole room and I can't look away.

"Right through here," Ty instructs. We enter the small administrative office that leads into an even smaller room. "Please, have a seat." He motions for me to take a chair across the desk from him. "Unreal, huh? It's a big change, but know that you are not alone. How are you feeling?"

"Stressed. Tired. Confused. Sick."

"Yeah, I bet. Thank you for an honest answer to an honest question." Ty adjusts his chair and allows me a moment to catch my breath. "Well, I'm just going to start by saying that it's normal to feel all of that, especially where you're coming from. In fact, if you weren't feeling that way, I'd be a lot more concerned—we don't need any more sociopaths in here!"

I expect Ty to laugh but he doesn't skip a beat.

Check in turns out to be quite the process. I watch as Ty pulls out a new client file loaded with medical releases, liability waivers, health insurance documents, food-stamp applications and privacy consents.

I do my best to keep up the pace as each form is explained. Ty patiently and unhurriedly walks me through each application, skipping nothing.

"We'll get through this together," he promises more than once. As he pulls out the final chart, labeled "Chronological History," I realize we're just beginning.

"Okay, thank you so much for your cooperation and hanging in there. This is the big one. We can take a break if you need to smoke a cigarette or use the bathroom. After this, I promise, you'll have time to relax."

I take him up on his offer. He hands me a cigarette and we head outside to smoke. I lean in as he holds out a lighter and I'm trembling so bad that I nearly burn my upper lip. The sun warms the back of my neck while the menthol drags cool me down.

I prefer regular Camels but take what I can get. My hand shakes with every drag, and I'm too out of tune with my body to know if it's the nervousness or withdrawal symptoms. Ty is so relatable that I can't help but feel like I have a friend on my side.

Finally, near the end of the cigarette, I can breathe normally. I take a puff and hold it in, wanting to cherish any rush I can get. Finishing my cigarette before Ty does, I watch as he puts his out early and gestures to head back inside to resume our work. Following on his heels as we enter the office, I look down at his custom, bright green Nike's with the words "You Got It" emblazoned on the heel.

"Let's start at the beginning." Ty taps his pen on the table.

Is this a trick question? "The beginning *of*—?"

"Why don't you start with your using career? When you first got loaded, then we'll go over your life story as time permits."

I think for a second. "You know, it's one of those funny things —when you think you're doing the right thing, but inadvertently cause drastic side effects." I pick at the edge of the table with my thumbnail. "Sort of like when man interferes with nature and sets off a chain reaction."

"How so?"

"Well, all three of us boys had the same deal growing up, one proposed by my dad. If any of us could make it to age sixteen without smoking a cigarette or using any drugs, we'd each get a thousand dollars. I have no idea where the idea came from, but of all three of us, would you believe that I was the only one who pulled it off?"

"I will believe everything you tell me until you give me a reason not to."

"It's true." I scoot my seat forward and sit up. "Both of my brothers got caught smoking pot early in their teenage years and were cast out of the running. My oldest brother was taking bong rips in his bedroom and my dad took his door off the hinges for over a month." I laugh at the memory of a flag hanging in an open doorway at the end of a hall. "But I wanted the money so bad that I used the deal as a crutch and held out while all of my friends were experimenting. I also realized there was a loophole—the deal didn't include drinking."

"So you drank a lot?"

"More than that and I started to notice a pattern. I drank to the point of blacking out every time. I would be at a party where a bunch of my friends would pass a bong around and since I couldn't smoke with them, I would try to match their buzz through alcohol. Who knew I was chasing a ghost? My drinking sped up, and by the time my sixteenth birthday rolled around, I was unapologetically an alcoholic."

"But you still got the money?"

"Of course, which is a lot of money for a sixteen-year-old. Once that happened, it was a huge celebration and the flood gates burst wide open. I started smoking weed, cigarettes, whatever I wanted. I had the money to do it and no excuse to use as a crutch anymore. Friends that had experimented with cocaine shared with me and before I knew it, I quite literally blew through the cash. I didn't know how to say no. Plus, I was still drinking and within months, I had my first D.U.I. and lost my license for a year."

Ty looks confused. "A year? Why so long? Did you hurt someone?"

"No, I was just an asshole. I was drunk and refused to blow at the police station. The officer tried to help me out, saying a refusal was a mandatory year confiscation of my driver's license, but of course I didn't listen."

"Wait. You said that was your *first*?"

"Yeah, the first of two. After I got my license back, I lost it again with a second D.U.I. That time, I nearly crashed on the Pali Highway. Several drivers called in to report me, and I got pulled over in Kailua as I rolled through a stop sign.

"Before I had hopped in the car that night, I had left my friend Joel's house with a bottle of wine I stole from his mother's stash. Without a wine opener, the only way I could open the bottle was to jam the cork inside. While driving home, I tried to take a swig, but the cork clogged the wine. As I shook it over my mouth while swerving, the cork popped up and I dumped red wine all over my shirt. They literally caught me red-handed. That arrest got me a week in juvenile detention and a year on probation."

"So, did you complete probation?" he asks.

"Yeah. Also, around that time, I was kicked out of Punahou for receiving two F's in one semester and ended up transferring to A.O.P."

"Academy of the Pacific?"

"Yeah, or Assholes on Probation," I joke. "But from there, I pulled my act together, got straight A's and even received a scholarship for college—"

"Where the heroin addiction started?"

I catch my breath. "It definitely didn't start here. I continued to struggle with drinking for the first few years of college until I knew I needed to stop."

"But you just traded one addiction for another?" Ty looks like he wants to help me. "You're doing great. Now, let's go back to your teenage years. You mentioned a couple of areas I'd like you to expand on."

I continue to open up to Ty. He's an excellent interviewer and makes me feel comfortable. The more questions he asks, the more I seem to remember and want to share with him, up until he broaches the subject of relationships.

When I let it slip that I was engaged at one point, Ty locks onto it like a Pit Bull. I try to dodge his inquiries, but I can't slip much past him. As the words flow, memories flood in alongside them and start to drag me down.

"Do we really have to get into this?" I ask.

"I guess that depends on if you really want me to make an effective recovery plan for you or not." Ty lays down his pen and leans in toward the table. "Look, all of this is about me trying to understand any potential threats that may be waiting for you outside of these gates. We don't have to get into the specifics, but relationships, especially toxic ones, won't do you any good moving forward. So what's her name?"

"Lucy."

"Is Lucy an active user?"

I roll my head before letting it bounce to a stop. Ty picks up his pen again.

"Two users can do a lot of damage together," he says. "Are you still in touch with her?"

I chuckle uncomfortably. "Honestly, I don't think I was ever in touch with her. But to answer your question, no—it's been a while."

"So it's over?"

"Yeah, definitely."

"Any love interests since?"

I scoff at the idea. "Ty, I haven't had a sex drive in years."

"That's not uncommon," he reassures me. "Sexual dysfunction is a byproduct of opioid dependence. But don't worry about it—it'll come back. That said, would she know where to find you if she wanted to?"

I shake my head. "I doubt it. She probably doesn't even know if I'm alive. Either way, she's moved on, and I don't blame her."

Ty leaves it at that and tries to sniff out any deep-seated trauma that may help to define me. He prods deeper and deeper before I have to admit that I have no one to blame but myself. The only abuse I've ever encountered in life was self-inflicted. There was no sexual assault to speak of, violence or neglect to attribute to escapism. The assessment is worlds deeper than I expected, but with it comes relief with being able to talk so openly and freely.

Addiction, in one form or another, has long been an old familiar friend. It also feels pitiful to hear my story described, but not once do I sense any judgment. I watch Ty's pen almost predict my statements as if he's sat through the same story once or twice before.

My feet shuffle under the desk, polishing the linoleum with my soles. Ty got everything he asked for, and once he wraps up the assessment, he excuses himself and leaves me alone in the room. To my left are piles of donated clothes stacked on a bookshelf, white shirts in a pile that looks ready to topple over. I reach out and flip through them, but I don't see anything of value.

I hear laughing outside of the door as Ty returns with company. Feeling caught off guard, my hand springs back and flops into my lap. The guy he's joking with squeezes through the doorway, side steps around him and welcomes himself into the already cramped room. He reaches out to shake my hand.

"What's up, man? I'm your Shadow, Deacon. Nice to meet you."

"*Shadow?*" I ask.

Deacon opens his mouth to respond, but Ty beats him to it. "Jordan, every new client gets assigned a Shadow for the first week they're here. Deacon will show you the ropes, teach you the rules, keep you out of trouble and help you ease into the program until the dust settles. It's also in your best interest to have someone with you during your extended withdrawal. I think the two of you will be a good fit."

I look Deacon up and down. He is shorter than me and in much better shape. His tan muscles hang out of his wife-beater tank top.

The jailhouse tattoo on the side of his neck reads "Valerie," and when he speaks, it's through a cheek stuffed with chewing tobacco. We both have long hair, but his is pulled back into a blonde ponytail whereas mine drapes around my face like curtains, helping me hide from the world.

While Deacon and I make introductions, Ty packs me a paper bag full of toiletries. I watch him from the corner of my eye as he tosses in a toothbrush and other items that look like they came from the dollar store. All of my personal items that I can keep are dropped into the bag along with a blanket and some folded bedsheets. Ty apologizes as he exchanges my copy of *Papillon* by Henri Charrière for the *Alcoholics Anonymous Big Book*.

"This novel looks good, but we want you focused on your recovery while you're getting settled," he says with a smile. "Please don't hate me—I don't make the rules."

I watch Ty toss in a yellow pad of paper, a Ziplock bag stuffed with tobacco, matches and some rolling papers. Ty swings my bag around me as Deacon reaches for it, grabs it by the knot and lets it fall to his side.

"I got this for you, Jordan. Just take it easy. You look like you've seen better days."

Ty raises his eyebrows and shakes his head. "Trust me, I've seen worse. Jordan, you are in good hands. Deacon is a good guy who's come a long way himself. I'm really proud of him.

"If you need anything else, remember that the staff is here 24/7 and most of us, myself included, live on the property. I look forward to working with you over the next few days. Take it easy and hang in there." Ty flattens his parted hair and composes himself. "Oh, and Deacon, make sure you two go over the rules, okay? Give him a fighting chance."

"You got it, Ty," Deacon says.

I thank Ty for his help and turn to follow Deacon out of the room. Looking down at my belongings in the clear trash bag, I realize that I'm starting over from scratch, and maybe it's not such a bad thing. Inside the bag, my boxer shorts are on full display.

Reaching out to take my bag back from Deacon, my eyes are drawn up from his wrist to the back of his arm. A bold, blood-red Swastika is tattooed across his elbow. I pull my hand back and instinctively slow down, stopping to put some distance between us. He hooks a right out of the office and carries on. A few more steps and he spins around, realizes we've become separated and encourages me to keep moving.

"Catch up, man. Everyone here is cool. There's no reason to be scared."

I don't know if he's talking about himself or treatment, but I'm not keen on either at the moment. I hate that it feels too late to turn back now. I promised my mom to give the program a chance, and I can't give up the first day. I opt to stick it out and be open-minded.

Following Deacon, I walk up a wheelchair ramp and step down some stairs into what looks like a hangout area just outside the Rec Hall. A large, green pop-up tent that stands about ten-by-twenty feet, covers a raised wooden floor surrounded by a few feet of gravel for drainage. The deck is enclosed with plantation-style wooden fencing, and the faded white paint is brittle from years of assault from the sun. Cheap, mismatched patio furniture is scattered about and the opaque glass tables are littered with ashtrays. I only see male clients buzzing around, coming and going every which way. There are a few blank stares, but otherwise, I'm surprised how many of them are in good shape for being drug addicts. Each plastic chair is occupied and even more clients are hanging around, leaning on the railing and talking story. Almost everyone is smoking and has something to say.

"You smoke?" Deacon asks.

I nod.

"Okay, cool." He waves his hand in an arc near the canopy. "This is the men's smoking tent." He points behind the tent. "And that is the men's A.C. dorm."

"A.C. dorm?"

"Yeah—it's the only dorm in here with air-conditioning. Everywhere else is hot as balls. All new clients stay in there for the first thirty days, so it should help you out while you're kicking. It's crowded, but trust me, you'll miss it when they transfer you to the back."

His words send a shiver up my spine as I'm reminded of the shape I'm in. "So that's where I stay? What about you?"

"With you. We're together for the first week, remember? I'll move in and take the top bunk."

"Top bunk?" It reminds me of my childhood and brings back long-standing resentments. "Hold on. Why do you get the top?"

"I don't know, it's just standard policy. I guess too many new guys kept rolling off and hurting themselves." He laughs and I chuckle along with him. I can see that being a real headache. Laughter helps my apprehensions subside.

"Let's put your stuff up, then you can smoke a cigarette if you want."

We head up to the door, but Deacon stops me before he yanks it open. "By the way, there's no talking inside of the dorms. Also, we always take our shoes off outside, but bring them in with you if you want, so no one steals them. There are some squirrelly fuckers here."

I don't want to believe it's that bad here.

Following him inside, I see there are rows of bunk beds, all neatly made with the sheets tucked in. The lights are off, but enough sun leaks through the windows to see the one lonely, empty bunk. Deacon checks out a wooden locker next to the bed, but it's full of someone's belongings. He tries another and finds it empty, so he tosses my whole bag inside, staking my claim. Stepping forward, I remove the tobacco pouch and look around. Some clients are still sleeping even though it's early afternoon. Others are lying awake on their bed watching my every move.

"It's kind of cold in here, care if we go back out?"

"Shh. Yes, but remember, no talking in the dorms," Deacon whispers.

I rub my fingers through my hair, putting tension on my scalp. My legs are achy and I'm anxious to get settled in. I move with a purpose to grab my tobacco and slippers, then head back outside.

Deacon and I squeeze onto a bench next to one another while I keep my hands busy and roll a cigarette.

"You coming from jail?" a guy across from me asks, taking a drag from his spit-soaked cigarette. I take a moment to realize that he's talking to me, but speaking for everyone else.

"No." I look around at all the eyes on me and scrunch my shoulders.

Deacon takes it upon himself to chime in. "Walk-in," he says.

The guy nods. "Braddah, as white as you stay, you look like you come straight from the hole." He laughs out loud, showing off his missing teeth. "Well, never mind dat. Welcome to Sand Island. I'm Kaleo, and dis one good place. Eh, wat you stay here for? Ice?"

I shake my head. "No. Meth wasn't my thing. Heroin and cocaine, I guess—when I could swing it." I take a long drag and miss my love.

"Fuck dat." His scratchy voice trails off only to explode in curiosity. "Wat, you shoot it?" he asks, punching his forearm.

I nod.

"Mean." Kaleo draws out the word while he settles back in his seat and crosses his arms, licking his lips. He sticks his legs out in front of him then sits back up, leaning in toward my direction. "Brah, how you afford that shit here? It's so expensive, yeah?"

"Is it? I have no idea. I just flew in after being in Portland for too long."

"You're from Portland? Where? Oregon?" Kaleo asks.

"Yeah, but I'm originally from here. At least, since I was two. I moved away to go to college."

"College? Oh, okay. So, smart you, yeah? Fuck. Smart, but crazy to walk into one place like dis. Either dat, or someone wen lie to you," he says. "Cuzzin' . . . no one like be hea."

"Almost nobody," Deacon adds as he turns to me. "There's a couple of other guys here that are walk-ins also, so you're not alone."

"Yeah, maybe two, t'ree, tops . . . out of what? A hundred, hundred fiddy guys?" Kaleo scoffs at the idea like we're both crazy. "No maddah, it sounds like you stay in the right place. I tell you dis one good place, my braddah." He pauses for a second to look me up and down. "You're detoxing, huh?"

"I already medically detoxed for a week in preparation for coming here, but I still feel like shit."

"Just hang in there cuzzin'." He puts out his cigarette and throws me a Shaka. "If I can do it, you can do it. Stay in da boat."

As he walks away, other clients go through the motion of introducing themselves.

"Do you take any medication?" Deacon asks when there's a break.

I tell him no, but he responds that if I do get prescribed any, I need to be in line at the medical office by 5:15 a.m. After that, we line up for breakfast and can eat between 5:30 and 6:00. If I want to shave, Ty checks out razors at the men's bathroom from 6:00 to 6:30. He tells me not to worry, everybody gets assigned their own razor and Ty keeps them for safe keeping. We're not allowed to have razors or any other weapon.

I chain-smoke while he fills me in on the schedule.

At 6:45, everyone lines up for morning house jobs. I'm told I'll eventually get one, but not to worry about it for now. While everyone completes their chores, we can hang out and smoke if we want. Then every client in intensive treatment lines up in the parking lot for morning calisthenics.

The fifteen-minute stretch and flex leads into the "10th Step," a morning journal activity that takes place during quiet time. We also have the option to work on any homework that is assigned to us as long as we use the time productively. Afterward, we're allowed another smoke break, this time in the back of the facility where the weight room is.

The schedule is way more detailed than expected, so I grab a pencil and take notes. The first class runs from 8:00 to 9:15 and is either lecture style or open discussion. All clients, male and female, are present, though the room is split between the sexes by an invisible barrier. Then there's another fifteen-minute smoke break before the next class which runs until lunch. They serve lunch at 11:30, and the women always eat first. The men line up outside of the Rec Hall, wait their turn and get called in five guys at a time. All new clients—along with their Shadows—get to eat first. Lunchtime is also quiet time, and until 12:30 there is no talking anywhere on the facility if you're a client, unless you're speaking to staff.

I'm grateful to hear that coffee is again served after lunch, but that thought fades away as Deacon explains that another class follows. We can smoke from 2:00 to 2:15, and everyone gets to hang out for the rest of the day except for me. Until I reach the forty-five-day milestone, I'm required to attend yet another class creatively called Forty-Five-Day and Under.

They serve dinner at 5:00 and the rest of the day is mine. Unless it's a Monday, which also has a Graduate-led A.A. meeting from 6:30 to 7:30 p.m. A.A. meetings are mandatory and held on Wednesday, Friday and Saturday at varying times. Tuesdays and Thursdays both have Big Book Study in the evenings. The weekends have half day schedules followed by movies if I'm not allowed out on pass.

"On pass?" I ask.

"We'll cross that bridge later," Deacon says, reeling me in. "Let's get you through the thirty-day blackout period first, then you can set your eyes on the outside world."

I drop my pencil, realizing I can't process the many overlapping schedules. The program is more complicated than both my preparatory school and college curriculums combined. I hesitantly flip open the pamphlet Ty gave me labeled "Treatment Rules."

"Can I see that for a second?" Deacon asks as he plucks the paper out of my hand. I think he needs a quick refresher, but I soon realize he's trying to protect me from freaking out.

"For now, just know that there are so many rules here, your head will spin if I let you go through them all. So, let's start off with the cardinal rules first—these are the zero tolerance ones and will get you walked out to the gate if you violate any of them.

"First, no acts or threats of violence. No stealing. Trust me, if you commit any crime in here, they are willing to prosecute and you'll likely be arrested on top of being kicked out. No engaging in any exchange of monies or other material items. This includes gambling, loaning, borrowing money and giving away personal items. There is zero tolerance for the use or possession of alcohol or illicit substances. Cross-gender interactions and intimate relationships are strictly prohibited. No weapons are permitted on the facility grounds at any time. Makes sense, right?"

"Seems straightforward."

"We'll get to all the other ones, eventually. Most of them are common sense, while others are less obvious. You can't run or skip. Don't touch the feral cats or plants. Don't go into other people's dormitories or talk in the Rec Hall during breakfast or lunch. Speaking of talking, there is no talking out of badge."

"Out of badge?"

"Think of it like out of group. Once you're here for a week or two, you'll get assigned a counselor and put into a group. You'll get a badge with your picture on it and your group color. You can only talk to guys with the same color badge or transition clients.

"Those are working clients who are still living here, but no longer in intensive treatment. Most clients make it to transition within six months to a year. Anyway, the only time you can take your badge off is to shower, sleep or when you check out on pass.

"More than likely, they will assign Mike as your counselor and you'll be in the green group with me. Actually, since you're a white guy and here for opiates, I can almost guarantee you'll be in the green group. Just like they assign most Hawaiians to Saunoa, Asians to Uncle Stan, and older clients to Miss Carolyn. Mike was a heroin addict at one point too, so he knows where you're coming from."

Deacon lectures on. "Anyway, besides all this shit you can't do, there's also a lot of stuff you have to do. You have to make your bed each morning. Attend class. Take an observed drug test when asked and if you can't pee, figure it out. Participate when called upon. Shower and take your meds if they prescribe you any. The list goes on."

I look away, trying to listen, but I feel discouraged by the regulatory stranglehold.

"Look, just follow my lead, and if you ever don't know what to do, don't do anything at all. I know it seems excessive, but realize that every rule here exists because some donkey made it necessary. Can you believe it only takes one person getting stabbed in the throat with a butter knife ten years ago and we're still eating with plastic utensils?"

Deacon lets out a laugh and I smile uncomfortably.

16

THIRTY-DAY TABLE

After an endless night of staring into darkness, the sun finally rises. Leaving the A.C. dorm, Deacon escorts me to the bathroom, which is in its own building behind the Rec Hall. As we walk on the path, we turn a corner and nearly bump into two female clients. Deacon jerks back, stepping off the path and looking down, making room for them to pass. I follow his lead and excuse myself to the girls for getting in their way.

As soon as they're out of earshot, Deacon yanks me toward him.

"Never do that again," he scolds. "Remember, you can't say anything to them, for any reason. Not even a 'Thank you' or 'Excuse me.' In fact, you're not even supposed to look at them. I know it's hard, but as far as us guys are concerned, they don't exist. Now let's hope neither of them reports you for speaking to them, or we're both in deep shit. You may get a warning this time for being new, but once you're off Shadow—" Deacon slices his throat with his fingertips.

"I wonder if that's such a bad thing?"

He shrugs. "That's up to you, but like I tell everyone, give this program a chance. Remember, you just got here. It's a big change, and you're going to go through hell at first, but you know the saying: 'If you're going through Hell—'" he waits for me to complete his sentence long enough to realize I don't know the rest. "You keep going. If you're going through hell, keep going."

Once the morning rituals are complete, Deacon and I walk into the Rec Hall for my first class. The rectangular room is dated with large, vaulted ceilings supported by wooden posts and no interior walls, which adds an airy feeling. Sliding screen windows line the two long walls, and overhead fans circulate the sticky air as their pull chains clack away above a packed crowd. Connected to the back of the Rec Hall is the kitchen, which is entirely walled off except for a door that muffles the voices behind it. It appears that some combination of staff and clients are working in there at all hours, prepping the food that feeds the whole facility.

Toward the front of the room is the duty office and an open corridor with two large swinging doors that are always propped open. The green carpet below is weathered and worn out in spots, stained from pulling double duty over the years, acting as a catch-all three times a day when the Rec Hall becomes our cafeteria.

Deacon points up to the front of the class. "That round table up to the left, you see which one? That's the thirty-day table. Don't try to sit anywhere else in the room until you've been here a month. And see those four or five tables on the right? That's where the women sit. Their whole area is *Kapu*. Just avoid it altogether and steer clear. I'll be sitting here in the back and will meet you outside once we're let out on a break."

Behind the Rec Hall, a bell rings a handful of times.

"Okay, class is about to start. Pay attention, but don't ask any questions. Remember, there's nothing wrong with listening. If you need to go to the bathroom, just raise your hand and walk out the way you came in. I'll see you coming and meet you outside."

I snake my way up to the front of the class, weaving between large round tables as the room fills up. The closer I get to the front, the tighter the pathway becomes. Male clients outside finish their cigarettes and hurry inside to take their seat next to the notepads they've left on the tables as placeholders. The room is quickly packed. I'm surprised at how many clients call this place home. I take the last available seat at the thirty-day table, and of the six other guys sitting there, only a couple of them acknowledge me.

Across the way, a character who reminds me of the Grinch waves his hand.

"Howzit. I'm Eli. Nice to meet you," he whispers.

Even though he's sitting down, I can tell he is tall and lanky. A broad smile splashes across his face, pushing up on his puffy cheeks. He's haole like me and stands out in a room full of tattooed, hardened criminals.

The local guy to my right is doodling surfboards with surprising accuracy. Every shape is represented in his paper lineup of twenty or so boards. His quiver ranges from quad fish shortboards to single-fin longboards. He puts down his pencil and drops his hands into his lap. "I'm Cavin." He pauses a second and lifts an eyebrow. "And you smell like onions."

Eli lets out a laugh. "Brah, if you have Maui Onion chips, you'd better fucking share!" He reaches under the table and smacks my pocket, startling me and the guy across the way who is sleeping. "Reminds me of home."

I look at him and shake my head as Cavin wipes sweat off his brow. "Eli, you're from Maui?" Cavin asks.

Eli wiggles a Shaka against his chest.

"Really, though—what's that fucking smell?" Cavin pinches his nose and I realize he isn't joking. "It's strong. Pungent. Overwhelming. Stinks!"

I think for a second. Since I can't smell, I never know if my odor is offensive. "Could be me? I wasn't able to sleep last night—I just sort of stared at the mattress above me and sweat."

Eli acknowledges the feeling. "You're detoxing, huh?"

"Aren't we all?" I look around the table, confused.

"No." Cavin gives up on his drawing. "Most of us came here from jail or prison, so we've been clean since incarceration or at least cut down a lot. Still get plenty of dope in jail though cause the guards are all crooked."

Eli shakes his head. "Not me. I'm a walk-in, but I worked hard to wean myself off as much as possible before flying over."

"You're both walk-ins?" Cavin's eyes bounce back and forth. "Both you guys are crazy. Why the hell would anyone in their right mind come here?"

He has a good point. To commit to a two-year program with no idea of what that commitment means confirms we're as crazy as we're led to believe. Still though, crazy compared to what?

"I had no idea what I was walking into, but maybe this is what I need?" I turn to Eli. "Are you kicking heroin too?"

"Fuck that, brah! No way, that shit's so hard to find here." He wipes his nose. "Pills. They're way cheaper than dope, believe it or not, and for the most part, you know what you're gonna get."

"That's it! That's the smell! All of that junk must be leaking out of your pores!" Cavin looks me up and down and the other guys at the table take notice. "Brah, try scoot over."

I look around at the cramped table, with nowhere to move to either side. Cavin smiles back like he's just giving me a hard time, but his smile fades away as a female counselor enters the room. She skirts around the empty table only a few feet away from us and leans against the sharp edge. Eli nudges the sleeping client and the whole room quiets down.

Her voice, loud and clear, bellows throughout the halls. "Please open your Big Book to bottom of page eighty-two." She pauses to allow a hundred pages to flip before reading the text aloud. "The alcoholic is like a tornado roaring his way through the lives of others. Hearts are broken. Sweet relationships are dead. Affections have been uprooted. Selfish and inconsiderate habits have kept the home in turmoil. We feel a man is unthinking when he says that sobriety is enough. He is like the farmer who came up out of his cyclone cellar to find his home ruined. To his wife, he remarked, 'Don't see anything the matter here, Ma. Ain't it grand the wind stopped blowing?'" She waits for the echo of her voice to die down, allowing the words to sink in. "What does that mean to you?"

Hands fly up in the air. I scan the room and watch, surprised by the class participation. The counselor uncrosses her arm and lifts a finger, pointing toward a man in the back. He drops his hand as he begins to share.

"Yeah, for me, Miss Cats, I can relate to this part. My addiction was so destructive that all of my life I have left carnage behind me. Wherever I went, I left a path and mess for my wife and family to clean it up. That's all I got." He rubs his hands through his hair and takes a seat.

Miss Cats gives a nod and turns her back toward our table as she lifts her finger to pluck out the next client. Her full back tattoo is on display. Though hard to make out, it looks like two dueling beasts in a muddled splash of color.

"Good morning, Miss Cats. The part about relationships, I feel like that's true. You know, I don't have anyone left outside of here that gives a fuck if I make it or not. My wife left me and my kids don't want to talk to me. But you know what? I don't blame them. I deserve it, and honestly, I think the only person who cares about how I'm doing today is my probation officer . . . and only because that's her job."

Around the room, heads nod in agreement. The sharing continues until the last hand is called, and once everyone has said their piece, Miss Cats takes over. I can't help but hang on her every word.

"You know, I hear this chapter, and I don't know about all of you, but I can relate. 'The alcoholic is like a tornado roaring his way through the lives of others. Hearts are broken. Sweet relationships are dead.' Look, I've been sober over twenty years, and there are still relationships that I cannot repair. I may have earned forgiveness from a handful of people, but there are still family and friends who will never speak to me again." She takes a sip of her water. "None of us can go back in time and repair all the damage we have caused. Look, you guys know! It doesn't matter what your drug of choice was—can you relate?"

She casts her hand over her shoulder. Her words ring out and echo as the whole room listens intently. "And for all you parents out there, you don't need me to tell you that kids are smart. Or that they have the best memories. Or that they never, ever, forget. In fact, they remember all of it. Shit. Things you don't even remember. Even years later, don't be surprised when they come up to you and say, 'Mommy, remember when you did this! Daddy, remember when you did that?' And you'll look at them like they're crazy until you remember how fucked up you was." She pauses for a second. "Unless they're making it up to take advantage of you, but how would you know?"

The class laughs along with her while she takes another sip.

"My point is, our loved ones suffered at the hands of our disease and that's fucked up. That's the shit we put them through." She shakes her head. "That's the nature of the disease—we get off easy, being medicated, high, intoxicated, loaded. Our families, not so easy. They have to live through our bullshit and deal with it. Or worse, they have to pick up after us. And when I think of that, all the shit we put our families through, it reminds me that we owe. Still, to this day, I owe. I owe it to my family to be there for them whenever they need me."

Miss Cats pushes off the table edge and walks through the room, her water bottle crinkling in her hand.

"Now, the Big Book says that 'selfishness and self-centeredness, that was our problem.' If you want to change and are here to change, that's an excellent place to start. And like the reading said, selfish and inconsiderate habits have kept the home in turmoil. Turmoil means disturbed, in case you don't know."

She walks over to a basket on a table by the duty office and picks up a dictionary, holding it up for the class to see.

"No shame to always better yourself. Anyway, today, I don't have the right to be selfish, but there's one exception." She barks the next sentence loud at the class. "Each one of you pay close attention. You need to know that the only time you have the right to be selfish is when it comes to your recovery and that there is nothing in this world more important, period! Not your wife, not your husband, not your family." Her eyes scan the room, landing on the ladies. "Not even your kids. Recovery comes first, always, or you won't make it. It has to be your number one priority, and you have to protect it because without it, you will be useless. It's the same reason you put the oxygen mask on yourself first if there is an emergency mid-flight. You can't help others around you if you are dead!"

She brushes aside her short bangs. A client raises a hand to ask a question, but she waves it down without batting an eye.

"And that's what we are fighting here—that's the severity of this situation. Your disease wants you dead, and if you don't believe me, look around. Congratulations, ladies and gentlemen, you are among the worst of the worst. Now, I don't take pleasure in this, but I will always be real with you guys. Do me a favor and look down at your seat. Every one of you in here today has earned that seat you are sitting in. But you are not special, because before you, there was someone once sitting in that exact same seat with the same opportunity that you have today.

"I look around the room and see we have a full house today. There's maybe a hundred and fifty of you here? That means, statistically speaking, by this time next year, about five or six of you guys will no longer be with us." She takes her final sip. "And I don't just mean no longer in the room." Her words sink in. "Sand Island has been helping alcoholics and addicts recover from this hopeless condition for over fifty years. Do the math, and if you need help, ask the guy next to you. Five deaths a year for fifty years, and that's just the clients who relapse that we know about. What I'm saying is, your disease is trying to kill you."

She walks back to her table in the front and center of the Rec Hall, pulls out the only chair situated there and takes a seat. Her voice, once blunt, calms down to a sincere utterance.

"You have a chance here today to change your future. Don't be another sad story we share about in class. Be selfish and protect your recovery." She twists the cap back onto her water bottle. "Protect it every single day. You know, even with all the years of sobriety I have under my belt, I know that the fight isn't over. It never will be. I know that regardless of how far I've come, or how far I go, I am always just one hit away from losing everything. I'm just one hit away from losing my seat. One hit—that's all it takes. One hit and I'm right back in. One hit, I'm back in jail, back on the run. One hit, I lose my family. Poof. My children. *Poof.* My grandchildren. My job. My house. My car. My friends. My world. Everything. You name it. It's all dust!"

As her words sink in, she looks back overhead at the wall clock and checks the time.

"And I'm not willing to lose everything today." She shakes her head. "Look, I don't know about all of you, but for me, I don't have another run in me. Some of you guys are young and have to go back out there and learn the hard way. You may or may not make it back." She shrugs her shoulders. "That's okay, but that's on you. For everyone else, know that relapse is not an option and fuck whoever tells you otherwise! Your disease, like my disease, is trying to kill you! And I'm no different. I'm not special. Twenty-plus years of sobriety and just like you, I'm still one hit away."

Her words are powerful and moving. They make me realize that the staff here are not merely academics. Every counselor has at one point or another gone through this program. Most entered through the court system and stuck around long enough for the miracle to happen. They've lived through this program and survived it, each of them continuing on to pursue a Certified Substance Abuse Counselor degree. When they speak, I know I can relate, and when my turn comes to share, I know they will understand.

17

BLACKOUT

I can't wait for this first week to be over. Impatience has set in and too much depends on which counselor I am assigned to. I do my best to follow along with the regimen and head into the Rec Hall to sit down and write out my Tenth Step. The introspective process of discovering where my mind is at always gets the blood pumping. Journaling is a means to allocate time and energy to hash out my inner doubts, anxieties and fears, as well as document my growth.

I read a leading question posed for those who've hit writer's block: *If I had to thank God, what would I be thankful for?*

"Being alive and being somewhere that I can get the help I need" is my answer, though I know that often my thoughts and wishes would contradict one another. Among the feelings of appreciation for a safe place to lay my head, I still wallow in poisonous thoughts of wanting to use. Trying to find a groove and learn the program is forcing me to face the fallout of my addiction.

Since I'm no longer running, everything is catching up to me, and I no longer have the numbing safety net of being high. I resent losing so much time to using, knowing that I can never get those best years of my life back. Some staff here have also made it a point to remind me of the financial burden my addiction has cost my family, starting at the six grand it cost just to buy my way into the program. It's a debt I have no means to pay back.

As I write, I imagine what the future will hold. In time, I know my parents will heal with me and I expect to be granted family visits. The corner of a baby photo sticks out of my Big Book. I pull out the picture and study it. Dad is dressed in scrubs, holding me in the delivery room with my head nestled to his chest. It's amazing what parents will do for the love of a child, and though I can't communicate with them, I am still grateful for their continuing support. I think of my family and blame myself for not reaching out for help earlier. When I think of all the pain I have caused my mother, father and brothers, my imagination runs wild.

Full of uncomfortable remorse, I trust that recovery gets better with age, but I feel the need to speed up the process. On top of being unable to sleep, I am hit with the reality that for years I have manipulated and misled those who love me most. Those who didn't deserve it—those who didn't understand it. It makes me accept that I belong here with the lowest of the lows. I wonder how some of them around me can sleep so peacefully. I pray for sleep. I am thankful for Deacon and his free advice to curtail caffeine and take warm showers before going to bed. One day, I will be thankful to relax and drift away instead of incessantly licking my wounds.

I keep my head down, wipe my mouth and flip the page.

Dear Dad,

Thank you for saving my life. How I got to this point is something that I'm working on. I was looking at these pictures Mom sent me of you holding me as a baby and I couldn't help but cry. How did I get here? Why did I fight and resist getting here? All that love, yet so much hate. I don't know why. I stopped loving myself and once I stopped caring, it was easy to self-destruct. I worked hard to get here and earned my misery and pain. But I brought it for others too. You raised me to be a good person. I know right from wrong and am smart enough to know better. So there are no excuses why—

Tears tickle my cheeks and drop onto the notepad. I pinch my nose to hold back the sobs, not wanting to attract attention. One gasp rings out while my jaw trembles and I realize that I can't continue writing. I'm not strong enough to crack open the flood-gates and hold back the surge. Not here. Not now. Perhaps, not ever.

A hand drapes over the edge of the top bunk as Deacon rolls over in his sleep and I debate waking him up once again. It's not his fault that I can't sleep, and though he has never once complained, I feel selfish dragging him with me while I stretch my achy legs. I decide he deserves sleep and slip out the dormitory door, quietly closing it behind me.

The facility is a different beast at night, dimly lit and deserted. Only a few clients are still up at this hour, and all but one are wearing the mandated white t-shirt required after sunset. I rest my feet under the stars and drop a pinch of tobacco onto a rolling paper.

"Want a real one?"

I look up and see a transition client pulling a pack of Marlboro's from his breast pocket. His work shirt reads "The Cheese-cake Factory."

"I'd love one, thanks." I dump my tobacco back into my bag along with the rolling paper and reach out for the cigarette.

"Need a light too?" he asks.

I wave him off. Bending a paper match, I snap it on the striking strip, light my cigarette and blow the flame out with a puff of smoke. I leave it attached with the other burned matches and stuff the sulfur-laden matchbook back into my pocket.

"You must be new, huh?" he asks. It's a small island and an even smaller treatment center.

"Yeah, just got here a few days ago. I'm Jordan."

"Who's your Shadow?"

"Deacon," I say, blowing smoke out of the side of my mouth.

"Right on. He's a good guy." He looks around. "But where is he?"

I sniff the night air. "Asleep. I didn't want to wake him up again. I haven't slept since I've been here and think he deserves at least some rest."

He takes a long drag. "Well, that's on you, just make sure you don't get caught wandering around without him or you'll both catch a restriction." He stands up to leave, leaving two cigarettes on the table in front of me. "Trust me, you don't want to make your life here any harder than it needs to be."

Swiping the cigarettes off the table, I head back to bed before Deacon realizes I'm gone.

My finger highlights the text in the Big Book as Deacon reads Step Four aloud. I repeat after him, hoping to commit the first four steps to memory. I shake my head and face the fact that we both have very different ideas of how to best take advantage of our downtime. I close my Big Book and begin to roll a cigarette on the cover and notice Ty heading my way. He brings with him the excitement of a break in the routine.

"Mr. Barnes, congratulations!" Ty smiles, handing me a piece of paper before hurrying on, looking for the remaining new clients. Brushing my hair out of my face, I study the laminated photo of me on my first day during intake. Next to it is a large green dot.

"Green group! Called it!" Deacon says proudly. "Welcome to Mike's group! Now, take a look around—you can only talk to other guys that have the same color badge. You can still talk to any transition client and staff member, but that's it. And remember, no talking in dorms. Work on that."

He's right. I've been struggling with not only talking in the dorms, but with talking more than I am listening. "Thanks,

Deacon. I know that I'll be off Shadow soon and I feel like there's so much to this program I still don't understand. You've done a great job explaining everything, so I hope it's a smooth ride."

"You'll be fine," Deacon promises. "You're in a good group. Just take it day by day, say the Serenity Prayer if you need to, and remember, if you don't know what to do, don't do anything at all." He smiles and sucks tobacco juices through his teeth, allowing his eyes to trail off in the distance.

I turn around and see Mike approaching with a clipboard in hand. I've sat through one of his classes before and found his energy to be in-your-face infectious. He has a passion for recovery and a short temper for having his time wasted. With a chest like a barrel of apples, he stands at least six-foot-four. He's in his fifties, though in better shape than most clients here who are half his age. Bobbing as he walks, his long arms swing through the air like he's paddling through a sea of bullshit. His dark tan skin and blonde hair pay homage to his Californian youth.

"Is there a Mr. Barnes here?" he asks, looking around.

I jump up and catch my reflection in his sunglasses.

"I love it," he says. "Follow me." Mike turns and I scramble to gather my stuff and catch up. I speed walk, making sure not to run and break a rule. We zigzag along the path to the back of the property, stopping outside of a white shipping container with jalousie windows and an aged screen door.

"Step inside. Please remove your shoes." He kicks off his slippers and takes one large step inside, skipping the two wooden steps that lead up to his doorway.

"Please. Have a seat. Welcome to my office and my Hale," he says. In the corner is a Hawaiian day bed that looks too short for him. There is a small TV with streaks on the screen and a stack of surfing DVDs leaning against it. On the wall is a horizontal rack of surfboards of varying shapes and sizes. A large Koa steering paddle leans against the wall and next to it is a framed photo of a surfer deep inside a double-overhead barrel at Sunset beach.

"Is that you?" I ask, leaning in closer, moving my head to see past my reflection in the glass. The stance in the photo is low and powerful.

"Hell yeah! And you know what? That could be you too! Once you're off Blackout, you'll be able to go out to the beach and get in the water. Swim, workout, train." He flips open a manila folder, splaying it out on the desk in front of him. "So, what do we have here?" His finger draws an "S" across the paper. "Heroin, huh?" He sucks in air through his teeth. "That's a tough one. How are you holding up?" While waiting for my response, he crosses his feet and extends them out past the side of my chair. They look like flippers.

"It's okay, I guess. I'm weak and always hungry, but mostly, I just wish I could sleep."

"You will, in time. I can promise you that," he says. Mike slides on a pair of reading glasses and buries his nose into my folder. "It says that you detoxed before you came?" He leans back in his chair. "Lucky."

"Yeah, for a week back in Portland."

"Good, that's good. Because it's a beast of a drug to kick." His eyes light up. "Be thankful you're not going cold turkey though, like I had to." He lets out a guttural laugh and slaps the desk. "I wouldn't wish that on anyone!" He cranks his neck back and looks up toward the ceiling for so long that my gaze follows suit. "Yeah, you'll be okay. I'm excited to work with you."

If I had any guard up, I let it down immediately. I believe I can trust Mike, knowing that he understands what I'm going through. He's old enough to play the father figure, but talks to me like a friend with my best interest at heart.

"We're not going to get into too much today, but that's okay—recovery is a lifelong process. Do you need anything?"

I think for a second. "I could use some tobacco."

He gives me a couple of cigarettes out of his own pack. I'm surprised that for a treatment center, almost every person here smokes. As I get up to leave, Mike thanks me for the opportunity to work with me.

"Oh, hang on a second." He fumbles through a stack of letters on his desk. "I think you have mail. I just need you to open it in front of me and you're good to go." He hands me a letter from my mom, and I rip it open with the edge of my finger. Pulling out the paper, Mike spreads the envelope open with his fingers and peers inside. Satisfied it's only the letter, he sends me off.

As I walk away, I hear the door creak open behind me. "Oh, and you're officially off Shadow. Good luck."

On my way back to the dorm, Deacon sees me coming and simply asks, "Off Shadow?" He gives a thumbs up as I smile to confirm. Hooking a right, I head back into the dorm and flop onto the bed, unfolding the typed letter onto my pillow.

Dear Jordan,

Your father and I were talking about you yesterday as we were kayaking on the bay. Son, I am so grateful that you came home with us and that you embraced all that we did. I look back on our time in Portland and how it all fell into place. The sauna/hot tub, Japanese dinner, time spent together whether waiting for our plane or being in our hotel room and even the plane ride home, was a treasure. We were open and honest, and it started the healing process for us all.

I'm hoping that you are taking this time to learn about you. There is no rush—we are not going anywhere and this time will help you help yourself. I hope that you are not like me when I was at your age—I lived in the future and did not embrace the present. Time is now your friend. You are safe, well fed and cared for. It is time to work on you and to be honest, so you can get the help that you need to have a wonderful life!

Jordan, you are so precious to all of us. It was refreshing to see your sense of humor back as we were going to work and needed to dump the trash at the top of the hill. Jonathan said he would gladly get out to take the trash out of the truck bed, but he was stuck because his door didn't open and you said you would take care of it. And then you get out and walked past the trash, around the back of the truck and released Jonathan . . . that was too funny! We are looking forward to the next time we can see you!

Eiji asked about you on Saturday and said that he enjoyed meeting you. I put your herb tea in the freezer where he said it would keep well. Last time I went, he put the acupuncture needles inside my ear. Didn't like that one very much. He left tiny little gold dots in my ear to help my thyroid—now that is styling because you can only see them when I turn just right. We'll see if that helps. Eiji's little chicks are not so little anymore. The black chick is the most social and will hop up on your hand to be carried. One of the yellow chicks looks like she has makeup on. It seems that everything Eiji touches flourishes!

Love, love, love, Mom.

Deacon steps into the dorm and begins to pack his belongings, filling his pillowcase with his clothes. Once everything is ready to go, he leans over and whispers into my ear, "I told you your first week here would be over before you knew it. You're going to be fine, and I'm here for you if you need anything." He shakes my foot with the same tattooed arm I was so quick to judge him on. I realize that perhaps this is a place where people can change, then let my thoughts fall back onto the letter.

P.S. I'm honoring my promise to you that we will work on getting healthy just as you are doing so. Keep up the good work son. Please know and accept that this will not be a quick solution for you. This is your life, Jordan. You are very bright, funny and loving. Take time for yourself—be honest with yourself and others. Always remember what I taught you: do the right thing for the right reason when no one is looking, and life will be very good back to you. Trust me, this works, and you will feel so good about yourself!

I fold the letter up and store it safely in my locker. My eyes are wet as I know what she is doing. She is reminding me of normalcy and showing me that I have options. The pot at the end of the rainbow is the promise of a good life.

I turn on my side, clutch my pillow and pray that my mind may finally rest. Every night, I collapse into bed in an exhausted mess and wear myself thin with an endless fit of kicking, tossing and turning. Since my arrival, sleep has evaded me and this mental turmoil has depleted my energy. The food here is all that keeps me going, and though each meal is a healthy portion, they are never enough to offset the number of calories I am burning off by sweating each night.

I hop out of bed, hungry and sore. No longer on Shadow, I can come and go as I please. Heading into the Rec Hall, I see a couple of clients watching late night TV, and pull up a chair beside them. A handful of transition workers who have returned from work are stuffing their faces with plate lunches from L&L Barbecue. Deacon mentioned that when I start working, I'll be allowed to bring home food or store non-perishable foods in my dorm, as long as they fit inside an air-tight container.

My elbows and chin flop onto the table closest to the TV and my stomach tightens. Having self-medicated for so long, I am not accustomed to any form of uneasiness. Hunger pangs are no exception.

I crank my head to the side. "Any of you guys know where to get a bite to eat at this hour?"

One of them lifts up his badge and taps the yellow dot. He's not interested in talking out of badge and catching a restriction, so my eyes bounce to the guy seated next to him. He gazes to me, back to the TV then back to me again. Leaning forward, he speaks softly and talks away from me.

"You can ask the transition guys for some of their dinner, but they'll probably say no." He scratches his cheek. "I shouldn't be telling you this, but there are peanut butter and jelly sandwiches in the white cooler up there." He points up toward the front of the

Rec Hall, just outside of the duty office, to an area that's off limits. "They're for clients who are diabetic or on a special diet. Otherwise, there's no food until breakfast, unless you know someone with a stash of oranges or apples."

I push back from my seat. I'm a veteran thief who supported a habit for years under the watchful eyes of loss prevention and the eyes in the sky. I've even stolen merchandise while being tailed by loss prevention after they had spotted me heading into their store. Looking around, I see there are no cameras and head outside of the Rec Hall. Waiting until the coast is clear, I sneak up toward the duty office and step inside the corridor where I don't belong. The clients who were watching TV are now duly entertained, and I snap open the lid to the white cooler. Inside, on top of a frozen chunk of ice, are a pile of sandwiches, each one in a labeled Ziploc bag. I slip a sandwich into my waistband and feel the sting of cold water dripping down my leg.

"Can I help you?" a voice calls out from behind me.

My stomach cinches. Pulling down my shirt, I turn around and know I am caught dead in my tracks. Russel, who daylights as head of the nursing staff, is making his rounds as tonight's Ninja. He's the lone staff member on patrol and this is my first encounter with him since he checked me in and medically cleared me. Somewhere behind me, a faint chuckle rings out in the Rec Hall.

"Or did you already help yourself?" Russel steps forward and sizes me up. His beady eyes look me up and down from behind his glasses. Without asking, he lifts my shirt, rips the sandwich out from my waistband and tosses it on the ground. "Ahh. *Stealing!?* Not in my house! Come with me," he says. He takes two steps to his right, opens the door to the duty office and pushes me in from behind. "Sit on your hands. Do not touch anything. I'll be right back." He slams the door shut and disappears.

It's hard to breathe. Like a bottom-feeder in a fishbowl, I'm on full display to the Rec Hall with nowhere to go. Staring down at the carpet, I close my eyes and imagine the conversation with my parents trying to justify why I got kicked out of here. Just when I think Russel has forgotten me, I hear his animated voice in the distance. He's with another counselor and they're heading my way.

Uncle Stan is the first in the room. "This better be good. Do you have any idea how much I cherish my sleep?" he asks. His heavy breath whistles under a thick, silver mustache. As a retired sheriff turned client, then counselor, he's seen it all. He rubs his eyes, takes a seat and crosses his arms over his belly.

Russel squeezes around him and drops the sandwich on a table. "Mr. Barnes took it upon himself to steal this and stuff it inside his boxers. Evidently, he has yet to learn that recovery is all about changing old habits and learning new ones."

"Thank you, Russel. I'll take it from here. Can you excuse us for a moment?" Uncle Stan asks.

"You got it," Russel says. He exits the duty office and closes the door behind him.

Uncle Stan scoots up closer to my leg. "You know, we have a zero tolerance policy for stealing." He lets that sink in for a moment and exhales. "You're not diabetic, are you?"

I lift my hands up and let them fall to my side.

"*Hui.* Look at me like a man. You trying to get kicked out?"

"No. Not at all. I'm just starving and—"

"Figured you'd help yourself," he says. "Look, we're all addicts here. We know all the tricks. Most of us even helped write the rules. Russel is right—recovery is all about changing behaviors and thinking differently." He thinks for a moment. "When did you get off Shadow?" he asks.

"Today."

"Just today?" He stretches his jaw. "Your Shadow was Deacon, right? Did he go over all the rules with you?"

"Yes." I look around for a way out of this mess.

"Do you need to go back on Shadow?" he asks.

"I don't think so. I know what I did was wrong."

"Good. Then maybe you stand a chance."

Thoughts scatter through my head. I realize I'm not about to be kicked out and press my forehead into my palm. Had he shown me the door, I don't know where it would lead me.

Uncle Stan takes advantage of my receptiveness. "I'm not going to kick you out, because I think if I do, you will go right back to using and kill yourself. You're fortunate you're a walk-in, though. Otherwise, I'd send you back to jail to remind you how good you have it here. Consider yourself lucky." He pauses for a second. "But what you're feeling right now—don't get used to it. No one here will cut you slack again. You're a smart kid, Jordan. Please don't throw it all away over something as stupid as this." He holds up the sandwich. "You'll regret it forever. Now go, take this and eat, but never, ever steal anything again. Okay?"

I don't even have to think. "I promise, Uncle Stan."

He breathes in through his nose. "Keep your promises. Words mean nothing. Show me action. Now, get the hell out of here."

18

STEP ONE

For days, I am known around the facility as a joke, the new guy that stuffed a sandwich into his pants. But not everyone thinks it's funny, especially those who've watched a friend get kicked out of the program or sent back to jail for an infraction much less severe. Deacon takes it upon himself to keep an eye on me even though he's no longer obligated to. Mike, who initially thought I was off to a good start, reminds me I no longer have to keep proving others wrong.

Because seating is limited, Deacon and I each grab a folding white chair and head to the back of the facility. He doesn't need to attend the Forty-Five-Day and Under class with me, but prefers it to sitting around bored. This is the one class Russel leads and he welcomes us in. I anticipate being made an example of or being put on the spot, but he doesn't hold resentments and greets me as an opportunity to excel. He reels in the stragglers as well as their Shadows who were hoping to leave him on babysitting duties for the next hour.

"I got to say, I love working with you guys. I can almost smell the disease in the room today." Russel's nose sniffs a rainbow across the room and lands on his Big Book. "Remember, it's the first drink that gets you drunk, not the last. It's the first hit that gets you loaded. So how do you prevent that, you ask?" His voice is loud and confident. "Good question! You prevent that by being honest with yourself, starting today. Today, you are going to create your Step One, which is, in my opinion, the most important step. This will save your ass, so it has to be strong." His fist slams the table. The water in my cup rocks back and forth. "It has to be real! It has to be raw! Who here knows Step One? Anyone?"

Eli raises his hand and speaks before he is called. "Step One is powerlessness," he says, dropping his hand.

"Powerlessness, yes! But do you know the actual step? No half-stepping from here on out. You can't afford to wing it!" Russel looks around the room, hoping for a response.

"We admitted we were powerless ove—"

"Ah, ah, Deacon, I already know you know it. You've been here long enough. I want to hear it from the new guys. What about you, Mr. Barnes?" Russel's eyes lock onto mine.

I clear my throat. "We admitted we were powerless over alcohol and that our lives are unmanageable?"

"Had become unmanageable," Russel says, correcting me. "We admitted we were powerless over alcohol, that our lives had become unmanageable. Say it with me."

A choir of criminals rings out, repeating the phrase.

"Good, and if alcohol wasn't your drug of choice, just replace it with your vice. Simple! Now, all of you in this room, I need you to pay very close attention. If I ask you to define *unmanageable*, you would probably think of it as out of control, right? No can handle, eh?"

Around the room, heads nod in agreement.

"So we know that our addiction, our *disease*, was out of control. Otherwise, you wouldn't be here, yeah? So I want you to ask your-self how bad it was. I want you all to think back, and you don't have to share it, but think back and remember a time that you were truly powerless. How did that make you feel? You don't need to write it down, but you need to know it right here."

His trigger finger drills his temple. "It's critical that each one of you has a strong Step One—something to remember, someplace you never want to go back to. Something you hate about your disease. Only you will know it, whatever that is. Now, take as much time as you need." Russel stands up and leaves the room.

With a sip of my water, I think for a second and watch Deacon step out of the room. Regrets flash through my mind, along with close calls and days I wished I could have reversed. Homelessness. Hate. Being chased through a mall by a mob. Fights. Each one worse than the last. Each one I wish I could forget.

Then it hits me with the force of a Mack Truck.

I'm back in Portland, alone in my college dorm and sicker than the day is long. There is no dealer working at this hour or money in my pocket even if there were. I went to the library to look for a laptop to steal, but returned a failure. It's almost midnight, and I can barely make it through the next minute, let alone until morning. The chills are coming and it's not through an open window. My legs twitch restlessly and my bones creak. My spine struggles to support the weight of my upper body.

I dig through my trash, hoping to find some used dope wrapper with the tiniest bit of residue left, but I know I'll come up empty-handed. I tear apart the room, hoping any other addict I've let shoot up in here was more careless than I. Finding nothing, I drop to my hands and knees, then search the carpet for a fallen crumble of hope.

A shiver creeps up my neck and a ring invades my ear canals. I'll do anything for a hit. Opening my safe, I pull out a bundle of used needles along with a pile of spoons and cookers. I start by doing a rinse of my collection of used cottons, adding water and smashing them with the plunger to extract any remaining dope. The pieces of cotton are filled with remnants of cut and contaminants. I know this is pointless since I've rinsed them before. The water that seeps into the needle is clear and useless—

even though it won't do the trick—I let the shot ring out and move on.

I look at the pile of needles on the carpet next to me and stop counting at twenty. These are mostly mine, but I stockpile any used needles I can get my hands on to trade in at the needle exchange. There's no way to tell them apart, except for this one. This one is not like the others.

I hold the syringe in front of my eyes. By the size of it, it looks like it could take down an elephant. The large, 23-gauge syringe with a screw-on needle tip is only used by one person I know. He has collapsed every vein from his neck to his toes.

An open, black hole in his thigh next to his groin is all that stands between Jason and muscling every shot from here on out. He gave up on this shot and left this here with about 10cc of coagulated blood that hardened in the syringe when he accidentally spiked his femoral artery instead of his great saphenous vein. Nothing burns hotter than a shot into an artery, and the pushback of blood can fill a syringe and harden if you're not quick enough.

I stare at it for a second, then point the barbed end toward the cooker and squeeze on the plunger. I push harder, bending the thin plastic to the side. Shaking my head, I remove the needle tip, thrust both thumbs on the plunger until they turn white and the blockage explodes, shooting the curdled fluid into the cooker with a pop. Lifting the tiny cauldron to eye level, I gently heat it with a lighter and watch wisps of smoke rise from the soup like a voodoo concoction. Gagging aloud, I scoop out the coagulate with the tip of the needle and let it dangle in time like a persistent memory. A moment later, my hand twists and lets the fried globule flop onto the carpet below.

Here we go—I'm taking this to the grave and dig for a vein. The shot hits me, but I feel nothing. The burned blood coursing through me gives me the chills. Sick to my stomach, I drop my head and know it will be another long night. I feel the onslaught of uncontrollable bowel movements and clench my stomach. Cocking my head back, I look up to the ceiling and curse God.

That's when I see it. I squint at the miracle. All along the ceiling are faint spray patterns that look like blood splatter from self-inflicted gunshots. But nobody has killed themselves here. Not yet. I know those patterns well. They can only occur from one thing—cleaning syringes. After a hit, we always squirt out the last bit of fluid left to prevent clogging in the needle shaft. The colors are a deep burgundy brown and they're mine for the taking.

What goes up, must come down.

Balancing on my desk, I reach up to the ceiling on wobbly legs. With a wet cotton in hand, I wipe it along the ceiling, checking it after a few smears and realize it's working. The cotton is picking up color, along with a light chalkiness from the paint. I continue cleaning the ceiling, laughing out loud with surprise at my brilliance.

Jumping down on the floor, I drop the cotton into the cooker. Again, I begin a rinse and this time, my needle extracts water with the slightest tinge of brown. I ask God to standby until I spike a vein, and once I see the red flash of blood, I pop the tourniquet and feel faith restored. A large exhale is followed by the slightest release of pressure, yet I am nowhere close to out of the woods. It will still be an endless night, but if that first pass can take the edge off, I know the rest of my ceiling can hold me over until morning.

Russel steps back into the room. "So did you guys get it?"

A couple of guys nod and I wipe sweat off my brow. I need to return to that room.

"Anyone care to share?"

I close my eyes and keep my mouth shut.

"Mike . . . I feel so confused," I say. My eyes squint in the bright rays of sunlight slicing through his window. I adjust my seat and retreat into the shadows.

"Confused about what?" he asks, ever invested in my mental health.

"I don't know. All of this. I haven't been thinking straight lately and am finding it's hard to even talk." I desperately need sleep and wish I had medical clearance from the nursing staff to stay in bed during classes.

"I remember the confusion. It's to be expected as your mind adjusts to reality." He thinks for a second, his mouth dangling partially open. "Let me try to point you in the right direction, like a road map." His mention of travel reminds me that I have a temporary driver's license in my locker along with a one-way flight voucher if I ever decide to push the eject button. My license expires in two weeks, and until that day, I know I can still return to my old life and habits. It's my backup plan, and depending on my physical mood, it brings me comfort knowing that I have something to fall back on.

I try to focus as Mike spells the program milestones out for me in plain English. My personal treatment plan in intensive will follow the first five steps of the Alcoholics Anonymous program. It is fitting that Sand Island still exclusively works the Alcoholics Anonymous Twelve-Step Program after fifty years in the game. Narcotics Anonymous isn't practiced here because apparently the recovery concepts for all addictions are the same. Regardless of your drug of choice, it's a level playing field once we toss our ego out of the game. Mike asks me to follow along as he reads the steps from the book.

He waits for my shaky hand to flip to the correct page and begins. Step One: We admitted we were powerless over alcohol—that our lives had become unmanageable.

"I know you have a history of alcoholism, so just add cocaine and heroin to the list along with any other addiction," Mike explains. "Like I tell all my guys—the very nature of your existence in this program means that your addiction was out of control because otherwise, we wouldn't have let you through the gates. But despite being in a two-year drug treatment program, you'd be surprised how many guys here don't believe they are the problem. They think the world is against them and struggle to accept responsibility for their own life decisions."

I cut him off. "My life has been out of control for as long as I can remember."

"I'm sure, but even if you don't need convincing, we ask that you take some time to settle into it. Take a month and study the homework I'll give to you. No rush."

Step Two: Came to believe that a Power greater than ourselves could restore us to sanity.

"I'm sure you've heard the term Higher Power before—this could be God, Jesus, Odin—doesn't matter. Most people defer to Jesus, but we don't care what you decide for yourself, just try and put some thought into it. It's not about who or what you believe in, but that you believe in something that works for you."

"And what if I don't believe in God?" I ask, or perhaps confess.

"Not *believe* in God? Haven't you lived through Hell? Haven't you seen the devil?" Mike shakes his head. "Either way, remember, it's not necessarily about any particular god. A lot of people get hung up on that, so they draw a line between spirituality and religion. You'll hear the quote in class often: 'Religion is for people who're afraid of going to Hell, spirituality is for those who've already been there.' For me though, it's always God first, but I'll tell you from experience to give it time. You probably have a lot of walls up and that's okay. Eventually though, I think that if you're honest with yourself, you'll realize that someone was always looking out for you."

Greater than myself? I knew this was coming. "What if I always felt abandoned?"

"Trust me, if you were abandoned, you wouldn't be here. But let's not get too hung up on this step right now. Just know that, in time, people change."

I agree with putting it off for now. I know my mind isn't thinking clearly yet, but I can't help recalling the morning of Simon's passing, which solidified in my mind that no God could exist in a world so cold. As I stared at his dead body, it was so clear to me there was nothing beyond that moment except the end of another sad story. A chill stings my spine.

Step Three: Made a decision to turn our will and our lives over to the care of God as we understood Him.

"Step Three is all about relinquishing control to take yourself out of the driver's seat. You'll hear us constantly say that 'your best thinking got you here,' meaning it's about time to let someone else take the reins and drive for a while. It's all about a willingness to let go of control and trust the process."

"And how is that determined?" I ask, trying to quantify the unquantifiable.

"On a case-by-case basis, but we've been doing this a long time." Mike laughs a little. "Look, none of this is anything magical you can capture in a bottle, but you can expect each step to take about a month. Here's a tip though—when my guys try to rush through these steps, they only seem to delay the process. You'll move on when you're ready."

I slump back in my hard, plastic chair. From the sound of it, I don't have a choice but to relinquish control, starting now.

Step Four: Made a searching and fearless moral inventory of ourselves.

"You are going to make a resentment list, including everything and anything you can think of that you regret or wish to make amends for. People you've hurt, those who have hurt you, people you've wronged, things you wish you could take back. Everything that is wrong with you and holding you back from moving forward, including your deepest, darkest secrets."

"What's the point of that?" I ask, feeling interested again.

"You have to know what you harbor to dispose of it properly, and resentments are the number one offender. The danger of not letting go of all that bullshit is that over time it can build into an excuse to relapse. Don't let your past poison your future. You have to learn how to forgive yourself and others."

Step Five: Admitted to God, to ourselves, and to another human being the exact nature of our wrongs.

"This is the last step in intensive treatment. Once you have everything written on paper, you get to pour it all out to a Holy Man. You're Catholic, right?" Mike asks.

"Raised Catholic, but wouldn't consider myself a practicing one. After being burned out as a kid being an Altar Boy and going to Catholic School, the moment I got old enough to decide to stay home from church, I did. Then, as I got older, the sexual abuse scandals and hypocritical moral compass of the institution sickened me, and I never looked at church the same."

"Okay, well, I'll still probably send you to a Catholic Church to perform your Fifth Step unless you tell me otherwise. When you sit down with the priest, you'll go through your list line by line, reading it aloud like confession. This is where you let go and leave all of that baggage behind. After that, you're ready to move on to transition with a clean slate. You will feel like a new man, and from that point forward, the rest of the program is considered maintenance steps."

I inhale, taking in the whole process. "Thanks, Mike. That was helpful. I appreciate you walking me through all this."

"Well, I've had a lot of practice."

"So when is Deacon doing his Fifth Step and going to work?" I ask.

"He'll do his step when he's ready, but he won't be going to work."

"Why not?" I ask. "I thought everyone goes to work after Step Five?"

"Almost everyone. Some people can't, because they are court-ordered to stay on property or are a danger to themselves or others. But Deacon is Drug Court so he's on a different path."

I give Mike a blank stare.

"Drug Court is a whole other curriculum for clients who are ordered here by a judge, usually after violating terms of the court or failing a drug test. It's like a last-chance opportunity before being sentenced to prison. There's a handful of them here, and they take about eight months to work through an expedited treatment plan."

The gears up top start turning as I wonder if there is a way for me to work it out so I can be done in eight months as well.

"I know what you're thinking, but it's not going to work for you. You have to be sentenced here as part of Drug Court. As a walk-in, you're no different from all the other guys here in intensive." Mike pauses for a moment. "Don't get hung up on the time —there's no shortcut to any place worth going. This program will be as good as you make it and gets better after thirty days because once you're off Blackout, you can go to the beach or store. If you can avoid drama, learn to say, 'You got it,' and keep a positive attitude, you'll be fine."

"You got it?"

"Huh? I'm surprised Ty didn't tell you that." He ponders a second, raising his eyebrows. "It's like a magical phrase. If staff ever asks you to do something, just say, 'You got it' and do it. It doesn't matter if you agree or even want to. What you'll find is that it gets easier to do things you don't want to do, like volunteer for a shift or chore. It takes you out of self and forces you to think differently. In time, you'll learn that sobriety often requires you to do things you don't want to do."

"Okay. Got it," I say.

"No, it's 'You got it!'" he says. Mike laughs aloud and slaps the cover of his book shut. "Anyway, remember, this whole thing is a process that takes time to navigate, but if you put in the effort, you'll get out tenfold of what you put in. If you like, you can always meditate on the Serenity Prayer, if you find that works for you."

It's a lot to take in, and I realize that my attitude will be the driving force between success and failure. I wonder if I will find the strength to commit and be honest. I know where I would still be if I weren't here right now.

"Something else to keep an eye on is self-sabotaging. Try not to worry too much about the future," Mike says. He leans back in his chair, extending out his long legs.

"I can't help it. I can't imagine a life where every day feels like this!"

"That's a lie and you know it. Every day is not going to feel like this. I'm telling you, all of this will pass and it will get better. Much, much better, if you take a step back and let God do his work."

I exhale and look out the window. A cat is napping on the warm sidewalk. "Mike, I can't sleep. It's torture. All I do is lie awake in misery. I want to leave, use and—" I cut myself off.

I don't want to die, do I?

"Jordan, I know what you're going through. I've been there and I'm here with you. The physical side, the Post-Acute Withdrawal Symptoms that we talked about, these are going to be uncomfortable, but manageable. You will get there, I promise, but only if you control your thinking. The negative thoughts will come, but you have to let them go. Don't dwell on them. Tonight, when you're lying in your bed and hating life, remember, each day that passes will be better than the last. Tomorrow, will not be worse than today."

The cat outside stirs, flops over and stretches its legs.

"Sobriety is a lifelong commitment, but I didn't tell you that to freak you out. I told you that to give you hope." Mike looks up to the photo of him surfing the barrel at Sunset. "Do you think I would still be sober after all these years if every day was a struggle?" He starts the motion of laughing, but only a heaving breath escapes. "Every day is a blessing, and I love my life today. I have the freedom to toss any board in my car, drive to the North Shore and paddle into the largest barrel of the set. I can live life and you can, too."

The look on his face in the photo is seriousness mixed with thrill.

"This will pass, and if you do the work, you will get the right results. You'll probably always have an addictive personality and anti-social traits, but in time you'll discover how to manage those character defects. But for now, you're feeling powerless because you're burned out and are only starting to heal. Everything is coming at you all at once—don't expect to catch it all." He leans back in his chair. "Yeah, it fucking hurts, but trust me, it can't hurt forever. I'm telling you from experience." He slaps the arms of his chair. "Oh, and before I forget, you have mail."

I hope he's right about the pain subsiding. After thanking him, I take the letter back to my bunk where I can read it semi-privately.

Dear Jordan,

I've been thinking about you and sending good thoughts your way. What a welcomed relief that you are in a safe place where you can get help on so many levels. Your brother and I are going to either an A.A. or Al-Anon meeting this week. A lot of changes are going on here—I bet there are a lot of changes going on with you also! I think of you often, and I am grateful that you are in a place where you can be safe, talk about yourself and get help to move forward.

Do you remember when your father and I stayed at Saint Stephen's and you came to pick us up at the end of the weekend? You looked at the small room we had and asked how could we have stayed there comfortably. You couldn't have known, but that was one of my favorite weekends. Although we were with a group of twenty other couples, that weekend was all about each couple reconnecting with themselves and God. It was a time to work out issues, learn new coping skills and find peace within. Your father and I felt renewed, reinvigorated and refocused. It was a time for ourselves without outside worries, money concerns and family issues. It reminds me of what I think you must have.

When your brother was in rehab, he called me during the last week to say he was ready to come home and that he had everything in perspective. I told him he should wait until the end of his program and listen to when his counselors thought it was time for him to come home. Time is to learn about yourself and how to cope—to physically, mentally and spiritually heal. Please take this gift of time for what it is: a wonderful gift. You are so creative and smart—I can't imagine how grand it is to apply yourself for the sake of yourself.

I went to work on Saturday and then to Eiji. I was surprised not to see his four chicks in the yard and heard the sad news. Eiji thinks a mongoose got them because he found nothing in the caged area when he went out to bring them in for the night. Eiji was so heartbroken and looked guilty. He had put out all kinds of plants along the fence to shade the chicks and they had grown so fast. There were no real words to make Eiji feel better though I tried.

I went to church with Auntie Chris this morning. She noticed that I had a tiny silk bag that I held during church and took to communion. I told her the story about you making me the clay piece when you were eight-years-old and when you gave it to me, you told me it had all of your good thoughts inside! She thought that was so sweet and couldn't help but cry. We walked out of church and Father Keenan asked about your father and you. I told him that I keep you near me in thoughts and prayers, then showed him the small silk bag and he blessed that bag, your Good Thoughts and you!

Jordan, keep doing what needs to be done to get you back to real health. You have so many family members and friends that are caring for you in thought and prayer.

We're very proud that you are doing the right thing. Your father's birthday is coming up this Friday and mine is Saturday. I can't think of a better present right now than having you in a safe place, knowing that you are getting help in so many areas to better yourself and make your life something you will truly look forward to. Jordan, you are very special to all of us, and I look forward to having a simple lunch with you one day, or even just going to a movie or the beach together.

I drove to the Coast Guard base the other day after work and saw a group of men running. They did not appear to be Coast

Guard, but they all looked clean and healthy. Some were running fast—some not so quickly, but still trying. I let my mind venture to see you running or playing soccer again. In the past few years, I never allowed myself to think of you doing those things, but now those thoughts come to my mind. Jordan, take good care of our son—we love him very much. Keep moving in the right direction. I'm very proud of you for conquering yourself.

Love, love, love, Mom.

19

BREATH OF LIFE

M y palm rubs circles on my forehead as a silent yawn
stretches my jaw. Morning has broken, and with it, the
dorm light flickers on. I pull my sheet up over my face, letting my
eyelashes flicker against the thin cotton. Through it, I can see
shadows of clients as they launch off their upper bunks, ignoring
their ladders.

Waking up has never felt so good. After a month of lying
awake in bed night after night, my mind finally tapped out last
evening. I don't remember the moment I drifted off, but I am
refreshed to realize I victoriously cast away. Having slept through
breakfast, I hold onto my pillow for dear life until I'm torn away
from it, kicking and screaming, by house jobs.

Sleeping through breakfast is optional, but every client here
needs to suit up and show up for their daily chores. Living in the
here and now is a struggle for the handful of us who are assigned
shower duty, even when equipped with latex gloves. As we pull
the shower curtains off the rod and load them onto a wheelbarrow,
we are mindful not to let them brush our pants or touch our shoes.

At first glance they may look clean, but we all know they're
filthy, regardless if they were taken out front to be scrubbed and

hosed down on a tarp as recent as yesterday. When a hundred guys share only a handful of showers, it doesn't take much imagination to envision how quickly they can get dirty. Despite the policy not to shave anywhere but your face, some men still shave their bodies from head to toe, leaving a mess behind to be cleaned up by others. In a shared living space, the showers are also the only private areas available—besides the toilet stalls—and nobody in their right mind would ever step foot into either without slippers, let alone touch the walls.

As our cleaning crew gets to work, I pass a stall and spot red bloodworms blindly crawling up the tile. A client nudges me out of the way to hose the fly larvae back down the drain, and spritzes the walls with AJAX to sanitize the piss, hair and semen caked on the walls from the previous day.

I take my time cleaning the mirrors and sinks while others finish off the stalls. If I time it correctly, we can all finish about the same time and wrap up with a quick scrub of the floors. From what I can tell, the arrangement works well for the time being. Two of the guys on our crew take on the showers each day with pride because it's the first real job they've ever had. We let one guy paint himself into a corner with a scrub mop, then jump out of the way as he uses a hose to flush out the floor, spraying everything toward a drain outside. The whole corridor gets coned off for a half hour to let everything dry.

I wash my hands and walk back into the Rec Hall to journal my Tenth Step and take personal inventory of my life. Meanwhile, staff and interns sweep the dormitories looking for stragglers hiding out in their bunks. I journey inward to become intimate with my thoughts, which is a terrifying space to wander.

Pulling out the Tenth Step questionnaire helps to keep me focused, reminding me to dive deeper and be reflective about my fears, attitude and resentments. The guide takes me on a brief, fifteen-minute journey each morning of honesty and focus. Some of the most straightforward questions leave me with a sore writing hand. Once I start writing, it's hard to stop.

Like a ship exiting the fog, I look behind me and see the wake I've been churning up all these years. I know I've been selfish lately, writing a letter to Mom asking her to drop off tobacco for me at the front gate. I've also been fearful of my outstanding warrants and the eventual blood test for diseases I'll have to take. Some of my biggest resentments don't have an immediate solution —there are so many things I gave up on long ago because I didn't expect to be around this long to suffer the consequences. My teeth hurt and I wish I took better care of them. I think I'm going to try my hand at getting into shape once I receive medical clearance to use the weight room.

The things I am willing to try today are surprising. As my pencil scribbles away, I mouth the words I write. Almost everyone here is trying to grow along spiritual lines and I am no different. Talking to God before meals is a start and at the very least proof that I can try new things. The mind is unfathomably powerful, and I love setting it free to chase after it.

My attention turns next to my Step One homework. Opening the manila folder that Mike gave me, I pull out a five-page handout titled "My First Step: Knowing My Problem." It starts:

There are three fundamental questions that you, while using the Big Book as your guide, must answer to have a program of recovery from alcoholism or other addictions. They are:

- What is the problem?
- What is the solution?
- What can I do to use that solution in my own life?

At first glance, the concept seems rudimentary. Can it all be as simple as recognizing the problem? If so, I may stand a fighting chance. The rest of the handout seems tailored to those who need convincing that they are where they need to be. Diving deeper into the work, I encounter a list of descriptors that define an addict to see if I fit the bill. "I will often drink or use when no one else is."

Check. "I may drink or use any time of the day or night." Check. "I hide the amount consumed or used." Check. "I will lie to . . ." Check. "I will continue to . . ." Check. "I . . ." Check. Check. Check. Check. Check.

Skimming through the rest of the packet, I chew my lower lip and look around the room. I'm not in denial and flip the folder shut. I want to get through the step work as painlessly and quickly as possible, but I know I'll have to wait my turn. Things take time here. There's no question that I'm an addict—it's in my nature, embedded in my personality—and I am grateful to be in a place where I can seek the help and skills I need, especially since self-awareness of powerlessness alone won't override the deep desire to get loaded. I belong here, even though if everything goes according to plan, I'll be walking out the gate by tomorrow afternoon.

"So, we have to do this each time?" I ask.

"Well, you know what they say—failing to plan is planning to fail." Deacon hands out four blank "Plan of Actions" for each one of us to fill out. Eli, Cavin, Deacon and I all pull our chairs together and stare at our small piece of paper while we learn how the P.O.A.s work.

"Men's day out and women's day out alternate every other day. During the week, passes are allowed after last class, and you have to be back on the property by 7:30 p.m. Not a second later—no matter what. On weekends, men and women alternate Saturdays and Sundays."

I can't believe I'm finally off Blackout.

Deacon enjoys playing teacher. "You can only leave the property if your pass is approved. If you want to go out, you need to submit this P.O.A. the day before, and James will either approve it or not. Passes get shut down for any number of reasons: you got caught breaking a rule, you have a shitty attitude, your counselor thinks your focus should be elsewhere. Or sometimes one bad apple ruins it for everyone. You guys can only go out with other members of our group or a transition client if they're down to hang out, but usually, they're too busy to fellowship. Here—just fill out your name, admit date, 'Mike' as your counselor and who else is going."

I look at the paper and fill it out, writing "Sand Island Beach Park" under activity. Leaning over Eli's shoulder, I see that great minds think alike and run my fingers along the page as if sealing an envelope.

"I'll be the escort, meaning I'm liable to make sure no one deviates," Deacon says. He reaches out and grabs our P.O.A.s, one by one. "That also means if my pass gets shut down, the whole group doesn't go, but if one of you guys gets your pass shut down, the rest will have fun for you." Deacon snatches the pass out of my hand. "I'm going to turn these into the office."

"Brah, it's gonna be so fucking nice going to the beach and getting out of here," Eli says.

"Have you been to Sand Island Beach Park?" Cavin asks. "It's pretty shitty. Lots of rocks. Crumbly surf. Get plenty of feral cats with tons of fleas living in the jetty."

Cavin shivers. He's a former professional bodyboarder who traveled the world chasing the best breaks. He might just have a tad bit of a higher standard than I do when it comes to surf breaks.

"Who cares?" I say. "I can't wait to get into the ocean. It's been years." I draw a blank trying to think of the last time I wiggled my toes in the sand. "Do they give out sunscreen?"

"What you really need is soap, onion boy!" Cavin jokes as I swipe my hand over his head, pretending to roughhouse.

I smile and laugh. Over the past few weeks, we've all bonded in a way that can only occur when people go through tough times together. We're fighting the same fight, and whether we would have been friends outside of this program or not, it doesn't matter much in here.

"I'm excited too, but I'll watch from the shore—I can't go in the water," Eli says.

"Can't swim? Sharks?" I ask.

"Worse. I suffer from seizures. They're medically controlled but still dangerous. I can't risk it, which is the same reason I can never drive a car."

I feel bad for him, but I don't want to show it. "Well, it's still going to be a lot of fun getting out of here!"

Deacon returns. "All right fellas. Fingers crossed. They'll call out passes tomorrow. You guys know the drill. Don't be late, and don't get caught doing anything stupid between now and then!"

Running down the beach toward the water, I only manage a few high steps before my knees clip the surface and I trip into a shallow dive. Breaking my fall with my palms, my mouth parts and my breath swells deep within my chest. I plant both feet against the seafloor and explode out of the ocean, spitting a mist and throwing my arms up to my side. My long hair whips left to right until I wipe it away from my face.

The shock is alarming at first, tingling senses I haven't felt activated in years and trickling shivers down my spine. Overhead, a warm sun looks down on me, illuminating my pale flesh, giving me chicken skin. Once the shock has passed, a light wind tickles my torso and I slump back down into the water until only my head is exposed. Dipping the crown of my head backward, I reach both arms overhead and float on my arching back.

Last night I could barely sleep, but for once it was not because I was hating life or combating restlessness—I was looking forward to this first pass. When Mike moved me on from Step One, he handed me Step Two and Three's homework simultaneously and told me that survival in recovery requires rewiring my thinking and controlling my emotions. His advice was to work toward maintaining a positive attitude at all times, and how fellowshipping with peers can fast track the gratitude that's needed to grow.

As I float on the water, the current licks my cheeks. I feel what Mike was talking about—the ocean is healing and freeing. There are no rules or boundaries out here, a stark contrast to the confines of the facility, where no matter which way I turn, someone is always checking up on me, asking me to recite the Steps or wondering what I did to strengthen my sobriety today.

I can't catch a break, but as much as I go back and forth about wanting to leave, I realize that I must be making progress because I have no aversion to trying new things. Staff constantly challenges me to always progress, from realms as intangible as mastering my attitude down to functions as autonomous as controlling my breathing. What I am discovering is that every day, I perform and function better than the day before, which boosts my confidence to reconsider certain boundaries.

Talking to God still feels unnatural, but no more so than being sober. I think back to last night, when I tried my hand at praying and asked God to keep my head in the here and now, and also to let my pass get approved if he was feeling extra generous. I didn't even bother going through the motions—my hands weren't clasped in prayer and my lips didn't move.

Baby steps.

Deacon and Eli are joking on the beach, but I tune them out by reciting Step Two aloud. "Came to believe that a Power greater than ourselves can restore us to *sanity*." The words are muffled by the water in my ears. "Came to believe. Power? Restore us to sanity? Restore. Sanity. Crazy?"

Am I insane?

The ocean crackles in my ears.

If I'm honest with myself, I would admit that the insanity of my actions led me here, and that I am still acting selfishly by asking my mom for money and tobacco, even though I don't need either. I don't need a dictionary to know that the definition of insanity is doing the same thing repeatedly, expecting different results. I close my eyes as a wave washes over my face.

I breathe deeply to increase my buoyancy, taking larger and larger breaths to fill my lungs. My belly stretches as my navel reaches toward the sky and my palms flap on the surface of the water. I breathe deeper, calm my heart rate and hear the soothing voice of Auntie Mae lecturing the class about the "Hā" breathing technique. I focus on the breath of life, and as I float, movement and motion beyond my control engulfs me.

"In, two, three, four, five, six, seven. Out, two, three, four, five, six, seven." I mimic the Hawaiian exercise for the full seven rounds and am mindful of what I can and cannot control. My body rocks with the current and I relax my shoulders, letting my arms sink to my sides. For the first time in weeks, I am not surrounded by distractions, only by vastness. Looking up, my gaze has nowhere to fall but inward. The sounds on the beach fade away and the sun overhead sears my body. I relax my squinting eyes and float.

I am not insane.

This mind of mine is a gold mine, a treasure I am beyond grateful to still possess. I may have lost everything, yet nothing unrecoverable, nothing more than stuff. Material matters come and go like the tide. A wave licks my face and water flows out of the corners of my eyes like tears.

I know I can be so much more than an anxious hermit who makes his home inside of a broken bottle, or a shell of a spooked man who wanders the streets tarred and feathered yet unwilling to change. I no longer have to bathe in blood or wallow in self-pity to make it through the day.

Surrounded by the most powerful force on this planet, I aim to lose orientation and forget which way I am pointed.

I let go and find myself at Her mercy.

The current dictates my bearing while the deepest burdens I harbor bubble to the surface. I am a blot on the horizon that will rise again.

Only after my skin heats up and starts to burn do I lift my head out of the water and realize I have barely drifted away.

Walking up the beach, I tug on my board shorts to cover my pale knees and reach for my shirt half buried in the sand by Eli's feet.

He scoffs a little laugh. "Welcome back to reality, brah. You all right?"

I dab the salt out of the corner my eyes and head for the shower. "You know what? I think I will be."

20

LUCK OF THE DRAW

"Damnit! Okay, okay . . . let's try the other hand once more, but first, let me grab a heat pack." The phlebotomist pops the tourniquet off my wrist and hangs it on the armrest of the blood drawing chair.

When the medical team announced this morning that I had a scheduled blood test appointment, I felt both relieved and nervous. Sanchez, the facilities driver, shuttled a couple of other clients and me here to the Diagnostic Laboratory Services clinic for our mandatory blood tests. It's a step in the process I've long dreaded. I'm almost sure that somewhere along the line I've contracted Hepatitis C. When I first started using, I swore I would never share cookers or needles, but as times got harder, the hardest decisions got easier.

The phlebotomist returns and slaps a heat pack on the back of my hand. "Here, do me a favor and hold this for a second." He is the second technician this morning hoping to get a sample from me today. The first had to stop due to policy that restricted him to two attempts. I don't know who felt worse for who, but he kept apologizing after each miss, as if I didn't do this to myself. My arms—like a safe—are impossible to crack. My veins are shot, scarred and collapsed.

The second phlebotomist is ready to take a stab. "Okay, let me see," he says. His gloved hands twist my arm in the bright light as he inspects the lack of plumbing beneath the surface. "You said you would go here?" He taps the top of my knuckle, gently squishing for any bounce-back from a hidden vein beneath the skin.

"Yeah, just a little lower," I confirm.

He twists the latex tourniquet around my wrist and applies pressure to the heat pack over my knuckle. "Don't worry, we'll spike this. I don't quit."

"Me neither," I half-heartedly joke, staring down at my forearm.

The phlebotomist clasps a tiny needle with butterfly wings between his thumb and middle finger. He asks if I'm ready, as if I haven't been poked a million times before, though it's different when I'm not in control. As the needle tears a hole, we both hope for flashback, but watch as the flexible clear tubing remains clear. Had he spiked a vein, the pressure would force blood through it and into his specimen vial, but we're not there yet. Slowly, he pulls it back most of the way out, adjusts his angle, then tries again. He takes one more attempt before he pulls the needle out and pops off the tourniquet.

"Shit," he whispers. "Where else would you go?" He places a band-aid over my knuckle in a spot where we both know it won't stay.

I tap the inside of my arm, just below my armpit and above the scar from the abscess surgery. "Right here worked for me the last time."

He clicks his tongue. "We can't go there," he says. "It's policy." He thinks for a second. "But you know what? Let me try over here."

I remind myself of that famous Winston Churchill quote Deacon taught me: "If you're going through hell . . . keep going."

He repeats the process, warming up my other hand. I control my breathing and pull myself together in the most sterile of places. I watch as he fishes for a vein, and to my surprise, blood trickles out.

"Damn I'm good! Now, don't you move," he says, widening his stance.

I wonder where these magical heat packs have been all my life. I had no idea they helped so much, and if I had, I would have gone in for blood tests every few weeks just to leave with a few in my pocket.

He pops a vial into the other end of the tube and lets the blood dribble in, careful not to move either the needle or my arm. Once the vial is about half full, he pops it out and replaces it with another.

"That should be enough for that test, but we need two more. Come on little guy!" he coaxes.

Blood seeps into the vial and I remind myself to breathe. When the last vial is full, he pops the tourniquet and smiles with his eyes. "Told you I'd get it." He slaps a Mickey Mouse band-aid on my hand, making the grand total six. "Take your time getting up, okay?"

Staring down at my arms, I can't help but laugh—I look as though I'm about to walk out of the happiest place on earth.

"Push. Push. *Push*!" Deacon stands over me, demanding that I dig deeper.

My heels lift off the floor while I summon all the strength in the world from the balls of my feet. I bare my teeth and tremble, not wanting to ask for help. Deacon gives me another second, then reaches down with four fingers to assist the rusty bench press bar upwards. With a light clink, the forty-four-pound Olympic bar lands safely on the rack.

"Just keep at it man, you'll get there."

I lift my knees to my chest and thrust them forward, rocking myself to my feet. While Deacon loads the bench press bar with weights, I steal a glance in the mirror and see that my arms are literally shot to shit. Healing takes time, and that's about all I seem to have here, but I expected that the purple undertones in my flesh would have faded by now. By the time I turn around and look up, Deacon is smacking his chest with his fist and emptying his lungs.

"Let's do this! Stand behind me and spot me!"

My head scans the bar from left to right and I can't even imagine how much weight there is. "You're crazy! There's no way I can lift that."

"You won't have to," he insists between heavy breaths. "Just act like you're spotting me so we don't get kicked out. Trust me, I know my limits. Ready?"

With every rep, Deacon's breath explodes into the air like a geyser. I would have never imagined that in less than sixty days of treatment, I'd be working out in the hand-me-down gym. If I had to guess, I'd say every piece of machinery here was donated. It makes no difference though—weight is weight—and I enjoy the setup.

The large tarp that covers the open-air gym billows in the breeze. We call it a weight room, but it's not actually a room at all. Eight clients, the maximum allowable amount in the weight room, run through their routines as the guys on the wait-list smoke around the outskirts. Deacon and I have about fifteen minutes left of our one-hour time slot, then I'll sign us both out and let the next guys on the list have at it. Until then, moving my body and getting the blood flowing helps get me to a better state. Besides the camaraderie, the makeshift gym doubles as a coping mechanism for most of the population who need a method to vent. The privilege to work out is so sought after that it's the first privilege taken away when a restriction is sanctioned, which has resulted in a client or two walking out the gate since my time being here.

"Can you believe Mike moved me on to—" I cover my mouth with my hand, catching a thread of drool that almost drips onto Deacon's face. I remind myself to be more careful when I speak. I stand up straight and try not to distract him further while he finishes his set of nearly twice my body weight. He racks the bar, shaking the facility. He's right—he didn't need a spotter.

"So, can you believe Mike moved me on to Step Three?" We both start stripping weights off the bar, leaning them against the rack on the ground. "He told me to say the Third Step Prayer three times daily, read 'We Agnostics' and 'More about Alcoholism' from the Big Book."

"Sounds like Mike. Do you know the Third Step Prayer by heart yet?"

I shake my head. I sit down on the bench, protect the back of my head from hitting the bar with my hand and lean back. "What about you? You don't pray much, do you? In fact, come to think of it, you don't talk about God ever, huh?"

"What's there to talk about?" he asks.

I look up as Deacon leans over and enters my field of view.

"Running my mouth only gets me into trouble," he says. "Besides, you'll learn that talk is cheap, especially in here. Just watch. Like clockwork, the guys that run their mouths the most will run themselves right out the gate. Talking the talk isn't the same as walking the walk. Ready?" He helps lift the bar off the rack and barely lets go. "Keep it level, keep it level!" Deacon coaches, reaching out to cup my left elbow.

Out of the corner of my eye, I see a pair of guys to our left stop their workout to enjoy my struggle.

"Don't mind them," Deacon whispers as he squeezes my elbows in to help me complete the rep. "Remember, the only person in here you ever need to impress is yourself."

Staring up at the bunk above me, I close my eyes and shake my head, having never expected to be put in this position. In my mind, there was never a possible outcome that resulted in me leaving Portland alive, yet here I am, genuinely hoping God hasn't forgotten about me. I'm coming to terms with living long enough that I'm forced to face my fears. Every bad decision that was based on not being around long enough to pay the price is catching up to me. And while most of the guys in here are scared to death of relapsing or returning to a six by eight cell, I toss and turn each night praying that I'm not HIV positive. With my labs results pending, I shudder as I think back to Portland where I've dodged this bullet once before.

It was one of those rare days when I was questioning my future after my entire world had collapsed. "Needle in the Hay" by Elliott Smith was stuck in my head like a recurring nightmare. When I first heard the lyrics, I knew I had found the perfect song to die to and I couldn't help but adopt it as the solemn soundtrack to my tragedy.

To avoid the line at the entrance, I made my way over to Outside In an hour after they opened, so the crowd had time to dissipate. Haven, the passionate coordinator who ran the show, smiled when she saw me stepping into the needle exchange and wanted to show me some complimentary rapid oral HIV tests. If I could spare a few minutes, the tests were free and going fast.

I took care of business first because I didn't have a choice and counted out my needles on the transfer table, slipping them into a square opening to fall away into a large sharps container below. Haven counted along and filled a brown paper bag with new needles, topped it off with cookers, cotton, twist ties and a tourniquet. I completed my internal battle and agreed to take the test. I took a seat and proceeded to sign my life away while she closed the door behind me.

The familiar room seemed smaller than usual. I looked at the posters on the wall until our knees bumped when she pulled up a chair. Opening my mouth, I held my breath to avoid sharing it with her as her gloved hands swabbed my gums. I remember how easily my gums bled and I sucked the blood between my teeth before answering any of her questions. The test was over before I knew it and I anxiously awaited the results.

Haven swallowed.

Hard.

Her ever-present smile faded away as she turned around to read the results.

It read positive.

"There's no way," I stuttered. I couldn't let the words sink in. It can't be right.

Haven had to be sure, but as far as I was concerned, it didn't matter. Nothing mattered in that panic. I knew I had done it—I had lost everything. I crossed the threshold where there was no redemption and no turning back. The walls started moving and crumbled around me. Haven began preparing to take a confirmation blood test, but couldn't convince me that it mattered. I wanted to overdose on the spot. She wanted to calm me down.

Calm down? I was calm like a bomb. The blood test was mandatory? Why the fuck did it matter? She had to know? How would I tell my mom! I had to leave. Disappear. Fade away. I would make a clean escape or maybe rob a bank—but not until I found whoever gave it to me.

Haven spiked a vein to take another sample before I could push her away.

"Jordan. *Jordan*. Can you hear me?" she asked. "Don't let this make you crazy, okay?" She was waiting for a response to make sure I could hear her. "You can stay here as long as you need to, but once you leave, I need you to come back and see me in a few days for the confirmation blood results. In the meantime be safe, and please don't share needles or cookers. If you're sexually active, protect yourself and others. You will be okay. I promise you. If you need to talk, you know you can always find me here."

The memory tears me up inside as I recall how cruel life can be and how quickly things can fall apart. I close my eyes again and remember that it didn't take more than a week before I became the luckiest man alive.

"What do you mean a mistake?" I lost balance, fell backward and slumped against Haven's office door. The fall should have hurt, but the pain didn't register. The stale taste of confusion puddled in my mouth and I fought how to form a complete thought. "A mistake?" I whimpered, shaking my head to clear the clutter. "A false positive isn't 'a mistake' Haven."

I couldn't believe it. It had been a week since I last saw Haven, and instead of spending it coming to terms with my new positive outlook on life, I lusted over ways to end it all. The only thing between me and a fatal overdose was not being able to scrape together enough dope. I buried my face in my hands. Fuck my life —I even told people!

"I don't know what to say, except that I've been looking for you everywhere. I wanted to tell you sooner, but I couldn't find you. You were supposed to come back in for your blood test results days ago. Why'd you wait so long?" she asked.

"I don't know. I guess I was afraid of the test being confirmed."

Haven stared up through the ceiling. "I'm so sorry you had to go through that." She reached out to help me to my feet, even though we both knew I could get up on my own. As she took my hand, I realized it was the first time we'd ever made human contact. She took it a step further and clenched my shoulders before pulling me in for a hug. Who was she trying to comfort more?

"I don't know what to say, other than we don't understand how this happened. It sounds like we received a bad batch of tests, but I promise you—we're investigating it and will find out. Oh, and just so you know, right after your labs contradicted the swab test, we immediately ceased all testing." Haven wiped her hair out of her face. "I haven't slept in days, Jordan. I've been worried sick about you, driving circles around the city and waiting for you to come back. I even put the word out if anybody saw you to send you our way, but I couldn't tell them why because of our strict confidentiality laws."

I scrambled to keep up with her words before a thought sucker-punched me. "Haven, how many times has this happened before?" I asked.

"Since I've been here? Never. At least, not until last week."

"But what if the blood test was wrong and the swab test was right? How do we know that—"

She cut me off as if she had already walked through this in her head. "Jordan, the oral swab was a false positive. A hundred percent. We know this because not only is the blood test way more accurate than a swab test, but also because you weren't the only one who received a false positive."

I turned my back on Haven. Never in my life had I found someone else's personal turmoil so reassuring. It's incredible how often antisocial addicts find themselves in the same boat, convening on the verge of life and death. Regardless of how we got there, I wasn't mad at Haven or the program. I was shaking inside, but not from anger. In fact, I felt like the luckiest man alive. It was the sort of thing that only happened in books or movies or when God has a sense of humor. I'm thankful I summoned up the strength to return to the clinic, even if I only went back for new needles.

As Haven prepared to cut me loose on the world, she plead with me to not let this one experience violate my trust in the health care system, though it wasn't a promise I was in a position to keep.

I clear the machine and let the memory fade away. Sitting up in my bunk, I regret my ability to ruin a good thing if God lets me. I had sworn that I would never vandalize the clean slate I was handed and that I would protect myself at all costs. That promise only lasted about a week, until the next time I was dope sick and needed any needle I could find. Now, here I am once again, bracing for results that will determine what misery the future holds. Cracking my knuckles, I exhale into my palms and fear the worst. Pulling my sheet over my head, I curl up into a ball. I can't believe I put myself back into this position.

• • •

While Mike flips through some paperwork, I watch as Russel hands Dr. Lai my lab results and a three-ring medical binder with my last name scrawled across the spine. Regardless of what happens next, I am exhausted and committed to returning to my bunk and going back to sleep. Last night, I swear the yellow lights outside burned brighter as the chorus of snoring throughout the dormitory was relentless. Seated in front of me, the doctor reminds me of an Asian Yoda, if Yoda wore a blank stare, round spectacles, ignored my presence and imparted no sage advice.

When I first met the doctor, I felt more like a number than a human. It was only after Deacon pointed out the gun he was under that I felt a sense of empathy for the man. Every time he steps foot on the property, it is a nonstop marathon for the medical team since he meets with most of the clients and even the staff when necessary. Today it works in my favor—I'm ready to get it over with. These past four days have dragged on forever, and it's time to square up with my past.

"Okay, it looks like your lab results are—," he flips the paper open, "—Hepatitis C, positive. HIV, negative." He looks up at me from his seat behind his desk.

I throw my head back like a PEZ dispenser. This is the turning point I needed—a glowing light at the end of a tunnel. The results sink in and send a deep shiver through my core like a vessel suffering propeller cavitation. In this moment, one of my most die-hard reservations instantly becomes obsolete, as the perfect excuse to relapse evaporates.

And even though I've never tested for Hepatitis C before, I have to say I expected this. No one who shoots dope the way I did could reasonably expect to come out clean on the other side. I despise myself that I wasn't very safe, but once I accepted my life would be short-lived, I had no reason to protect myself. After crossing a very real line, the results of my actions weren't of conse-quence because I wasn't expecting to live long enough to see them.

I realize I need to learn more about Hepatitis C, and Russel must have read my mind because he hands me a tri-fold paper explaining all the facts and frequently asked questions. "Everything you need to know is in here," he says.

I snatch the pamphlet and wipe my mouth.

"It could have been a lot worse, right?" Russel nods, inviting me to follow along. "Just don't spin yourself out. Hep C is curable."

Mike stands up and towers over me. "Russel's right. I've lived with it for years, but you won't have to."

"You didn't tell me you went through treatment."

"That's because I haven't." He puts one hand on my shoulder and uses the other to motion for Russel to wrap it up. "You guys keep us so busy, I haven't found the time. But trust me, it's on my bucket list." His laughter fills the room like a smoke bomb.

When the smoke dissipates, Dr. Lai hands me a referral to Queens Medical Center and instructs Russel to schedule a sonogram to check for liver damage or scarring. While I'm there, they'll also send me upstairs to add my name to the long wait-list of clients hoping to squeeze into the Hepatitis treatment program. Until today, I've never had a reason to care that Queen's liver center is world-renowned.

I turn toward Mike. "I guess I'll hope for the best?"

"I wouldn't waste your time hoping—try praying instead. You never know. You're young enough to have a healthy and happy life. All you have to do is ask."

21

SHAKING THE TREE

A familiar bell rings out in the distance, rousing me from a nap. Covering a yawn, I relax my jaw and realize something doesn't sit well. Unless I'm confused or the wall clock is broken, class isn't supposed to start for at least another hour. Through the thin metal walls of our shipping container dormitory, I hear the flapping of rubber slippers fast approaching. The sound stops just outside of our door, when a heavy knock bursts it open, slamming the edge into the side of my bunk.

"Everyone inside the Rec Hall now! You guys got three minutes or catch a restriction!" The staff member yells through the opening.

"What's this about?" Keoki's question goes unanswered as the door wobbles in the wind.

I press the book I was reading to my chest and sit up in my bunk. After I dog-ear the last page I had read, I slip the novel under my pillow and jam on a pair of shoes. Tossing on a shirt, I'm the first one out of our dorm and fall in with a sea of other clients in churned-up confusion. Some are clutching their Big Books while staff continue to herd up clients, calling into the showers and bathrooms to wrap it up.

I bump shoulders as we filter into the Rec Hall and ask if anyone knows what's going on.

"They're shaking the tree," a transition client says, "but no worries—you're good."

I take a seat as the crowded room fills up with intensive and transition clients alike. The only women present are staff—all the female clients have been ordered to their dorms. I see a few interns as well—they're clients stuck in limbo who have been plucked from treatment and promoted to staff in training. They start at the bottom, running errands and paying dues whether they want to or not. The bell rings a final time and the interns note every client who enters late from this point on.

Ambient murmurs die down as Saunoa walks in and jerks back a chair at the head table. He wields a massive body, remnants from a life of prison, powerlifting and hard knocks. Even though I see him around the facility almost every day, I've done a decent job at avoiding him so far. We all know that any counselor can tune up any client at any given time for rules violations.

Saunoa is the leader of the yellow group, comprised of all the Polynesian and Asian clients, USO gang members and any other institutionalized client in the program who might not stand a chance. Saunoa keeps his head shaved and a white beard trimmed under his round eyeglasses. Though today he can say he's changed his life for the better, nobody dares take the remission of his bad side for granted. His past lies dormant, ready to erupt and shake the whole facility to its core.

"Everyone, listen up," he begins. "I'm going to speak to all you bitches, man to man, and I'm not going to repeat myself." Saunoa doesn't raise his voice and doesn't need to. His words carry weight and hit home through some combination of fear and respect. As he talks, interns scan the room to see which clients aren't paying attention to add to their restriction list.

"Look, I don't know what's gotten into you assholes, but we've had a lot of shit go down in the past couple days, yeah?" Heads around the room nod in agreement. "But gang graffiti in the bathroom? *Really?* In my fuckin' house?" He removes his glasses and gently lays them on the table. "I'm only going to ask once—I want to know which one of you little bitch-ass, gang-bangin', mutha-fukkas wrote that illiterate chickenshit on my walls!?" He raises an eyebrow as his head scans the room and makes a couple passes.

"Well, who did it? I know it didn't write itself, assholes."

Even at 3 a.m., the Rec Hall isn't ever this silent.

"Listen carefully. If you want to rep your set or claim your gang, then this is your chance to man up. So?" Saunoa takes a deep whiff. "Then mutha-fuck your gang!" he bellows, blowing half of the room back in their seats. "Whoever wrote that, they should kick you out of the set for being a spineless bitch. But more impor-tantly, you're in the wrong fuckin' house if you want to rep your little prison gang. You need to take that shit back to Halawa or O.C.C.C. because there's no place for it here."

Saunoa calmly stands up, lays his knuckles on the table and leans forward.

"Make no mistake, this will always be my house, but as long as you're a client living here, this is your house too. I wonder, would you tag your own bathroom at home?"

He doesn't wait for a response from the class and lets out a laugh.

"Maybe some of you would, but that's why we're here. We're here to change, and if change isn't in your immediate future, then you all know where the fuck our gate is. Go ahead and find out for yourself where it leads. But don't waste our time, the same way we don't waste yours. And if you're here to play games, I'm telling you right now that the house always wins. Don't you know that there's only enough room in this bitch for one gang, and that's the Sand Island family!

"We don't ask for much, but keep fucking around, and you'll end up just like, what's his fuckin' name?" Saunoa's fingertips tap the table in front of him. "Oh, right, Bronson? Well, we walked his bitch-ass out the gate yesterday for giving these assholes attitude." Saunoa marks out the C.R.s. "He wasn't so tough when he was begging for another chance, was he? Well, *fuck that!*" His massive hand stops beating the table and points to the interns standing in the back of the room as they glance up from their notepad.

"Another chance? You know, twenty years ago, he'd be crawling out of that gate after we had our way with him." His eyes twinkle as he riles himself up. "Look, the bottom line is that we don't need to take any shit from any of you assholes in here. We're working too damn hard to help you have a better life." He wipes a slick of sweat off his forehead. "I'm getting too old for this petty bullshit, but guess what? So are you!"

Saunoa pauses for a second to let his words sink in. As tough as he seems, I know that if he didn't care, he wouldn't still be here decades after first entering the program himself.

"All right, with that shit out of the way, everyone in my group raise your hands." About twenty-five hands shoot into the air like celebratory gunfire. "You're all on thirty-day restriction. No weight room, no phones, no passes, no nothing."

A chorus of sighs rings out as hands slump back down, slapping thighs and raining casualties throughout the room.

"That's for the four assholes from my group who deviated yesterday and were stupid enough to get caught. Good luck explaining that to the rest of your group. And the next time the thought crosses your—"

I wonder if that's what this is all about? When I returned with my group from pass yesterday, I checked in while four clients from Saunoa's group were being split up in the duty office. Interns had collected urine samples and each client was writing down his own version of their story. Two of the guys were already on thin ice and will probably get kicked out or sent back to jail for a time-out. I took their misery as a learning opportunity for myself and a swift reminder to stick to my Plan of Action.

"And let me make this clear in case any of you assholes forgot —no one else is fighting inside my fuckin' house." Saunoa's hand slams the table and sends a shock wave throughout the room. "At least, not on your own terms. So here's what I got for all you badass shot callers—if any of you men have a problem with someone else in the room, I want you to stand up, call him out and you two can duke it out right here in front of everyone before I throw both of your bitch-asses back in jail."

A few nervous laughs bounce off the walls.

"Anyone?" Saunoa tests the waters and motions for the Client Representatives to step forward. The C.R.s are guns for hire, a handful of men and women in intensive treatment themselves who become the eyes and ears of the staff. Their job is to write-up any infraction they witness and hand in their papers to the staff for a small weekly stipend. If they see a rule being broken, they can ruin your week and have your passes shut down. To their credit, they didn't ask for the job, but some go overboard with their newfound power and make a lot of enemies.

"No!?" Saunoa continues with a chuckle. "You sure? Come on, you can't all be this soft. This is your last chance! No one? Okay, good—that means you all have hope. Now, C.R.s, pass that shit out."

The C.R.s circle the room like sharks, slapping Post-it notes on the table in front of every client in the room.

Saunoa leans over his desk. "Here's the deal—today we are 'Shaking the Tree.' Some of you transition clients may remember the last time we did this. Some of you may have forgotten. That tells me it's been too long."

As Saunoa explains the directions, it reminds me of *Survivor*, except if you get voted out of the facility, your ass is probably headed back to prison. Saunoa instructs us to write the names of the three clients that we think deserve to be here the least. Voting is required but anonymous—there is no opting out of this one. The decision is based on who I think is taking advantage of this opportunity and breaking the rules. Who is the dead weight? Who is the biggest asshole?

Seconds before the voting begins, a client stands up and asks to address the class. Before Saunoa can say no, the client launches into a frantic plea to the room, begging us not to vote him out. He is shaking and convincing. He doesn't want to leave before the miracle happens. He knows he's an asshole, but just doesn't know why.

"Thank you for sharing. Now sit the fuck down," Saunoa demands.

Once all the papers are filled out, the C.R.s collect them and leave the room with Saunoa. They return to the main office to count the votes and let us torture ourselves. As soon as they are out of sight, the room starts comparing who voted for who as the worst offenders begin to sweat.

Moments later, Jerome is called up to the office by a C.R. and escorted back to his dorm to pack his belongings. I guess that's all it takes here sometimes. Two other guys are switched out of their groups and now have Saunoa as their counselor. Their ghastly faces tell it all—they have no idea if they just dodged a bullet or not.

Once we are dismissed from the Rec Hall, I let the other men fight for the exit and take my time getting out of my seat. Looking down at the worn carpet, I feel guilty about casting my vote for the guy who was kicked out. And though my vote was only one of many, I take no pleasure in knowing Jerome may or may not make it. I add this to my list of depressors, including the thrill of not having HIV wearing off faster than I expected. I've been riding high for a while, but now I have to face the fact that Hepatitis C isn't going to be a walk in the park. The more I've educated myself, the more I wish I hadn't.

As I head outside to the smoker's tent, I remind myself that in recovery, I can look forward to getting back the things I've lost to my addiction and that's not just the material items. Pawning a drum set or laptop is one thing, but after facing death, those aren't the things that truly matter. I'm looking forward to developing and renewing my faith, joining my family again as a loving son and brother, and having healthy relationships built on trust. Most importantly, I'm looking forward to loving myself, which starts with facing my hurdles and tackling them one at a time.

The holidays are coming up. People are already murmuring about leaving treatment for them. And though I don't want to be here either, it's easy to see that these are the clients who are short-sighted. I'll watch them go while knowing that staying here is the best gift that I can ever give my family. I roll a cigarette and stare at my poor wrapping job. For the past few years, I was like most of the guys here—I cared more about calling my dope dealers than calling home for the holidays.

I light the cigarette and let the tobacco scratch my throat. At least this year, my family can celebrate knowing where I am, that I'm safe and that I love them enough to love myself for once.

22

THE HAND-OFF

I anxiously peel a couple of paint chips off the handrail I'm
leaning against and let them float down to the gravel. Though
I've never known Sand Island Beach Park as one of the nicer
beaches on the island, slowly but surely it has become everything
to me, and I'm keeping my fingers crossed that my pass has been
approved. I'm surrounded by other clients packed tightly under
the smoker's tent waiting to learn our fate—the only exception
being those on permanent restriction who no longer even bother
applying. There are also those who don't trust themselves enough
to step outside of the facility and endure a self-imposed restriction.

Right on time, Scott the intern exits the office and approaches
the far corner of the deck. Holding a freshly printed list in his
hand, he peers over his glasses and calls out names.

"Kimo, Sean, Grant. Approved."

Kimo claps his hands one time as his hips swing an imaginary
hula hoop.

"Ikaika, Diego, Jeremy. Approved."

Ikaika splits to go wake up his group mates.

"Eli, Billy, Jordan. Approved."

The three of us smile at each other.

Scott calls a handful of other groups until abruptly finishing and smugly retreats into the office. It's obvious he enjoys the sense of power he has over his former group mates, having recently been promoted from C.R. to Intern. From the looks of it, he's not in it for the small monthly stipend or sixteen-hour days.

Some groups around me are obviously displeased and begin grumbling as towels are flipped back over shoulders and they retreat to their dorms. It's always a gamble when you fill out your pass because it feels like everything is riding on it.

What a beautiful day. It will be an opportunity to feel normal and get some much-needed sun. Before we leave, one of the transition clients quietly offers to let me borrow a mask and snorkel, which I wrap in my towel to conceal it. I can't wait to cool off in the clear ocean. I hope the ice cream truck will be in the parking lot. To me, passes are great for a lot of reasons and it's worth waiting for all week, which makes the day trip more enjoyable. It also makes sense from the facilities perspective—these excursions are a great incentive to help keep the client population on track. Sure, I still break rules here and there, but a carrot on the end of a stick gives most of us a reason to focus and work hard.

Next to me, Billy, a middle-age surfer still stuck in the seventies, is talking incessantly, but I tune him out. The walk to the beach is a slow fifteen-minute stroll, which I use to consider what I'm doing with my life. I suppose that as a client in an intensive inpatient treatment, I could make the argument that I'm not technically in recovery yet, but just like this slow stroll to the beach, I'll get there eventually.

"Brah, did you hear what happened to Mike?"

As we approach the gate to Sand Island Beach Park, I think to myself that no good news ever starts like this. I listen to Eli describing the newest rumor that's weaving its way through Sand Island and kick a rock with my slipper, watching it take an odd turn, bounce off the curb and slink into the bushes.

"I heard that Mike had a surfing injury and somehow managed to perforate his intestines. I guess he was doing a cutback and his foot slipped off the tail. The nose of his surfboard popped up and smacked a bulging hernia." Eli grabs his stomach and cocks his neck.

"No way." I pause for a second. "Wait, Mike's been surfing with a hernia?"

Eli raises his eyebrow. "Come on, man—*it's Mike!* You should know by now that nothing will keep him out of the water. Besides, that's not even the worst part. I heard that when he first went to the emergency room, they turned him away because they misdiagnosed him, thinking it was something minor. So he came back to Sand Island, and put up with the pain getting worse before driving himself back to the ER. He begged to see a doctor and refused to leave, and was almost thrown out by security for causing a scene. He's lucky that a doctor intervened and heard him out, then rushed him into emergency surgery."

"He's lucky they didn't kill him."

"Nah, they'd have to try a lot fucking harder than that." Eli hawks a loogie and wipes his mouth with the back of his hand.

I'm pretty sure he's right—most addicts in recovery might not be superheroes, but they are damn sure good fighters. Mike takes it one step further as a waterman and a warrior who commits what little free time he has to training his body, mind and spirit.

Eli fills me in on a few more details. It sounds like Mike will have his work cut out for him, where he'll be fighting a whole new type of recovery, one that includes physical therapy plus a temporary drainage bag. I hope he's okay and I feel like I should say a prayer for him, even though we're still a little rocky after he threw away my entire Step One homework binder after I worked on it for over a month. Maybe that's his tough love way of showing me that the exercise was really intended to be for my own benefit.

Trust the process.

My towel kicks up a puff of sand as I drop it next to Eli and head toward the water. Mike's situation reminds me of a class where I listened to another counselor describe the only way an addict should respond to finding himself in a similar situation. He promised that Sand Island would always have our back, as long as we remained sober. I sit down at the shoreline, let the water push and pull me, and imagine what it would be like to live through his example.

Once I graduate, if I am ever in some freak accident and come to in a hospital bed on a Dilaudid drip, I know I can ring the buzzer, admit to the nurse I'm a heroin addict in recovery, then ask her to call Sand Island on my behalf and speak with Dr. Lai. On my way out of the hospital, they'll have a taxi waiting to deliver me back to Sand Island, where I would have the pleasure of being placed in Isolation inside a musty trailer in the back of the facility.

The goal is to protect me from myself, and if I ever find myself in that situation, this is their commitment to me as long as I meet them halfway and protect my sobriety at all cost. Like the ocean that changes so quickly, curve balls are hard to predict, but it's how I would respond to these situations that will make or break me.

Our trip to the beach is short, but it's just what I needed to clear my mind. Stepping out of the shore break, water peels off of my pale skin and I bury my face in my towel, smiling and knowing I will always have a safe place to return to, unless I decide I no longer need it.

We return from our beach trip to find the facility in chaos and I observe our group being torn apart like a foster family. The men who opted to stay behind or had their passes denied were doing their best to adapt to the sudden change, but I knew this was coming. As a metal detector swipes my pockets, I learn that Mike is back on Shadow with Ty and in Isolation. Someone saw him earlier, and there's no way he'll be in working order while recovering from surgery. Since the doctors removed a large portion of Mike's intestines, he is also heavily medicated and being monitored by the medical team to ensure he's taking his medication per his doctor's orders.

I learn there are different schools of thought about taking narcotics when you're an addict. I seem to side with the consensus that the facility is making the right decision. Nothing good comes from enduring severe pain, and it's not like Mike asked for this surgery. From what I see, the staff are playing it smart, maintaining control over his pain pills. The body needs to be relaxed to heal, and besides, it won't hurt Mike to cool it for a bit.

While Mike is out of commission, the other counselors have no choice but to step up and take a handful of us under their wing. Eli and Cavin are adopted into Carolyn's group, and just like that, I can no longer talk to two of my closest friends. My new temporary counselor is Tony, and as soon as I hear this, I prepare myself for some changes.

From what I've seen, Tony keeps recovery . . . *simple*. He is a deep-sea fisherman and a counselor known for only allotting the bare necessities to members of his group. His school of thought is if you don't need it to survive, you don't need it at all. Other counselors let their clients have MP3 players, diving gear and some even allow surfboards. But not Tony. I've watched as a client of his opened a package with cash inside and Tony made him return it to the sender. Tony separates the needs from the wants, and as far as he is concerned, all of our needs here are taken care of.

So, I'm surprised when Tony calls me back to his office to sit down for an expedited one-on-one and hands me an opened package with some cigarettes and thirty-five dollars that my mom mailed in. Tony is one of the few counselors who doesn't live on property and comes and goes when his work is complete. His shipping container office is sparse and cluttered with images of the catches that didn't get away. It is an organized mess with stacks of confiscated parcels and packages lining the walls. He hoards these unnecessary niceties like a dragon in a lair, waiting until the timing is right to dispatch them to his clients, usually once they level up into transition.

Tony looks down at the money and sniffs. "Would Mike let you keep it?" His gravelly voice is straight to the point.

I answer without hesitation. "Yeah, definitely. He knew this was on its way."

"You're not on restriction, are you?" Tony stares me down—his dark skin is flanked by tan lines from his Oakley sunglasses. He's been in the sun a lot lately and probably can't wait to get back out on the water.

I shake my head. "No, never have been."

Tony holds out the package for me to take but keeps the money, all except five dollars. I place the box on the floor next to my chair and remind myself not to forget it.

"I'll put this money on your books. You can request your weekly allowance next Wednesday from Yvonne. So tell me, how have you been feeling?" Tony asks.

Five bucks a week doesn't seem like much, but it goes a long way on pass when all we want is ice cream or to split a pack of cigarettes. I'll take it and be grateful, even knowing Mike would have let me have the loot all at once. I let off and dig into my thinking, explaining to Tony that I've been clear-headed lately. The obsessive thoughts about using aren't as loud as they normally feel.

As I speak, I realize that I'm learning to be honest with myself in the presence of others, though I still hold back about ever mentioning wanting to leave. Mike has had me focused for so long on trying to assess how I can work toward controlling my emotions versus the other way around, and I think it serves me better to appear stronger than I really am. That said, I can't help but feel overly emotional, still bumming around every now and then as if trying to glide through the everyday motions.

I've been here long enough that I can handle the rough days without seriously considering leaving, though I often entertain the idea and embrace my vivid imagination. I think back to when I was using and how every day felt like Groundhog Day, only to stare at the schedule and realize that not much has changed. On the bright side though, time seems to fly, whereas before I felt as if I was stuck in a black hole.

Tony thinks before he responds and I'm relaxed in his presence. "Jordan, I don't know much about you, but I do know that if you get this, I promise you, you will have the freedom to never feel stuck in any situation again. In fact, you're already there. You're a walk-in, right?"

"Yeah."

"You know that almost without fail, most of your peers here are converting at least one criminal sentence, the most common being an open five or ten-year term. In exchange for receiving a clinical discharge from the facility, they'll either earn a reduced sentence, or sometimes, even a dismissal."

"I know that, Tony. It must make it hard to determine which guys to focus on since you don't know who wants to be here versus those who prefer it to the obvious alternative."

"That's not how it works. I treat you all the same, because most people come here for the wrong reason. My job is to help you dig down and uncover the right reason to stay for yourself."

"Well, you would think that two years in an inpatient facility where you get to go to the beach and even see your family is a sweet deal compared to being locked up." I think for a second. "To be honest, I guess I don't feel stuck, but I also don't feel free. I know I can leave anytime, but there's a lot of pressure to stay as well. I'm learning what reverse peer-pressure is, where people try to talk you out of doing the wrong thing for once.

"I also feel committed to being here by my family, or rather, for my family. Besides, even if I left, I know I don't have anywhere to go. Both of my parents have their sights set on seeing me complete this more than I think I do. I also have a good idea that Oregon is just glad that I left their state and haven't caught wind of them pursuing me for extradition."

"You have outstanding warrants? I didn't know you had an open case."

"I don't like to think about it even though it's always on my mind. The drugs that kept me a prisoner in Oregon are the same reason I'll have to go back. I'm so glad I could break away, but I know I'll never be free until I clear my name."

"All of those loose ends will be handled in time. The main thing is that you do this for you, or you can never expect it to last. You're right, there are guys here that know this is easier than prison. That's okay because people change, so they may come in for one reason, but learn the truth in time.

"You're not here for community service, and you're not here for repentance. You're not here to make right by your victims, family or community. Those things may happen while you're in here, but don't confuse that with your purpose. My advice is this: do not convince yourself that you're here for any other reason than to save your life or I promise you, you'll resent your time here and your time here will be short."

23

HEAVY WEIGHT TO BEAR

I've given up on questioning whether or not the wall clock in the Rec Hall is broken. Tuning out the speaker in the background, my pencil doodles in my hand, pretending to take notes while the class discusses the same old topic. I've always struggled with the idea that addiction is a disease, ever since I tried playing that card in high school and my mother called me out on it.

One evening, I came home knowing everything, drunk and stoned. As I approached our front door, I fumbled for my house key until I noticed the glow of a reading lamp. At that point, I didn't even bother sneaking in, and twisted the unlocked doorknob. There she sat, tired yet awake, waiting for me in the living room. She stood up from the couch and moved in for an unsolicited hug. My arms hung at my side. I felt the silent whiff from her nostrils as she absorbed the hooligan in me. The night was seeping out of my pores, wafting off of my tongue and tangled in my hair.

A mother at her wit's end is an unpleasant sight, and when she pushed me back, I could see the fight inside her was wavering. She didn't need to remind me we'd been going down this road for far too long. She'd given up on grounding me, knowing I'd sneak out. She couldn't take away my car—the cops did that already when they stripped me of my license.

She looked me up and down. "I don't know what to do with you." Her face wasn't angry—she had moved past that stage of grief.

It was my move. "I don't know, Mom. What do you expect? Maybe I have a disease and can't help it?"

I swallowed my slurred words and stared down at the carpet. When I looked up, I could see her shaking. It was a low blow whether or not I intended it to be. I was talking to a woman whose own mother died from cancer when she was only nine years old. The doctors first amputated a leg, then removed a lung. My poor mother helped give my grandmother her morphine injections every day to ease the intense pain.

Mom cleared her throat. "You cut that out." Her cheeks puffed with frustration. "Don't you dare try that with me!" she said through gritted teeth, shaking her finger in my face.

It was her left hand, which is about half the size of her right. It's easy to miss that she had polio as a girl, when she never allowed it to define her as an adult.

"Do you honestly believe that you have a disease? *AIDS* is a disease! *Cancer is a disease!* There are so many poor mothers out there watching their child fighting leukemia at any God-given hour that it breaks my heart. You wouldn't tell them that a decision to party is in the same realm as their little angel dying, would you?

"Of course, you wouldn't! I raised you better!" The words hung in the air while she waited for eye contact that never came. "Don't hide behind 'having a disease!' You have a choice, and I wish you would grow up and start making the right one!"

Sometimes parents just don't understand.

"Oh, come on. What do you know about addiction?" I challenged.

She shifted her weight and crossed her arms for a second before the fingers started flying. "Enough to know that quitting smoking was one of the hardest things I've ever done, and to this day, the thought crosses my mind to go back whenever I smell a cigarette.

"I know that your father almost divorced me when I couldn't quit after he did. And no matter how hard I tried, I couldn't resist. And I knew how powerful my cravings were when I was okay with the thought of him leaving me as long as I could still smoke. But I did manage to quit, and ultimately, it came down to finding my backbone and making a decision."

"So, you think you know better than all the professionals? Then explain to me why almost every man in our family is an alcoholic?"

"Well, for starters, your father's not!"

"Dad's an exception to the rule!" I shouted.

She took her time to respond, and in doing so, grabbed my ankle and pulled me back down to earth. "Jordan, you will never know what your dad went through growing up with an alcoholic father. He swore that he would never be like that, especially to his own kids. I admit that alcoholics may have a predisposition, but don't hide behind that and let it become your purpose. I pray you don't let it define you. You have so much going for you, and God gave you so much."

"Mom, stop."

"I can't stop. It's my job to care and I will never stop loving you, which is why it hurts to see you keep doing this to yourself. You know who you remind me of?" She grabbed my shoulder and shoved me into the couch. "You're just like your uncle Johnny. He was so smart and talented and loved, but he was also troubled. He let his addiction spiral out of control, and it took his life from him.

"I never told you this, but when he was in high school, he drank a lot and discovered he also loved codeine cough medicine. He once had me go into the drug store to pick up his prescription, which was in a large glass bottle and—"

I tried to press myself off the couch, but she towered over me.

"—and I was just a young girl! I brought it out to his car in the paper bag and watched as Johnny transferred the cough medicine to another bottle, put the cap back on the empty bottle and returned it to the paper bag. He then smashed the empty bottle against the pavement, which shattered broken glass inside the bag."

I tried to push her away, but she deflected my arm.

"I was first stunned, then scared when he told me to go back into the drug store and tell the pharmacist that I accidentally broke the bottle. Pink, sticky liquid oozed out of the bag and onto my hands. I was crying so hard and afraid of getting cut that I could barely talk. The pharmacist came around from behind the counter, got down to my eye level and told me not to cry—he would give me a new bottle.

"He comforted me, telling me that accidents happen. It wasn't my fault. He then took me to the sink to wash my hands. I was disgusted. I felt so used, small and taken advantage of, but I loved Johnny and would do whatever he told me to. Later in the week, I had to go to confession to ask for forgiveness for lying even though I didn't say anything to the pharmacist.

"That is how I feel looking at you right now. I love you so much and am so hurt by your decisions. I promise, you may think addiction may be hard on you, but it's hell on me!"

All around me, clients push back their chairs as class ends for lunch. Scooping my things, I fly out of my seat and realize my best thinking got me here.

As soon as I hit the door, I beeline it back to the weight room, willing to replace another skipped meal for a workout. A creature of habit, I step up to the scale and tap the weights with my finger until I zero it out. I jump on the base, wait for the needle to balance, then step off, surprised that I've put on fifteen pounds since I've arrived. When I first checked in, I weighed almost as much as a middleweight, somewhere right around a hundred and sixty pounds. I made it a goal to eat every meal and work out daily, before realizing I often had to sacrifice one for the other. If it were up to me, I'd be a regular in the gym, but because of its popularity, it's hit or miss more often than I would like. So lately I've replaced my lunchtime meal with an extra apple or orange that I saved from our morning snack, so I don't starve before dinner.

Overall, my attitude has been consistently decent, and I attribute the stabilization to working out. I begin my routine by jumping rope, amazed at the progress my body has made in healing itself. With my heart pumping, I hang up the rope and inspect my arms in the mirror. While my track marks have scarred over, some color seems to be flushing itself out of my skin like a body rejecting a bad tattoo. My left forearm is still a muddled purple color, but at least it's getting better, not worse.

Even though it's quiet time for the rest of the facility, I hear the clients behind me discussing how grateful they are that staff reopened the weight room yesterday. It's been shut down for a week thanks to a couple of clients who took it upon themselves to ruin it for the rest of us. Since the number of clients who want to work out always exceed the amount allowed in the gym at any given time, it's always a mad dash to the back of the facility after class to be one of the lucky eight.

It's usually the same guys who pick their seats in the Rec Hall to be closest to the exit, ready with their bags packed. The moment we're excused, a mass of men power walk toward the back of the facility since running isn't allowed. As soon as they're out of sight of staff—blocked by the rows of dormitories—they sprint toward the gym like their lives depend on it.

The day they got caught, they hooked a corner and nearly trampled Miss Cats. Since she had already warned everyone to be mindful of their own stupidity, she shut the gym down and confiscated the red gym binder we use to list our names. It was bound to happen—a devastating blow that left us all pointing fingers and blaming one another.

Two interns with fluid loyalty slipped us the word of her plans to shut the gym down for a month, which made tensions run thick. Working out has become such a necessary part of my routine, and like everyone else, I depend on this outlet. I also had a hard time believing it would really be shut down for so long because the staff knew how critical it was for us to vent.

Most of the guys who work out throw weights around like footballs, ridding the tension with an explosive energy that has to go somewhere. As cooped up as we are, this place can be a powder keg, with the capacity to explode into a madhouse. We're constantly reminded that we are only in control of our own thoughts and actions, yet it's hard to process how often we are collectively punished. It makes me believe that staff have learned long ago that, ironically, a bunch of criminals are the best ones to police themselves.

A couple of older guys from Carolyn's group are doing light presses on the bench and I ask to join in. Since a spotter is always required, the weight room is one of the few places where we're allowed to communicate with clients from other groups.

I jump into their conversation, and it's obvious that I'm not the only one excited about the gym being reopened. I step into a discussion of benchmarks and goals, and it's pointed out that it's impressive I'm benching thirty-five-pound plates because my arms look like they've died inside. I laugh with them as I lay down on the bench, but deep down, wonder how long it will take to physically recover?

Lifting the bar off the rack, I'm encouraged by the thought that if I keep it up, I'll be at the forty-five-pound plates in no time. I've only been allowed into the gym recently, and the promise of quick progress is enticing.

I sit, roll my neck, drop my chin to my chest and take pride in respecting my body again. I'm doing a lot of things lately that point me in the right direction. Yesterday, I was sent to get vaccinated for both Hepatitis A and B. I expect that I'll be scheduled for my sonogram to check out my liver for any damage. With Mike still in the hospital, I'm preparing for some delays with my treatment plan and figure it's best to use my time wisely. Rotating into the spotter's position to return the favor, I feel my stomach growl and know I won't get where I want to be without a little sacrifice along the way.

Stepping into the shower, I let cool water run off my face and massage the cheap shampoo into my tangled hair. With Thanksgiving around the corner, I consider what I'm most thankful for. I'm reminded almost daily that my focus should always revolve around the practice of being grateful, starting with gratitude for simply being alive. For me, the list doesn't stop there: I am truly grateful for my family, a chance to save myself, my health—for what it's worth—and the friends I've made in here. I figure I'm smart enough to know I would never have gotten this far alone.

I'm also thankful I've surprised a lot of people—myself included—at sticking it out for these past few months. I'm nearing the point where my family can come visit, assuming they're approved.

I cut the water and dry off in the stall, careful not to let my towel touch the tile. I can't remember the last holiday I spent with my family, and though it's too early in my treatment for them to be allowed to visit tomorrow, at least they know where I am and what I'm up to. I have a good idea what they will be thankful for, and know it starts with me being where I need to be.

Staff warned us earlier that tensions always run high around the holidays. Some of my fellow clients aren't even allowed to leave the facility, being on permanent restriction or supervised release as mandated by the courts. For those who have family visits, the holidays are tough, but manageable. For others, either from a neighbor island or practically disowned, the holidays are a sour reminder of what they've lost.

Thankful that I still have family willing to have me in their lives, I rush out of the shower and sign my name on the phone list, then take a seat under the smoker's tent while I wait for my turn to use the payphone. When my turn finally comes, the phone clerk starts my five-minute countdown. I drop fifty cents into the slot and hope for someone to pick up.

"Hello?"

I lean into the receiver. "Happy Thanksgiving and Mele Kalikimaka!"

"Jordan?! Merry Christmas to you too, son! It's so good to hear from you! Hold on a second." I hear Dad call out to Mom a few times to tell her I'm on the line.

"Dad, it's okay. I don't really have a lot of time here."

"Oh, that's right! You know, your mother and I were just talking about how proud we are of you. We've been trying to schedule an interview with Yvonne to get started with family visits."

"Really!? I appreciate that."

As much as I love them and look forward to our time together, I still feel guilty when I hear them say they're proud of me. How proud can any parent really be when their son is a drug addict in treatment? They've been nothing but supportive. I'd be a fool to downplay the pain, worry and turmoil I've inflicted on them. I get that I'm doing the right thing, but I still feel ashamed of all my actions that led me to this point.

When we start to discuss Christmas, I know that I'm not yet eligible to apply for a day pass at home. Families must attend at least four meetings before a client can return home for either a day pass or an overnighter, and there aren't enough Wednesday family meetings between now and then to qualify.

"You know, even though your mom and I are so thankful that you're in treatment, to be honest, it's much harder for us than what we had expected. It's just, you've been out of our lives for so long, it hurts not to be together as a family, especially now that you're so close."

I hear him sniff through the receiver.

"Well, I'm not quite out of the woods yet."

"Yo! Two minutes," the time monitor calls out. I know that if I were in his group, he'd play favorites and run my time loosely.

"We have to wrap this up."

"So soon, huh?"

"Tell me about it."

"Well, you won't hear any complaints from me, son. It's good to hear your voice. Wait. What's that? Son, hold on a second." I hear some ruffling on his end and look back to see the next guy in line pacing in front of the booth. My time is quickly counting down. "Okay, Jordan, you still there? Your mom wants you to know that she is moving swiftly to fax over the paperwork for our family visits. She can't wait."

"Me neither."

I'm excited yet nervous about them coming. I've heard some things about what this place will say to family members. My parents will be educated in areas like boundaries and why they should never trust us. James will pound into them that all addicts are selfish and manipulative. I've even heard that he will make them promise to get a Temporary Restraining Order against us if we ever relapse.

"You know, Dad, the sooner you both get cleared for visits and we complete the four family classes, the sooner I can come home on day passes."

"We can't wait. We're so proud of you, son."

One day, I hope to make them proud, but not because I've stopped doing the wrong things. When I can do the right thing for the right reason when no one is looking, then I'll feel adequate and proud of myself. The irony is that Sand Island teaches the same lessons my parents tried to hammer home as a child.

I keep the thought to myself, let them both know I love them and wait for him to hang up first. Stepping out of the phone booth,

I don't feel like a superhero even though I'm making leaps and bounds. I am not empowered. Instead, I am learning that the good times often mingle with the bittersweet. Not being able to return home for Christmas is just another drag on my willingness to stay here, but it's not like I'm the only one.

24

ALL IN THE FAMILY

The chase is on. A tiny yellow puffer fish with brown spots introduces itself and fills the lens of my dive mask, appearing to enjoy his newfound company. I smile as wide as I can while biting a snorkel mouthpiece and make my way to the underwater bunkers at the West end of Sand Island Beach Park. Looking down, the water doesn't get very deep out here, maybe fifteen feet where the coral heads open up to the rocky ocean floor below. It's a calm day to bob on the surface, clear my head and purge the pent-up holiday excitement.

The pursuit continues as I swim toward the breakers. The little fish is so slow I find myself swimming backward at times. I have no problem tailing him and I even propel him forward by swimming behind him. With nowhere to be or go, I follow the fish for a few minutes as we pass over sea cucumbers and urchins.

Beneath me, something catches my eye, and I dive deep, equalize my ears and return to the surface with a wooden string of prayer beads draped over my fingers. Stuffing them into the back pocket of my board shorts, I spin in a circle, but it appears my new friend has left me for greener coral.

I forgot how much I loved the ocean. I'm falling in love with diving all over again. It's more than fun—it's peaceful and refreshing. There is nothing like plunging my face beneath the surface of the water and separating myself from the world and its distractions. I find a priceless tranquility beneath the disturbance of the surface. Concentrating on my breathing has paid dividends as I regain control of my body. While I swim up to the concrete bunkers that are half-submerged beneath the surface, I see an older client from another group prying some Opihi off of the surface of the bunker with a dive knife.

As I pull myself up onto the slippery concrete bunker, Balavan hands me an Opihi. I confess I've never tried the shellfish, even though I grew up on the islands. The shell has dark black ridges that radiate outward like a volcano. The raw meat, though chewy, tastes like I've been missing out all my life. I couldn't eat too many of them though, with the notable salty grit and sandy aftertaste.

Balavan uses almost every available pass to come diving along with his group mate and dive buddy, Chris. They're known for finding large cowrie shells, somewhere around four inches long with bright tiger stripes. I watch as Balavan dons his mask, slips through a small opening in the wall and enters the submerged bunker. I wait for him to come back out, but he doesn't reappear.

"There's a trapped air pocket inside," Chris says with a smile. "Follow me if you want!"

Chris times the waves and swims for the hole. I follow right behind him. Inside the bunker, the air is stale and dry, with little room to move around. The echo is loud, and the walls are covered with black, spiny sea urchins wedged into crevices and corners. We hear the waves crash outside, and with each surge, the air pocket overhead shrinks then expands while we bob closer to the ceiling.

Between gasps for air, I'm learning how to smile again.

When it's time to exit the bunker, I'm the first one to dive down and swim toward the light, but a sudden wave surges and pushes me back into the opening, pinning me against the wall for a split second. Were I wearing dive fins, I doubt I would have kicked the wall or the urchin, but I feel a spine prick my big toe and I grunt in pain. Immediately, numbness ensues—the tingling sensation—a reaction to the poison in the urchin's spine. I pull my pale foot up to my mask in an attempt to assess the damage. The last thing I want is to see is a piece of spine broken off beneath my skin. I twist my foot to get a better angle but have to let go as I start to flip over. It's going to be a long walk back to the facility, but I wouldn't change a thing.

"Let's take it outside then!"

I bite my tongue and puff my cheeks. I have nothing to prove to this bastard.

"You want some? Let's go, bitch!" he snarls.

Bennett locks eyes on me as he stands up and backs himself out of the Rec Hall. Shuffling toward the exit, he continues to taunt me, begging me to step outside and toe up with him. My feet are firmly planted.

How did I go from having such a beautiful day at the beach to this?

"Come on haole! I'll fuck you up!"

I spit out a laugh. "You won't do shit," I promise, correcting him.

There's about as much sense in reasoning with him as there is in stooping to his level. My body begins to shake with anger and embarrassment. I need to calm down and not take his bait, while controlling my breathing. Today is my turn dealing with him.

A couple days ago, it was Balavan's, but we're not the only two here who think he must have a death wish. Bennett seems keen on picking fights even though the scar on his chest from open heart surgery has barely healed. One wrong hit could ruin two lives in the blink of an eye.

"I'm right here, white boy." He holds his arms out, but isn't asking for a hug.

I hold up my swollen fist like Hellboy. "You don't have the

heart, punk." A pointer finger springs out of my balled-up fist. "Don't fuck with me! I don't have jail hanging over my head."

All of this is because he came in to class late and stole my seat while I took a quick bathroom break. The entitled bastard should walk to the back of the property and fetch his own chair like the rest of us do when class is full.

"Let's fucking go!" By now, Bennett has got the attention of the whole Rec Hall, minus any staff or interns who are uncharacteristically absent. Embarrassed, irritated and frustrated, I hear him repeat himself and realize there's no winning this either way.

Until, once again, I'm proved wrong. His fire is put out as Uncle Stan rounds the corner, steps in front of him, cuts him off and casts a shadow over his tirade. Uncle Stan doesn't even check to see who Bennett is instigating a scrap with. With an arm pointing over his shoulder, Uncle Stan grabs his collar and jerks him down the sidewalk.

Moments later, Uncle Stan returns, huffing and puffing. "All right, who's the second half to this story?"

I understand where Bennett is coming from. I remember how lonely it was walking around full of spite and always being pissed off at the world. Those were the times when I couldn't count on anyone, except for them to cast judgment. So as upset as I am, a part of me can't help but feel bad for the guy.

I shadow Uncle Stan into the duty office, take a seat and uncomfortably wait for him to return. He didn't even bother asking how the confrontation started—his mind must already be made up. It's been obvious that Bennett has been asking to go back to jail, and I expect he'll get what he wants soon enough. I remember Ty's warning that Sand Island has no problem providing us with all the rope we need to hang ourselves.

When Uncle Stan returns, he slumps into a chair and pauses a moment to catch his breath.

"You okay?" he asks.

I tap my chest. "Me? Yeah, just a little confused why he blew up like he did." I let out an audible breath and strike my fingers through my hair.

"You said you're 'confused?'" He scoots his chair forward. "'Confused' about what? It's simple—he's an asshole. That's all it is."

"Yeah, but we've never had a run-in before."

"Doesn't matter. Guys like him walk around locked and loaded, and he knows he's not willing to change. If it's not you, it's someone else. That's why I don't even need to ask what happened."

"Either way it doesn't sit well. I feel bad this had to go down like that."

"What you mean 'feel bad!' You're not in a position where you can afford to *'feel bad!'* You need to focus on your recovery and watch out for stupid in here because it's everywhere. Some of these guys, it's all they know. Fighting comes naturally—it's bred into their bloodline.

"That's the normal way of solving differences. They use this." He balls up a fist. "Not this." He taps his temple. "So don't waste time worrying over things you can't control. And if he's not going to lose sleep over it, you shouldn't either." He pauses for a second and wiggles his mustache. "It also doesn't help that the holidays are here. It's hard on a lot of guys, who make it hard on everyone else. But that's the old way of thinking."

"Okay, so what's happens now?"

"Sheriffs are already on their way to pick him up and take him to jail."

I'm not surprised. But even though he brought this on himself, not everyone is going to feel that way. So while Bennett is readying himself for Christmas in jail, I need to remind myself that it was his choice to start something with me. Time-outs, as we call them, occur when the program contacts a parole or probation officer to take a client off of their hands when they are acting out. It's like a reset button, or better yet, a fresh and cruel reminder of how good some clients have it here.

Taking a lesson from Mike's playbook, I rack my brain to see what this event is trying to teach me. How do I make good of this situation?

I realize that I can fight for something without ever raising a fist. I can fight for myself and my sobriety without letting others stand in my way or knock me off track. Bennett challenged me to lose my cool, and for a moment, I did. I have to work on that self-control and remember to rise above the bullshit as Mike so eloquently puts it.

The altercation is a firm reminder that I am not only powerless over my addiction, but over others as well. I no longer have the right to lose my mind over anyone or dwell on whether Bennett's friends will blame me for his time-out. Worrying over things I can't control is a luxury I can no longer afford. This program is my one-way ticket to be reintegrated into society as well as my family. I have to protect this opportunity. Listening to myself think, I can barely believe how far I've come.

There's quite a sinking feeling navigating the emotional highs and lows in this program, especially when they occur one after the other. As my mom and dad enter the room, I'm still agitated about yesterday's close call with Bennett. Hugging both parents brings an unfamiliar smile to my face that hurts my cheeks. "So you guys passed the criminal background check, huh?"

They smile, but don't answer as they take a seat across from me. The plastic folding table between us gives us room to grow. While Mom looks me up and down, Dad takes in his surroundings.

The doors are open to allow a fresh breeze to flow in along with cigarette smoke from the guys outside. The room is small yet sparse with chipped, dated linoleum beneath our feet. Only a handful of clients are approved for family visits, which range from parents to wives and girlfriends, even children. Each family has their own table and space to get acquainted with. Cavin is across the room with his parents and I quietly point him out to Dad. He rocks his head back and forth, feigning interest. Next to us, another client covered in tattoos, pulls his chair around his table to sit next to his wife.

"So, this is it, huh?" Dad asks.

"You seem surprised."

"What was that?"

"You seem so surprised. I'm not sure what you were expecting," I say.

"I'm sorry, I'm having a hard time hearing you." He leans in toward me, hunkering over the table.

They have so many questions.

As we talk, my parents note how soft my voice has become. I didn't realize I had lost the confidence in my voice. Perhaps it's born of shame, or maybe it's that I don't want anyone to hear me since everyone in here is always so nosy. Occasionally, Mom cocks her head and cups her ear, reminding me to speak up and be proud. She wants to know how I'm doing.

"Something is changing deep within me, the smallest seeds of acceptance or gratitude sprouting right here." I tap my belly with my palm. "I no longer want to leave all the time, and I have stepped up to volunteer more often. I pick up shifts to keep busy, which is a distraction that helps me remain somewhat positive. The same way that lifting weights helps me feel relaxed." I flash a smile.

"You need to give it time, son. You did a lot of damage, and it's only natural you need a lot of recovery. But keep your head up—the difference I already see in you is like night and day. You look much stronger."

"Your father's right," Mom says. "I can see you've put on weight and your skin looks so much better."

We reintroduce ourselves, while catching up on life, business and the family. I've missed out on a lot these past few years and

I'm keenly aware that I can't make up that time. I'd be a fool to try, and even more foolish not to attempt to make the best of the time that I now have. Gratitude and calmness surround me as I appreciate the unwavering support of my parents. I can tell that when I hit the transition phase of treatment, I should be able to go back to work for them and learn the ins and outs of the family business.

Perhaps I'll be the prodigal son?

Dad is curious about the structure of the program and associates our endless rules here to his time in the service. I tell them about Mike, about his surgery and the subsequent recovery. Our group had just learned that he'll be returning to work in a few days. Mom wishes she had known—she would have brought Mike a cozy throw blanket and a home-cooked meal. Her motherly instinct has never abated, but is interrupted as conversation in the room comes to an abrupt halt.

We all know that sound and are used to hearing him coming before we see him. The familiar sputtering of an electric wheelchair rolls up the planks of the wooden ramp outside and I sit up straight. James hooks the corner then struggles to drive over the threshold and into the room. He backs up his wheelchair for a running start and powers through the entrance with a loud clunk, skidding to a stop at the front of the room.

"Hui!" he barks. His hand struggles to rise off his armrest. "Wrap it up."

We all stand up, slide our tables toward the wall, then arrange a half-circle of folding chairs into the center of the room.

James waits for our attention, then rolls into position in the center. He wears his ever-present dark sunglasses that shade his eyes from us. A wool beanie sits skewed on the crown of his balding head. For once, he is smiling and a silent shudder ripples through me.

"Looks like we have . . . a full class . . . this afternoon," James says, struggling with every word. "It's so nice of you all . . . to join us."

There is nobody here except the Director who is more potent

and powerful than James. Even though he suffers from a debilitating nerve disease that has robbed him of the use of his body, the former power lifter still commands the utmost respect. He has risen above the rank of staff or even Sand Island 'Ohana. Love him or hate him—he is a Sand Island legend.

"The purpose of today's class . . . is to help prevent you all . . . from doing more harm . . . than good." James looks at the loved ones in the room, ignoring us clients. "My job is to make you understand . . . that you can't save these men. Moving forward . . . they can only save themselves."

James terrifies us clients so much that most of us are even afraid to admit it. He has the power to shut down the entire facility to reel us back in and worse, he isn't afraid to do so. His voice often cracks when raised, but he can still bellow from one end of the facility to the other. By far, he expects more from us than anyone else here because he hates the disease. With a vengeance, he hates alcoholism and addiction. And as a proud Hawaiian, it pains him to see anyone, especially his people, decimated from the methamphetamine epidemic that ravages his community.

"*If* these men . . . graduate . . . they will walk out of the gate with all of the tools . . . 'Ike . . . resources . . . and support needed to stay clean . . . and sober. As a parent . . . wife . . . girlfriend . . . or child . . . your job is to give them *nothing!* It will only interfere . . . with their growth."

Like the other couple of clients in the family meeting, I am flanked by my loved ones. I soon realize that James is a different person in the family class than the staff member I know and fear. At the very least, he has more sides to him than I knew. I never saw him as either funny or likable, but my parents are instantly enamored.

As we listen to him lecture on the intricacies of loving an addict, I keep waiting for an outburst of cursing that sprays chewing tobacco in the air. Though somehow, he remains calm, but terrifying.

"You need to know . . . that . . . you can never trust an addict.

These men are all . . . master manipulators. They are selfish and conniving . . . and they will drag you down . . . if you let them. If you choose to allow them back into your lives . . . make sure to protect yourself and one another . . . at all costs."

"What's that mean?" Cavin's Mom asks.

"It means . . . if Cavin relapses . . . you call the police . . . and issue a T.R.O. against him."

She looks puzzled. "T.R.O.?"

"It's a 'Temporary Restraining Order' Mom," Cavin whispers.

"See? Smart kid. He already knows what you should do." James smiles at Cavin, then continues.

As James wraps up the class, I don't hate him for telling my parents the truth. If anything, I feel lucky that my parents are here beside me. Miss Cats only approved a handful of new clients for family visits, and there's over a hundred of us living here. I hope these classes will help rebuild my relationship with my parents, but I know that more than ever, it's all up to me.

25

FOURTH STEP

As I start a new day in my journal, I am grateful to be in a better mood. I wonder if praying for my attitude last night had any impact. I'm not sure, but I know that if I can't keep my spirits high, I'll be fighting a losing battle. In the middle of a thought, the tip of my pencil snaps off, so I lay it to rest on the table and watch it roll back and forth in a half arc.

Kai is sitting across from me, sketching waves instead of taking part in the required writing activity. I know that instead of being cooped up in this facility, he wishes he was off surfing some secret break. Young and energetic, he struggles the most with people telling him what to do and as he sees it, deciding his destiny on his behalf. It must be hard to be a free spirit when you have an open five-year sentence hanging over your head.

I think back to my conversation last night with him on the smoker's deck, and I'm baffled by how much he helped to put things into perspective. Usually comical and immature, he surprised me with the empowering statements extracted from his psyche under the open stars. If I can do this, he posited, I can do anything. He even took it one step further to say that contrary to popular belief, I don't have a choice—I *have* to do this. I need a program of recovery for a better life. Being pessimistic is the old way of thinking, the same thinking that brought me here.

It blew my mind that came from him, and not just because of how hypocritical it seemed from a guy who catches a new restriction every two weeks and has "fuck the world" tattooed on him. But I respect his maturity in acknowledging that waving the white flag is actually a sign of strength. There is no shame in tapping out when you know that continuing will only wreak havoc. And I agree with him, even though he makes it hard to see beyond his light-hearted self.

The more we talked, the more I learned from his saga of mistakes, and I realized that it takes less energy to give someone the benefit of the doubt and to trust the process. This helps to explain why negative thinking shows itself as the prevalent school of thought in here. Dropouts spiral downhill and drag other clients down, even when it takes more grit to be abrasive.

I dig inside my backpack for a new pencil and take another look at Kai. Last night he showed all the promise in the world, whereas today, he seems to no longer care. Or perhaps he's focused on news of the latest relapse and wondering who's next?

I've learned it takes a certain amount of faith to stay positive with what we're up against when it seems that nearly every person who has moved out in the last four months has relapsed. No one here wants to invest two years into a program that may or may not work. Many don't have a choice about being here, but I do, which adds to the frustration as to whether it's worth it or not.

Too many clients relapse and once they do, they aren't allowed to step back on the property. But if they're ordered to return by the courts, they'll come back as a "retread" to a program that makes life even harder on them the second or third go-around, especially when staff take away their amenities and privileges. I know a couple of retreads who say they are lucky to be alive and afforded another chance to stay out of prison, but who really wants to come back here to start intensive all over again?

To be fair, there are also countless graduates who never return.

There have to be those who take what they are taught to heart and never look back. But for those of us who want to see evidence, besides the staff, the only other real proof of lasting sobriety based on the principles taught here are the same few graduate students with five years or more of sobriety who come every Monday to run an A.A. meeting. They sit in the same chairs and tell the same stories, but for what it's worth, they are living proof that recovery is possible.

Mike wastes no time in getting back to work, and immediately upon his return, we have an expedited one-on-one where I'm advanced to the Fourth Step. My whole world will now revolve around making "a searching and fearless moral inventory of myself." As I understand it, what this means is that for the foreseeable future, I'll be making an honest and thorough catalog of resentments, fears and misconduct—going back farther than I care to remember.

I take his advice and head out to the smoker's tent to claim half of an open table, so I can spread out my paperwork. I've given up on finding a quiet place to write anywhere on the property, and use my palm to swipe a ring of water off the table left behind by someone's cup. Flipping through the sheets that Mike turned over to me, it looks like this will be the first tangible test of how deep I am willing to dig. Besides prayer and starting immediately, Mike's only other advice was that Alcoholics Anonymous is a program of action that requires doing the work. I'll get out whatever I put in, which is one of the few promises the program makes.

Ty walks out of the duty office, sparks a cigarette and joins me at the table. He knows as well as the rest of the staff the progression of every client, so he didn't need to see me laying out the skeleton of my Fourth Step to warrant congratulations.

"Mr. Barnes, I take great joy in seeing you make it this far."

I let out a quick laugh as he takes a drag. The men in the vicinity quiet down, and the attention isn't appreciated.

"I have to say that when I first checked you in, I thought you still had one more run left in you. I didn't sense that you were ready, and though I saw the fire in you, it was barely flickering. I thought after the first few weeks of not sleeping you would give up."

I recall my month-long extended version of Hell Week and shudder. "You're right. I came here kicking and didn't think it was possible to . . . escape. So much so, I was afraid to even try." I cast my hands out over my paperwork. "But as you can see, I'm moving on."

"You have no choice but to move forward." He snubs out his cigarette. "Come and find me if you need anything, okay?"

"You got it."

As he leaves, conversations pick back up and fly around my head. I lean in closer to the papers as though I have failing vision. Ashes from my cigarette scatter between the lines and I blow them off with a short burst of smoke. I've committed myself to honesty, so if any distractions approach, I wave them off. I'm not stopping for anyone and I'm not apologizing. I'll give whatever it takes to be thorough. I know that when I complete Step Four, the program will schedule me a date with a Catholic priest to fulfill Step Five. After I "admit to God, to ourselves, and to another human being the exact nature of our wrongs," I'll be off to transition.

This step is more than just symbolic—it's an exercise of cleansing myself of all the hurt that I've been clinging onto. The Big Book calls out resentments as "the number one offender" and this step is all about moving on with my life in the right direction. An addict like me cannot afford to harbor deep resentments that can deteriorate into an arsenal of excuses to feel sorry for myself. I have the feeling that most relapses start with self-pity, whether an addict recognizes it or not.

The time for feeling sorry for myself is over. This step will hopefully enlighten and provide awareness to prevent that trend of thinking. Understanding the errors in my thinking and how my defects lead me to feel as though I am being punished will become a strength. At least, that's the idea, and there's a part of me that knows I owe the people who love me and care about me the respect to no longer hurt them through my selfishness.

I remember when David once touched on this in class. He said that if he could use without there being any consequences, he would. Absolutely, and in a heartbeat. That's what addicts do best. We love the feeling of being high. But for every action there is a reaction, and our choices have severe and predictable consequences. It's a fallacy to believe that I could ever go back and only be hurting myself. With a clear head on my shoulders controlling my decisions today, I can't see myself consciously making the deliberate decision to hurt others. If I can manage to keep it that clear and distinct, I might be okay.

Tony began cultivating me for this step weeks ago when he advised me to pray and meditate over the type of life I wanted when moving forward. And as my writing hand grows tired, I am now realizing that the Fourth Step is also a tangible list of everything I don't want to bring along with me.

I apparently missed a spot on the table and my writing pad soaks up a ring of water. Tearing out the page, my brain enters auto-pilot as my pencil rattles off all the drugs I've experimented with.

Tobacco, alcohol, weed, cocaine, crack, ecstasy, mushrooms, heroin, methadone, ice, benzodiazepines, ketamine, Suboxone, Xanax and other prescription pills. I realize the real miracle in my life is that I'm somehow not surrounded by padded walls. I shake my head and allow memories to flood in along with warm gratitude that I've somehow preserved this fragile mind of mine. Perhaps my mind is damaged, but I am thankful it hasn't cracked beyond repair.

The list of my attempts at treatment and therapy is short and sweet, yet spread out enough to prove a pattern. Therapy with Dr. Makena as a misled teen began in early high school. Counseling with Sarah made me realize how selfless and caring professionals can be, even when working with challenging cases such as myself. Being an outpatient client at Tripler hospital after a drunken fight with my oldest brother on Christmas Eve one year when I stumbled upon a case of rum at my parents' house. An interview at Hina Mauka reaffirmed that I was a master of manipulation—I still can't believe my mother took me there and I somehow convinced them that she was the problem, not me. Hooper detox took a few tries before I found myself at Sand Island capping an eight-year odyssey through rehabs.

I focus on my thefts next and wonder how does one even begin to make amends to corporations? Old Navy. GAP. Express. Kohl's. Fred Meyer. Macy's. Target. Safeway. Marshalls. Sears. Rite-Aid. Dollar-Tree. Sports Authority. I write out my best estimate of times I've stolen from each store and give up after a thousand. A couple of times daily adds up quickly, so the only surprise there is how I avoided prison.

I don't know where to start for regrets and catch myself confusing them with blaming others. As a child, I often felt like the family business was the fourth kid that stole attention from my brothers and me. Looking back, I realize that while most of those feelings I harbored were valid, they were also short-sighted. Both of my parents sacrificed to provide us with top-notch education despite the cost. I erase the family business from the list.

Instead, I focus on my idiocies over the years and can barely write fast enough. I remember drunkenly running away from the cops at Bellows Beach one night and crashing straight into a tree, scarring my nose for life. Refusing a breathalyzer test at the police station cost me my license for a year where any high-school student craves independence the most. Flying signs and panhandling in Portland cost me my self-esteem. Stealing merchandise and selling food stamps cost me my morals. Codependency on my parents cost me my independence, and sharing needles cost me my health. I never thought I would find myself among such desperation.

I'm writing in the borders now, running out of room on the page as character flaws pour out of me like ink from a spilled well. The bad habits I can't bring with me range from biting my fingernails to smoking. Lying, poor hygiene, running from problems, anger, self-defeating thinking, self-medicating tendencies, self-fulfilling prophecies, denial. I'm on a roll and being honest is uplifting. Like my abscess, it feels good to let everything flow out instead of holding it in to boil and fester.

I'm a master of manipulation and a magician for making emotions disappear. Isolating and running away is a pattern dating back to childhood. I have no Higher Power or spiritual aspirations. Something deep inside of me stoked the flames of self-hatred. Spontaneity. Lack of confidence. Faithlessness. The need for instant gratification. Self-centeredness and selfishness—the root of my problems. Across the top of the page I scrawl, "I never stood a chance!" then stop to catch my breath.

I release my death grip on the pencil and watch as blood returns to my pale fingertips. Letting my heart rate slow down, my eyes scour the page and I swallow hard. I thought I understood the exercise, but realize I'm only just beginning. My character flaws, defects, pitfalls and shortcomings that were all stuffed deep down are now laid out, bare and honest with more to come. Every inch of the paper is filled with words. I stare at the full sheet, and I can only imagine how much potential I have with so much room to grow.

26

TIME BOMB

"Happy Aloha Friday!" Mom says, lighting up the room.

It never gets old to hear her say it. Mom stands and steps around the table, giving me a warm hug and a kiss on the cheek. Dad rises as well and bends at the hips to reach out across the table to me. We exchange a quick hug, patting one another on the back before plopping down into our plastic seats.

"Thanks for coming back," I say. "I really do appreciate these family visits. It's always great to see you guys."

"And it's always great to see you too." Her smile lingers on her face. "So, how are you doing?"

I reach out and rest my fingers on the table, drumming them as I choose my next words carefully. "Honestly? I think I'm ready to leave this place."

"Oh, not this again." Dad exhales, his eyes darting toward the ceiling. As he squeezes the bridge of his nose, I can tell his patience has run out. My mom stays quiet and stares into space. "Son, your mother and I don't want to keep hearing that. It worries us sick and we've told you that before."

"I know, and I don't mean to worry you, but you guys don't know what it's like in here. I feel like you two only see a glimpse of this program where everyone's on their best behavior." I lift the edge of my breakfast tray. "See this? They cook special meals for family visits. Trust me—the interns are never this nice, and the staff nev—"

Dad holds up a palm. "You know what? I'm just going to cut you off right there. Don't forget that as a retired Naval Intelligence Officer, I made a career of observing my surroundings. I've walked the property—I've overheard clients talking in the bathrooms. I know this can't be an easy program, but I thought we were past needing to remind you that you're here to save your life."

I look down at the table. "Dad—I get it—but this is a two-year program and you know it's only that long because everyone here is converting their sentences. That is, everyone but me! It was a mistake not to turn myself in when I had the chance, because my warrants won't just go away." I grind my teeth in frustration. "Whenever I bring it up with staff, I'm always reminded that now is not the right time to cross that bridge. Nobody wants me reaching out to Portland, and they all say the same thing—my main focus needs to be on recovery and saving my life. None of my legal issues are considered anywhere in my treatment plan, which doesn't work for me because I'm always looking ahead and can't make out the end game.

"Come on guys—think about it. Everyone else that makes it through this program will walk out of here with a clinical discharge and be able to move on with their life . . . except for me. In what world does that make sense? We're all doing the same work in here, even though it's not like I'm learning anything new anyway. I can only read the Big Book so many times and sit through the same exact class teaching the same exact thing. So please, I'm begging you, put yourself in my shoes—would either of you honestly stay in here if you were me?"

My dad gives it a second to make sure I've gotten in all out of my system before responding. "Son, I think I know the best way to help you." I watch as he reaches out and starts to pack up his belongings. "Your mother and I aren't going to do it anymore.

Every time we see you, you bring up leaving and seem fixated on convincing us this place is somehow holding you back. We're done, and if you mention it even one more time, we'll stop coming altogether." My mom shoots him a hard glance as he continues. "I don't know if you want to get high, but I do know that you can't come home if you walk out of those gates. Your mother and I are in agreement on that."

"Look, wanting to leave has nothing to do with wanting to use. I promise!" I reach down and pull my seat forward. "Do you know what the worst part about this place is? It's the *monotony*. New guys come in everyday, so the staff has to start the message all over again every week. It's like being shot in the face repeatedly. Same readings, same comments, same questions, same answers. I could probably teach a class by now if I wanted to." My arms raise in a "V," and I look around. "I can't believe I'm stuck in Groundhog Day all over again."

"Well, have you ever considered becoming a counselor? You're smart enough, Jordan. Imagine how many people you can help," Mom suggests.

I rub my forehead and give up.

"At least try and see the bigger picture," Mom urges. "Remember where you came from."

"I get it, Mom, but what more do I have to prove to convince you that—"

Dad cuts me off. "No one can keep you here. You know that. We know that. But I promise you, if you throw this opportunity away, know that even our endless support has limits."

My hands nosedive to my side. "Thanks, Dad, I really appreciate your unwavering support."

"You knock that off right now." He stands up to leave. "Stop trying to manipulate us and look around! I don't see anyone else in this room that loves you as much as we do."

"Gary, *please*." Mom pulls him down. "You guys, can't we just be normal for once and enjoy our breakfast together?"

"Dad, I didn't mean it like that. Look, I'm sorry. It's just that all day yesterday, I wanted to walk out of here. It was like an itch I couldn't scratch, so strong that I had to leave class and walk laps around the property to burn off steam. You know that with my warrants, I have no idea if me staying here will even mak—"

"What about that prayer they teach you about not worrying about things outside of your control? Did you try praying? Did you ask for peace? Because regarding your warrants, you'll cross that bridge when the time is right. As for right now though, it's a non-starter for us. We're not going to sit through every family visit debating whether or not you should leave. I don't have that energy, and it's not how I want to spend my Sunday mornings."

I stare into space, not wanting to admit Dad's right.

"Jordan, it's tough to come here and listen to you say that you want to leave," Mom says. "I take that home with me and worry about it until the next time I see you."

"Me too." Dad leans forward in his chair and props his forearm on the table. "Let me tell you about an experience I had when I was about your age that may change your perspective on time."

I glance at the clock and see we still have more time left.

"It was the winter of '75 and me and my class were in our final week of Aviation Officer Candidate School in Pensacola, Florida. We were living on the third floor of the barracks. A new class had just arrived and was moved into the first floor. No sooner after they settled in did all hell break loose. The drill instructors tore their rooms apart and PT'd those poor kids mercilessly.

"Once the smoke cleared, a few of us went down despite knowing the rules against fraternization between classes to check on the survivors. After eleven weeks of training we thought we had seen it all. As expected, we could see that the beds, furniture and even their personal belongs were scattered about the rooms as if a tornado had hit. That was normal, but then my classmate slapped my shoulder and pointed out boot marks on the ceilings of the hallways! See, there is an exercise called 'Frog Fuckers' where—"

"Gary." Mom places her hand on his forearm. My father rarely swears, but it often comes out when recalling his time in the military.

"Okay, there is an exercise called 'Frog . . . Effers' where you combine a jumping jack with a push up."

"Sort of like burpees?" I ask.

"What? Hey, can you guys just let me tell the story? Anyway, look, as the exercise intensified under the direction of a screaming D.I., the person working out literally had to dive to the ground, kicking their feet into the air as they dipped into a push up. We looked at the scuff marks on the ceiling and realized that they had brutalized these poor junior candidates worse than we had ever seen.

"The next day, we were relaxing in our rooms getting ready for our commissioning ceremony, which was only a couple of days away. We were finished with the physical training and enjoying life, feeling very much accomplished. Out of nowhere, the dreaded "Get On Line" order from a blasting voice shattered our peace. With lightning reaction, every member of our class jumped up and took a position of attention along the walls of the hallway. Our faces were striped with confusion like camouflage and our mood sank as we saw a stack of sandbags next to the drill instructor.

"He commented that, as we probably heard, the poor bastards on the first floor had failed their first inspection. He expressed his disappointment that we had not taken them under our wings and taught them better, but let me repeat, there was a rule against fraternization between classes. In fact, we weren't even allowed on their floor. Either way, at that point, he ordered all the doors and windows in the hallway closed.

"The Instructor then ordered the sandbags be passed up and down the hallway. 'Faster!' he screamed, and the more he yelled, the more oxygen he sucked from the room. When we could barely lift another bag, he called out 'Frog Fuckers!" and boots started flying. Imagine how difficult that was in a five-foot wide hallway crammed with people. Legs were everywhere and we were kicking and diving into each other, stepping on each other's hands. The instructors' version of rest was allowing us to hold planks in the upper push up position.

"After that, they ordered us to stand and pass the sandbags back and forth once more, up and down the hallway. Then we started the insanity all over again. Every muscle in my body was burning and screaming when I dropped to the floor, trying not to pass out. My nose plunged into a thick layer of sweat mixed with sand.

"Just when I learned the definition of misery, I heard someone laughing next to me. I lifted my chin to see my roommate Burt, who had a huge shit-eating smile on this face while his muscles trembled. I asked him why he was smiling. He responded with, 'You know, they can fuck with us all they want, but they can't stop the time.'

"I started to laugh and Burt joined in. The guys next to us heard him and the laughter became contagious. It lit up the hallway as if a fuse had been ignited and a taunting chorus of 'you can't stop the time' filled the corridor. The torture ended soon after that, and as we were all brought to our feet, every single one of us was standing there smiling. I learned that day, that no matter how bad it gets, there is always an end, even if it's not in sight. With the right attitude and armed with that knowledge, I promise you, you can get through anything."

27

LATE FOR THE SKY

I quickly snuff out my alarm before it wakes the entire dorm and press my bare feet against the cold linoleum. I shuffle through my locker for a plain white shirt, grab my pouch of tobacco, then head off to start my night patrol shift. It's five minutes to 11 p.m. and I know that whoever I am relieving is counting on me to be on time.

Stuffing my feet into rubber slippers, I shuffle toward the weight room area and pass by dim dorms that leak a choir of snores out of their bug screens. It's almost like there's a rule that each dorm must have one loud snorer. Thankfully, earplugs are available from the duty office if needed. I tried them once and I couldn't stand the silence.

I see Jon waiting for me. He steps out of his folding chair and pretends to brush the dust off. He holds out a pencil like a scepter and neatly arranges a clipboard, ashtray, pack of matches and a digital clock. I pick up the clipboard with a partially filled out chart and jot down my name in the next open row.

"Jordan B. 11 p.m. Begin Shift."

The chart has only two headers and needs the names of anyone who comes and goes along with the time they're passing by. I prop the cheap digital clock up on the weight bench to my left and press down the failing duct tape that holds a tear together. Besides noting the time, the only other thing expected of me is to walk a predetermined route every thirty minutes. It goes along a fence line, hooks a dorm, travels down a lonely path and circles back to my original starting point.

Our purpose here is to keep the people in that are supposed to stay in, but also to deter anyone from sneaking in that doesn't belong. I've heard of girlfriends hopping the fence, but thankfully nothing exciting has happened during any of my shifts, yet. If I were looking to get anyone in trouble, I wouldn't keep my eyes low and blinders up.

Adjusting my seat, I try to make this hard plastic chair as comfortable as it will get, and begin to count down the next few hours. Now and then, someone comes and goes on their way to the bathroom, but otherwise it's dead back here. If I don't know some-one's name, I have to ask them to remind me and embarrass myself with how bad my memory has become.

McDermott rounds a corner and methodically approaches, his long arms swinging from his shoulders like weighted pendulums. I sit up as he walks my way with his ever-present, close-lipped smile. A few weeks ago, he loaned me a book from his vast under-ground library that details the bonds between mentors and their apprentices in the scientific research industry. I've been sneaking in some reading during my free time and I can't put it down. In fact, I'd have it with me now if it weren't at risk of being confiscated as contraband.

McDermott's an enigma, defined more by what he's not than what he is. He's no longer a client, but also not an employee, though he's the closest thing to a landscaper we have. He's not a counselor either, but he has no aversion to counseling any client he sees promise in. And when staff asks, no one would ever out him as our black-market librarian, even though he scrawls his name across the leaves of every book with a Sharpie.

McDermott came here as a client over eight years ago and has called this facility home for longer than any of the staff. He's one of two former clients I know of who completed the program then requested to stick around. The other client that lingers in the back suffers from wet brain and may never leave, which may not be a bad thing for him. If there's a strong enough reason to stay, clients may remain on the property with permission from the Director just as long as they keep contributing something valuable to the program and remain sober.

I've heard that McDermott murdered a man with a brick, and once he transferred here from prison, he asked to live out the rest of his parole on property. If that's true, it makes sense to me, even though it's hard to see him as the same man capable of committing such a crime. I know him as a brilliant mind and realized long ago that one of his favorite pastimes is conversing intelligently with the clients if they're able to keep up.

"Night Patrol, huh? I guess someone has to do it. Ha! Look at you! So, you need a new book?" McDermott flashes a smile that emphasizes the gap between his front teeth.

"No, not yet, but I'm really enjoying this one lately," I say.

"I thought you'd like it. So, how far in are you?"

"Just finished the chapter about Candace Pert, you know, the neuroscientist who discovered the opiate receptor in 1971."

"Aww, the 'mother of psychoneuroimmunology.'"

"It's crazy to think that for a drug I couldn't live without, I had no understanding of how the chemicals metabolized in my body and brain. I mean, I knew about opiate receptors, agonists and antagonists, but I never understood how the drug actually worked, and definitely not on a molecular level. It makes me appreciate scientists like Pert because if it weren't for brilliant minds like hers, who paved the way for drugs like Narcan and Buprenorphine, I wouldn't be here today."

McDermott moves the clock and clipboard, then takes a seat on the bench. "So you had a close call? Tell me about it. Besides, I've got nothing else better to do than to feed my spiders."

I don't need much more prompting to start in.

"Long before I was homeless, I had just signed a lease with my fiancée for a small one-bedroom apartment near the Rose Garden back in Portland. We were both new addicts, and though we had jobs, we were still barely able to make ends meet and stop the bleeding. You know how it goes, sometimes never missing a hit meant sometimes being late on rent. I was working security at a concert venue in Portland called the Crystal Ballroom, but my hours were being cut back by a manager that was hoping I'd quit. Every week I brought home a smaller check and struggled to carry my own weight. Just like they say here, the highs and lows started stacking on top of one another, and eventually it became too much to handle for Lucy."

"Is that your fiancée?" McDermott asks.

"Yes, well, or was. Anyway, we were three days into a pact to both quit using, but I was sneaking shots behind her back. One night when I was at work, she was back at home in a fit of withdrawal and crawled into our bathtub then started cutting herself to release the tension. Considering suicide, she caved and reached out for help, but not to me. Instead, she called her best friend and told her everything."

"Fuck. So, she came clean?" McDermott asks.

"Yeah, I guess so." I resist laughing at the joke, pause to roll a cigarette and offer one to McDermott. "Her friend dropped everything and rushed over with backup, but Lucy refused to leave with them. She closed the door on them and didn't say a word about it once I got home. I flopped into bed because I had a final the next morning, but her tossing and turning kept me up all night. In the morning, we both awoke to a sharp rapping on our apartment door. When I opened it, I was excited to see Lucy's friend and sister until they demanded I take a walk for betraying them."

"All good things come to an end," McDermott says through a smile.

It's painful to recall what happened next.

"Lucy dug in her heels and again refused to leave with them, and as the three of them argued, our secrets rained out of an open window down onto the streets below. I ran back upstairs to try and calm them down before the cops were called, but my return didn't help the situation. As I closed the window, I could tell her sister wanted to push me out of it. She was totally blindsided by everything and blaming herself for not having any idea, but it wasn't her fault. You know how easy it is to hide addiction, right? At least, at first, before the weight loss and track marks betray us."

"Of course. We're masters of deceit."

"Yeah, well, there's some situations that are impossible to weasel out of. Since Lucy still refused to leave with them, her friend quietly got on her phone in the background while the two sisters argued. Moments later, their Plan B burst through the door —all three-hundred pounds of him."

"Yeah, you're fucked."

"You have no idea. In walks her stepdad, a monstrous, 6'4" tall behemoth in a tank top with a tattoo of the devil smoking a bong on his bicep. Immediately, all bickering stopped. And as he towered over me, he instructed the girls to pack all the belongings. He looked around the apartment and at all the former furniture of his we had decorating our pad. I'm sure he felt sick to his stomach.

"He told me, 'Well look at that! That's my fucking couch, you motherfucker, and you're getting my little baby high on that! You're a little piece of shit, huh?!' I prepared myself for a beating, but Lucy jumped in and claimed responsibility for her own actions. She wouldn't let him push her out of the way, so over her shoulder he warned me to never speak to her again. Then he reached out, pinned me to the wall and studied my face, in case I ever changed my appearance and shaved my beard."

"It sounds like you got off easy."

"I guess it depends on how you look at it. It wasn't easy to watch her pack, especially when she begged to say goodbye. Torn apart by the sadness and rage, it surprised me when her stepdad took the bag of clothes from her arm and stepped toward the apartment door. He told her to be quick and promised to return for his stuff after he talked to our landlord. Then he squeezed into the hallway with her sister, but left the door cracked open. Lucy apologized and told me she couldn't do it anymore, and together we cried in each other's arms.

"I was so sorry to have let her down, but she didn't blame me once. With a tearful kiss, she turned and walked out of the door and left me gutted. I looked around at the apartment we had just moved into two months prior and wrote everything off in my mind. Knowing I still had the keys to my old dorm room with rent paid through the semester, I started to pack up everything of value and anything incriminating. I gave them a few minutes to pull away and left the apartment behind, making sure I wasn't being followed."

McDermott was following along. "Wow, you're a lucky guy to have survived that, but when did you overdose?"

"Well, in this story, I wasn't the one who did. A few days later, I got a call from Lucy that she had made it into a treatment facility and was having a hard time kicking. She asked if I would mail her some shampoo with some dope stashed in the bottle so she could wean off easier. I could hear the pain in her voice when she swore she was getting clean after this, and that I had to do the same if we had any future together. I promised I would try, but neither of us stood a chance. She left rehab shortly after that and met me at my dorm. We went upstairs and did what we did best."

I pause for a moment, still unnerved about how close everything was to changing that night.

"I opened the safe, pulled out a cooker and fixed her a shot. I knew I had to be careful because her tolerance would have dropped, so I started off small. She asked me to shoot her up, which was usually the case. As the needle entered her silky arm, she leaned back a bit, then kept going."

McDermott stroked his hair back over his head and leaned forward. He knew where this was going.

"Her chin slumped, then her body gave out. I caught her just as she slid into the mini-fridge. Her face landed on the carpet and her breathing started to slow. I knew she was overdosing, and ran across the room, then started spinning the dial to my safe.

"By then I was panicking. Thank God that inside the safe was an overdose kit that the needle exchange had been giving out before their funding ran out. I pulled out the small glass vial of Narcan and a long intramuscular needle. Drawing one cc of clear fluid, I ran back to Lucy and flipped her on her side, jamming the needle into her arm. Then I rolled her onto her back, cocked her chin back and started to breathe for her. It took a couple of panicked breaths before I realized I needed to plug her nose for the oxygen to fill her lungs."

"You were lucky to have that Narcan, huh?" he asks.

"Not as lucky as she was. It took a minute before she came to, and in that time, all I could think of was that if her life was over, so was mine. I knew her stepdad would kill me. There was no way out of this mess. If she died in my dorm room, I think I would have joined her.

"But as her eyes opened, all of those fears fell away. She awoke in confusion, with absolutely no recollection of what had just transpired. When I brought her up to speed, she didn't believe me, even as blood trickled down her arm."

McDermott smiles in disbelief. "Modern medicine. Amazing, really. It's just too bad that society goes back and forth on getting a drug like Narcan to the people who need it most. It's such a lifesaver—harm reduction services really do save lives."

"I wouldn't be here today without it, because I had overdosed before that and nobody had Narcan except for the EMT's. Fortunately my friends took turns breathing for me until the paramedics arrived and injected me with it on the spot. Just like Lucy, I didn't remember anything when I came to."

I shake my head at the thought of how quickly life can be derailed. "You know what? The crazy thing was that within about fifteen minutes, Lucy was begging me to fix her another shot. I told her she was insane, and not because it would be a waste of a hit."

McDermott stands to his feet. "No, she's not insane," he says. "She's just powerless, like all of us in here are."

28

PUEO

(HAWAIIAN SHORT-EARED OWL)

"Thanks for picking me up, Mom." I open the car door and launch a mesh bag full of dirty laundry into the backseat. As I hop into the car, she hands me bottled water draped with condensation and a chocolate protein bar. I tear the package open and get to work.

"Seat belt," she reminds me as she puts the car in drive.

"Oh, right," I mumble with a full mouth, catching crumbs in my palm as I lick the melted chocolate off the wrapper. "So, how have you been?"

"I've been better. Happy to see you, but struggling."

"What's wrong?" I ask, swallowing my last bite.

She's in no rush to start, but once she does, my heart sinks with each passing word. "I'm just getting it from all angles. Your cousin's wife is battling cancer, but I think she'll be okay—it's your aunt that I'm most worried about. She's fighting lung cancer, and I don't think she's going to make it."

"What?! I'm so sorry."

"Me too. The worst part is I'm worried that she may have given up the fight."

"Given up? What do you mean?"

"My gut tells me it's her son, your cousin. He's her only child and is so lost in his addiction that I don't think she has a reason to live." The tears explode, dripping down her cheeks behind her sunglasses. I put a hand on her shoulder. It's the least I can do.

"Mom, pull over. I'll drive."

"You know you can't. No, I'll be okay. Can you pass me a tissue please?" She reaches for the glove box, but her arm comes up short.

I pop the lever and napkins flow out. Gathering a few, I place them in her hand and watch as she tucks one behind her sunglasses, drying her eyes.

We continue in silence that neither of us mind. I don't know a lot about cancer, only that Mom has seen too much of it in her life. It was only a few weeks ago when she told me she had learned about a tumor on her thyroid, though, thank God, it's benign. Then she admitted debating whether or not she should tell me at all because she feared I might overreact and blame myself for all the stress I've caused.

Riding next to her, I can only hope that her strength runs deep in my blood. She is so strong, even when she's weighed down with the likelihood of losing her sister. My heart breaks for my aunt. It troubles me to know that Mom has existed in a similar state throughout the entire duration of my addiction, going back as far as high school.

As we pull into her driveway, Mom collects her thoughts for a final time. She lifts her sunglasses to reveal red swollen eyes above a perfect smile. "We only have a few hours. Let's make the best of the time we have, okay?"

"Was it hard to come back?"

"Mike, you have no idea." I catch the audacity of my statement and let out a chuckle. "Okay, maybe you do, but either way it was great. Thanks for approving my day pass."

"Hey, I didn't make it happen. You did. Do the right thing—get the right results. Simple as that. Keep it up and you'll be able to go home on overnighters in no time. So, was the whole family there?"

"Yeah, they were all waiting for me. Both brothers said I look ripped compared to when I first got here." I flex my bicep and my smile. "They respect how hard I'm working to repair all the damage I've caused to my body." I pause for a second. "And while I was at it, I also told them about the Hep C."

"Honesty will set you free. I bet they were full of questions?"

"A couple, but it helped to have the results from my sonogram. They were glad to hear that I don't have any scarring or noticeable damage to my liver. I'm glad we caught it early."

"That's how, my braddah. You and I both know it could be a lot worse. You're good. So what else?"

"Well, Dad fired up the BBQ and we feasted like kings. After that, we hung out around the house and everything just felt normal—like a family again. Oh, and this happened!" I pull off my hat. "Finally cleaned up the rat nest!"

"Killahs. Looks great."

"And feels clean. I'm much less self-conscious," I admit as I slip my hat back on over my buzzed hair. "Words can't describe how enjoyable it was to be home."

"And they don't need to." Mike leans forward in his chair and uses a folded piece of paper to funnel chia seeds from a packet into a water bottle. He gives it a shake and lets the cyclone inside mix the contents. "It's important to rebuild the relationship with the 'Ohana. That's critical. Not only because they are good people, but also because you'll need their support. Keeping them close will help to keep you accountable and out of trouble." He unscrews the cap and downs half of the bottle in one swig. "I hope you realize how lucky you are to have the parents you do. Not too many of my guys have families that are still here for them."

"Yeah, I'm starting to get it." I give Mike a second to finish the rest of his drink. "But you know, oddly enough, it feels good to come back though. Almost like I hit a reset button and cleared the machine."

"That's good. You're drawn to the light." Mike flicks his fingers and motions for me to lean forward. "Never forget, brah, this is your home too, and you're part of our family as well. Our doors are always open for you. That is, unless you choose to close them."

Alone under a full moon, time is moving slower than normal. It's just me and the guard shack with nobody in their right mind coming or going. I prefer to take on night shifts where the air is more relaxed and there's less movement. The two-hour blocks may seem to stretch out longer, but I appreciate the extra time to think and write poetry. Spiritual growth happens in the darkness and I am no longer afraid of being alone with my thoughts.

My legs ache, so I venture out of the shack for a stretch. A thin trade wind scatters dead leaves across the driveway and slaps them against the fence. I embrace this quietness. It's so foreign to the daily rumblings of the facility. I see a rock that doesn't belong on the driveway, so my shoe sends it flying. I watch it take a bounce, ricocheting off the wall of the guard shack with a sharp crack that tears through the night.

At the same time, there is an explosion of leaves from the tree above and I instinctively jump back. A large white owl rockets out of the canopy and swoops over my head, forcing me to duck and drop to the ground. In a single motion, I spring to my feet and wipe bits of gravel off my palms while I take in the sight, watching the owl disappear over the wastewater treatment tanks next door.

My eyes drop when I hear footsteps approaching and I spin around to see a shadow nearing with a flashlight sweeping the ground. As he gets closer, I realize it's Kevin from his long black ponytail. He must be working Ninja tonight, making his periodic rounds throughout the facility as the lone staff member on duty. For all intents and purposes, Kevin is the Director's right hand man. During the few times we've talked, he's always been cool to me.

"Howzit!" he calls out.

"Please tell me you just saw that?"

"Saw what?"

"The Pueo that burst out of this tree. It flew that way."

"Oh, no way. That's a good omen, especially out here."

"You think so?" I look at Kevin, who is making a strange face with furrowed brows.

"Did you cut your hair?" he asks.

"Yeah, over a month ago. You're just noticing now?" I let out a snicker. "It feels great, you should try it." I skim my palm over my head, feeling the odd tingle of the short hairs flipping forward.

"Never going to happen." A smile crosses his face. "Dude, I'm sorry, but I thought you had left the program and that a new guy came in who looked a lot like you!"

"Well, that's mildly depressing."

"Sorry, but you know I spend a lot more time interacting with staff than clients." He scratches his cheek. "Remind me when you got here?"

"End of August."

"So that's what . . . seven months? Have you done your Fifth Step yet?"

"Nope. Still waiting."

"And your counselor is Mike, right?"

"Yeah."

"Cool, cool. And how are your parents doing? You know, you wouldn't be here if it weren't for them. You're a lucky man to have family that loves you so much."

"I know, though 'lucky' isn't something I've considered myself as for a long time. I've been angry, bored, stagnant, tired, num—"

"I don't blame you, but compare how you feel today to say, six months ago." Kevin cranks his head back to stare at the moon. "Are you hoping to work for them?"

"I would love to if you'd let me."

"That has to be between you and them, but I don't think anyone here will get in your way. Have a good one. I'll see you around."

. . .

I remain seated as our minivan rolls to a complete stop between two faded white stripes in the parking lot of St. Patrick's Catholic Church. Sanchez adjusts the rearview mirror until my face fills the frame. "Do you know who you're meeting?" he asks.

I nod and look away. After my brief conversation with Kevin, Mike had walked me through what to expect today after advancing me to my Fifth Step.

"Okay, I'll be waiting right here for you when you're pau, but don't return with any baggage. Remember, it takes courage to let it all go."

I clear my throat and slide the door open. "You got it, Sanchez."

Straightening out my collar, I head in toward my appointment with Father Tim.

The concrete steps leading up to the church are long and skinny, and from the parking lot, it looks as though the church is built in the shape of a cross. A large stone statue of Saint Patrick adorns the arched entrances, but I don't believe I'll be passing through them today. Instead, Mike had instructed me to check in with the receptionist in the offices attached to the side of the church.

They're waiting for me and already I'm expecting a different experience. Having looked forward to this day for months, I've conjured up images of a shadowed priest in a gilded robe on the other side of the confessional screen, receiving my innermost secrets. Instead, I'm seated in a well-lit room at a desk across from Father Tim like I'm here to apply for a job. He is Chinese-American, wearing a traditional Aloha Shirt, and gives a single, quick smile from beneath his bushy, silver eyebrows.

"Good morning." He shakes my hand and introduces himself. "Over the years, I've done many of these Fifth Steps. I think you should be very proud of making it this far. Please, begin."

I stare down at my stack of paperwork in my lap and wish I

had a drink of water. "How do I start? Do I just start reading you my list?"

"Whatever feels most comfortable for you." He interlocks his fingers and keeps smiling, but he doesn't lead me through the process like I envisioned he would. I was expecting some back story and build up on how I came to be here, including how much progress I've made to date. Jumping right into it feels too much like a formality and my heart sinks a little.

I place the stack of pages on his desk and sort them out. There are twelve sheets, each formatted into tables I have filled out by hand. My fingers flip through the first six pages titled "Review of Resentments." Each row specifies who or what I'm resentful at and why. Then there is a long list of implications I can check off that the resentment affects, including self-esteem, personal relationships and emotions.

I flash a quick smile before beginning down the list. "I'm resentful at Simon for overdosing and dying. I'm resentful that my childhood best friend moved away to Florida and left me behind. I'm resentful at Punahou school for kicking me out in the eleventh grade. The judge who placed me on probation for a year when I was sixteen. Jared for introducing me to heroin and Thomas for teaching me how to shoot up. My friend Shaun shot himself in the mouth in Alaska, taking his own life. I hate that I hate him for that."

I look up at the priest and receive no feedback either way, so I continue, skipping over the ones that don't seem particularly important. "My mother for hiring a nanny to watch us when I was a baby, and also for hoping I'd be her first girl instead of another boy."

I pause for a second as a random resentment pops into my mind.

"You know, she also once admitted that when she was pregnant with me, she talked to God and expressed that she felt strong enough to raise a special needs child if need be. In her mind, she was thankful to have already been gifted two healthy boys.

Always thinking of others more than herself, I guess she thought that perhaps God could arrange a trade if some other mother needed a healthy newborn more than she did."

I shrug my shoulders. "I'm not sure if I admire or resent her for that, but I do resent both of my parents for starting a company that took so much time away from the family. My brothers fought too much, and though I am the youngest son, I always felt stuck in the middle. And though I don't hold this against my mom and dad, there was also this $1,000 deal they offered me and my brothers that proved the road to Hell is paved with good intentions."

I flip the page and continue. "I've hurt a lot of people along the way, but hate how I've dragged others down with me. My ex-fiancée Lucy has never once blamed me for this, but I introduced her to heroin and showed her where to find it. I blindly led her down that path and couldn't protect her because I could barely fend for myself. I haven't seen her in years, and will probably never see her again. I wish I wasn't capable of being so selfish at the expense of others, because in the end, we all lose."

My eyes gloss over a few more resentments that pale in comparison. When I turn the page, I realize that all that's left is what I hold against myself. These are all mine and I own them. I wipe my brow and realize that the priest might as well not even be here.

"I am resentful at myself for being selfish and self-centered and for totaling my motorcycle in high school. For letting my drug use run rampant and for turning my back on God." I don't even look up to see his reaction. "For lying to myself and others, causing my family pain, problems and perpetual dissatisfaction. I distanced myself from everyone, yet it got me nowhere. I am resentful for selling or losing everything that mattered, hiding my drug and alcohol use and not valuing the women I've loved. I put dope on a pedestal and shunned all responsibility. I regret being lazy and running away from life's problems. And in hindsight, I can finally see that I did myself a terrible disservice by procrastinating and stuffing my emotions all through my life."

I flip the paper over and pick up the next list, four pages full of fears. It's in the same format, asking what I'm fearful of and why I have those fears.

"I'm fearful of my past coming back to haunt me, nobody coming to my funeral and being remembered as unmemorable. I'm fearful of not being able to make amends and raising a child that reminds me of myself. I don't know how my addiction will come back to haunt me or if I'll have to explain myself for the rest of my life. I'm fearful of not completing treatment, someone reading my journals and being hurt.

"Cancer. Hepatitis C. Liver Failure. Debt. Failure. Success. Being alone. Falling tree branches. Losing a loved one too soon. I'm fearful of being loved and being incarcerated."

The list goes on. After I rattle off all of the drugs I've ever enjoyed, I flip the page and finish.

Father Tim clears his throat. "I would think that you should be very proud of how far you've come," he says, commending my honesty. "And as you step into a life of faith and recovery, know that God is still with you, always by your side. Now, shall we pray?"

I clasp my hands in my lap, interlock my fingers beneath the edge of his desk and hang my head. I listen to his words carefully, hoping for a cleansing rush of energy that clears the way like a controlled burn in a forest. I squeeze my eyes and sit up straight, inviting God to build me back up after breaking myself down in His presence.

But the prayer ends abruptly, leaving me fragmented and stale. I thank Father Tim out of respect and return his smile, then collect my things matter-of-factly and show myself out.

Even though I just spilled my guts like seppuku, I walk out of the building full of regrets and remorse. There was no euphoria or eureka moment. No transcendence or clean slate. No promised rebirth—only disappointment that my experience didn't live up to that of my peers. Depending on their respective religion, some clients are taken to a rabbi, kahuna, monk or other type of minister with spiritual authority.

Even with that wide range of leadership, nearly all of them return to the facility reporting a life-changing experience, or at least report having a weight lifted from their shoulders. Guys in my group and transition clients describe feeling free, refreshed, cleansed and ready to start anew after their Fifth Step. The experience I just had felt like nothing more than a notch in the belt.

Sanchez welcomes me back into the minivan with a smile and reaches behind him to pat my knee. "Before you say anything, know that whatever happened in there is between you, the priest and the Lord. My advice is to take this time to pray and meditate. Don't feel any pressure to share unless you want to."

I bite my tongue and keep my thoughts to myself as I stare out the window, knowing that pressure has no impact upon a soul so deflated. But as we back out of the parking lot, I force myself to look at the bright side—now, more than ever, I'm ready to move on from this moment.

29

SHIVER THE WHOLE NIGHT THRU

"Jordan, I have someone I'd like you to meet." Ty's smile says it all and my stomach tightens when I realize that I won't be going to work anytime soon. He continues with a positive spirit that's not as infectious as I imagine he's hoping for.

Ty turns to the newcomer beside him. "Austin, this is Jordan, and I couldn't imagine a better Shadow for you since his drug of choice is also heroin. Jordan was homeless up in Oregon, but had enough of that life and decided to do something about it." Ty turns to me, smiles, then plucks my client badge off of my shirt. "And his progress here has been nothing short of amazing—just look at his intake photo!" He passes my badge off to Austin. "If he can do it, so can you."

Austin barely acknowledges me while I size up what's left of him.

"Jordan, Austin is a retread, so he's been here before and knows the drill. He should be very easy to get along with, especially since you two have so much in common."

I give Ty an asking glance, wondering if he's serious. He reads my face and speaks up to clarify, though he knows he isn't obligated to.

"Unfortunately, Isolation is full at the moment with sick clients, but I think the two of you are tough enough to manage. Austin is detoxing cold turkey, but trust me, he can do this. Jordan, this will also be really helpful for you—it's going to remind you how far you've come. And Austin, Jordan just went through what you're facing, so when times get tough, look to him as proof that you can do this."

Ty places a hand on Austin's shoulder and his frail frame nearly crumbles under the pressure.

I lean in toward Ty to avoid aiming my disappointment at Austin. With a quick wipe of my lips, I choose my words carefully. "You know, I've already had a couple of shadows before—is there no one else who could use the experience? Besides, I was under the impression that since I just did my Fifth Step, I'd be off to work soon."

Ty leans back in slight shock. "And you will be," he assures me, "but for now, I'd say you have a much more important job in your near future."

I hate how nothing in here is up for debate. "You got it, Ty."

"Great. Thank you. Now, why don't you two get acquainted? We'll move you both into the A.C. dorm right after lunch." Ty, content with his introductions, gives one last smile and leaves us alone to figure the rest out.

I smirk at Austin. My eyes are naturally drawn to his forearms, spotting the similar marks of a true junkie. Most addicts begin their shooting careers by aiming just below the high-water line of the elbow. Over time, the waters recede and shit rolls downhill to the forearms, wrists, hands and fingers. Austin sees me studying his tracks and lifts up his rotten limb so we can compare arms.

There's also a striking resemblance between him and Kurt Cobain. Nirvana has long been one of my favorite bands, and looking back, I wonder if the willingness to try heroin was seeded in my grunge days as a youth. I drummed in punk bands all throughout middle and high school, covering favorite anthems from Rancid, NOFX and the Suicide Machines. From an early age, something burned deep inside of me and I sense that Austin shared the same fire.

Austin's straggly blonde hair drapes in his face and clings to his slick, sweaty skin. All around us, clients look at him, then at me and do a double take. It's as though I'm staring down a ghost from my past. For those who knew me when I first came in, they think we're a match made in heaven.

The main difference between us is that his face is bloody and scabbed from picking. I don't know how I never developed that tick, but I see he isn't able to help himself. While he introduces himself to me and shakes my hand, he uses his other free hand to dab blood off his cheek with a spotted paper towel torn from his pocket.

If I'm to be his Shadow, I need to find a way to do so from a distance. I've only known him for a few minutes and am already uncomfortable for multiple reasons. Besides the in-your-face reminder of withdrawal, I don't want to befriend anyone here that has local ties to heroin. Perhaps the single biggest benefit to my leaving Portland was making a geographical change that left my dealers and connections in the dust.

An invaluable buffer—I have no business knowing where to go or who to call if I ever decide to toss in the towel. Even though I've met hundreds of addicts in my time here at the program, nearly all of them get their kicks off a different drug of choice than me.

For new clients, drugs seem to be all they know and there's nothing else substantive in their life to talk about. Their entire world revolves around dope. I squint my eyes to block out the sun, light a cigarette and wish that the facility didn't have a policy against wearing sunglasses on the premises. I remember asking Deacon about this. He told me it's because the staff doesn't want us hiding behind a mask. Since the eyes of any addict are the first giveaway of being high, staff members are always on the lookout for overactive eye movement, a deadened gaze or pinpoint pupils.

The muscles in my face are tense, my eyes squinting to filter out the brightness. I turn my back to the sun and do my best to censor our conversation, keeping it positive as we feel each other out. So far, Austin seems like a nice enough guy, but the fact that he can't stop squirming gives me the feeling that I won't ever be able to relax around him. I'm starting to understand what I put Deacon through.

On top of his heroin and meth addiction, he is also easing into a methadone withdrawal, which we both know is as bad as it gets, almost up there with alcohol and benzodiazepines. Austin is starting to complain of being sick and I'm scared not only for him, but for myself as well.

I'm not ready to feel his pain.

An intern comes over to take Austin into the medical unit to perform a physical. Because I'm handing over possession of him, I stay seated since he doesn't need a Shadow when with staff. I'm asked if I don't mind staying put until they're done and take the opportunity to light another cigarette. I tune out the conversations around me and accept I am powerless over the process.

Sitting on the bench with my back to the railing, I massage my spine like a bear and feel a light bump behind me as someone approaches. Turning to the right, I watch a pair of hands tap the handrail. I arc my neck to see Russel, then respectfully turn away to avoid blowing a cloud of smoke toward him.

"Mr. Barnes, I see you have a new Shadow, huh?"

I flick the ash off the tip of my cigarette. "Yeah, he seems like a nice guy."

"Yes, Austin and I go way back." Russel leans forward, dropping his elbows on the handrail. "And from the looks of it, he's a lot worse than the last time I saw him. Remember, the disease is strong and it always, always, *always* gets worse. Never better."

He pauses for a second. "Do me a favor—I want you to pay close attention to what he is going through, okay? I suggest you *feel* his detox and let it remind you why recovery is so important. Also, get ready for some long nights—we won't be giving him any Seroquel to help him sleep this time." He pinches a small gap between his thumb and pointer finger. "Every time a client comes back to the program, it's our job to make it just a little bit harder on them, so they remember the pain."

I press my cigarette to my lips, but I don't take a drag. Staring straight ahead, the smoke burns my eyes and I can't compute what I'm hearing. I know it's not uncommon for staff to take away privileges like weight room access and day passes, but how does exasperating someone's withdrawal symptoms on purpose help them get better faster? I wouldn't wish withdrawal on my worst enemy and I can't believe that any staff member, especially as an addict themselves, could do the same.

I turn to face Russel. "You honestly believe that will help him?"

"Of course it will. I mean, you remember your withdrawal, right? Do you ever want to suffer through that again?"

I cringe at the thought. "No—*fuck no*—but it's not the same thing. He's coming off the streets and doesn't get the benefit of going through a week-long medical detox first. And even if he did, if he's anything like me, he's not going to sleep for the first month."

"Maybe, maybe not. But you made it, and besides, it's not that different. Austin had it the easier, softer way the first time he was here. We're not trying to punish him, but we're also not going to put on kids gloves to handle him. He needs to fight for his recovery if he wants to make it and he'll need your support."

Russel thinks for a second. "Trust me, I want him to succeed, but we're not set up to have revolving doors here. And every time someone returns for a second or third time, that's one less bed we have available to save another life. So there's a lot on the line. Austin knows that relapse is not an option, yet he chose to walk out of the gates once before. That said, keep a close eye on him. You know what he's going through. If it gets too much to handle, come find me and we'll reassess him, then adjust our treatment plan if necessary."

I stomp on my cigarette, then pick it up and walk it over to the ashtray. I know that Russel has a kind heart—I don't question that for a second. His methods are tried and true and I see how seriously he takes our safety here. He always encourages us to get closer to sobriety, but sometimes it's too close for comfort. Having Austin on Shadow for the next week means I'm right there with him living through withdrawal all over again. I put Deacon through it, but heroin wasn't his drug so he couldn't entirely relate and it didn't tear him apart. So when Austin tells me he's ready to crash out, that's my cue to get ready for a long night.

Heading into the Rec Hall for breakfast, I don't even need to ask Austin how he slept. He was out like a baby as soon as he hit the pillow, proving once again that I'm often wrong. That's when I remember the methadone in his system and it makes sense. His withdrawal will be prolonged over the course of a few months, assuming he sticks it out. Unlike me, he doesn't get the benefit of ripping the band-aid off quickly.

I breathe down his neck as we stand in line for breakfast. Austin's restlessness has already begun to rub off on me, and the hungry line behind us keeps shuffling forward, compacting what little space I can squeeze between us. I grab my tray and hold it out in front of me as a spacer, then remember how Deacon always had my back.

"Hey man, you seem a little shaky. Why don't you let me hold your tray for you?" I ask.

"I g-g-got it," he eeks out, refusing my help. Some clients struggle to carry things in early recovery, but Austin is in good spirits as we make our way through the chow line.

Over his shoulder, I watch him set a shaky cup of coffee on his tray, pick his face and thrust the same fingers into the utensil tray to dig for a fork. It's quiet time in the Rec Hall, so I keep my thoughts to myself as we take a seat across from one another. I force a smile as he shovels a pile of watery eggs into his mouth— he would never be considered a picky eater were it not for his dermatillomania.

After breakfast, I watch Austin fidget through a few hours of class and wish I could hit a switch to turn off my sense of empathy. I know what he's going through and suffer alongside him from a distance. When the bell rings, I grab my things and wait for him outside of the Rec Hall. He bobs out of the doorway with an unlit cigarette dangling in his mouth, and I follow him to the smokers tent.

At least he makes my job easy since he's been down this road before. He knows the routine and how to keep us both out of trouble, and after a quick comparison, we realize that not much has changed since the last time he was here.

I lick the glue strip on my rolling paper and twist the freshly rolled cigarette in my fingers. "We got some time before lunch. Want to run through a quick refresher on the Twelve Steps?" I ask. "I can't think of much else to do when you're a new client on an automatic thirty-day restriction."

Austin doesn't even skip a beat. "Not really, unless you really want to. I can't fucking stand that book."

"Oh, okay then." I take a drag and exhale it into the air like a smoke signal, allowing the conversations around us to come to the rescue.

"C-can I ask you something," Austin wonders, unable to sit still long enough to enjoy a moment of silence.

"Of course man, anything."

"Do you miss it?"

I screw my face. *Do I tell him the truth, or what he wants to hear?* "No, not really. At least, not anymore."

Austin picks his face and scoots closer. "Bullshit. There's no way you don't still think about using."

I cock my head. "What's your problem? You didn't ask me if I still think about using. Of course I do, every day and then some. But that doesn't mean I miss it."

"So if you still think about it all the time, do you think you'll use when you get out of here?"

"Not if I have anything to say about it." I scoff in his face. "I'm not going through all of this just to have to do it again."

"I remember thinking the same thing the last time I was here."

"Where are you going with this?"

"I'm just wondering if there's hope."

"Of course there is. There's always hope, but hope won't take you all the way. You're going to have to put in the work, but you already know this, as well as what happens when you don't."

"You're starting to sound like staff." Austin applies pressure to a bleeding scab. "What about the feeling? Can you still remember it?"

"I'll never forget it, but not because I miss it. It haunts me." I put out my cigarette. "All of the pain I endured to shake it—I won't do it again."

"Well, if you do, just know that the dope here sucks compared to the West Coast. I've gotten high everywhere, and you're going to pay a lot of money for a whole lot of junk. So what were you getting in Oregon? Tar? Powder? China White?"

"Mostly Black Tar." I don't like where this conversation is going and want to tread lightly knowing that we both share common ground.

"Was it any good?"

I stand up to leave and realize we're tied at the hip.

"To answer your question, no, it was never any good to me."

Lunch rolls around, and once again we line up. Clients on Shadow get to eat first, and after the lunch worker calls for the next five, we walk to the line server station to grab our plate, tray and utensils. Austin stuffs his bloody paper towel into his pocket, then reaches out for the ice scoop and thrusts his whole hand into the ice bin. I look around to see who's watching and realize everyone in view is looking at us with disgust.

Yvonne approaches us after lunch and I already see what's coming. She is fit, short and in control at all times.

"Guys, I need a second. Okay, Jordan, this is how it's going to work from now on—Austin is not allowed to touch *anything*. No doors, no trays, no plates, no utensils, no face, no nothing. What-ever he needs, you get for him, okay?" She turns to Austin. "And Austin, know that I'm not trying to embarrass you, but I can't have you touching things with blood on your hands. It's a health hazard."

I feel horrible for him and look to catch a glimpse of his response. "Okay, Yvonne," he says. He appears to be one of the few and rare addicts who means no harm. "I'm sorry—I only pick when I'm kicking, and don't realize when I'm doing it most of the t-t-time." Austin bares his teeth. "And same thing with this damn stutter—I never mince my words when I'm high." He rubs his burgundy fingertips with his thumbs and stuffs his hands back into his pockets.

Within seconds of her walking away, his picking resumes. The fidgeting is incessant like a beast is literally scratching beneath the surface. I want to show him empathy, but it's nowhere in me to be found. When we go out to have a cigarette, I pass him my matches, then think twice before taking them back. I can hand him things, but don't want to take them back. I was fortunate enough to miss the bullet with HIV and am terrified of being exposed to blood.

When Austin complains over the soreness of his face, I can't take it anymore.

"Don't you ever get tired of picking yourself apart?! This ritual-istic mutilation you have going on is only making it worse on yourself." I take a drag from my cigarette. "The staff has already decided not to make this go-around any easier for you, so why add to your suffering?"

"The staff?" Austins asks. "What are you saying? What the fuck do you mean?"

I decide against better judgment to tell him about my conversa-tion with Russel, and before I'm even done, he's heard enough.

For once, he stops picking his face.

I scramble after him into the dorm and watch as dumps his pillow onto the floor. He starts packing his belongings into his pillowcase and is beyond restraint.

"You know what?" he mumbles. "Fuck this place! I might not need meds to sleep, but that doesn't mean some s-sick fuck should be going out of his way to get some perverse enjoyment out of my withdrawal."

"Austin. Stop. It's not like that. I take it back—I didn't mean to upset you. And no one wants to see you *suffer*. The medical staff—they just think that if you remember the pain this time around, you will have a better shot at—"

He cuts me off, determined to leave as quickly as he came. Every effort to change his mind moving forward is wasted energy. Watching him pack, I realize the selfishness on my part for setting him off on purpose. *Am I that weak?* I should have asked Ty to replace me, and admitted that I don't have the capacity to be within arm's reach of withdrawal. I should have been there for Austin like Deacon was for me, every step of the way, encouraging and patient.

Someone ran for Ty, who enters the dorm and tries to be the voice of reason, but Austin has already shut down and is on his way out. The door bounces on its hinges and there's only one place I imagine Austin is heading. I realize that my inability to endure just a few short days of unease could cost him everything, and that I haven't made nearly as much progress as I imagined.

I haven't just failed him—I've robbed him of the opportunity to save himself. When Ty asks what happened, I can barely look him in the eye. With shame, I head over to my own locker and begin to pack up my belongings. As I exit the A.C. dorm, I hope that if I ever cross paths with Austin again, he won't remember my face.

30

LIGHTS OUT

I return to the program from my weekend pass with my mind made up. Last night, I could tell that Mom wished Dad hadn't told me that he was surprised I had managed to stay in the program for almost a year. To be honest, I don't think he's the only one who feels that way, but he's the first to admit it to my face. Ultimately, he's half of the reason that I lasted here as long as I have. It was a major turning point when he told me that he would quit coming to visit unless I stopped talking about leaving.

Once I began working at the family business, it really hit home how hard it is to keep my head up with my legal issues still hanging over it. Every day that passes seems like a missed opportunity, as though I would be sticking my neck out to stay here any longer. With one foot in the free world, I'm always waiting for my warrants to run up on me. If I get pulled over as a passenger in a vehicle on the way to a job site, the police could run my record and find out I am a wanted man and take me by force. I'd rather turn myself in now and avoid having to explain why I hadn't.

I sign back into the facility and my finger runs down the list of names of those who've come before me. Many of them are friends by now, and I'm grateful for the time that I've been here and the gift of recovery that was so freely given to me. These past few months have been more than good. Working at the family business for an honest dollar proved my ability to carry my weight in this world. I admit that everyone was right after all—I miss the "vacation" that was intensive treatment. What was the point of rushing to work when I'll be chasing an honest dollar and playing catch-up for the rest of my life?

After checking in and getting my bags searched, I head to my dorm and belly-flop onto my bed. I've worked most of this out in my head during the car ride back from my parent's house. Pulling out my trusted notepad, I intend to do this the right way.

It's been a long time coming.

Mr. Mason,

I am submitting my notice of intention to move out of Sand Island Treatment Center. I plan to move in next door to my family and will continue attending A.A. meetings regularly. I have a strong support group, a good job working with my family and will have saved $3000 by the next pay period. I would be more than grateful to be allowed to return to Sand Island for meetings. I have nothing but good things to say about you and your staff, the program and all that has been done for me here. Thank you for opening your home to me.

Mahalo,

Jordan B.

I stare at the letter for a moment before making the long walk to the main office. When I look up from the path, my reflection in the door catches my eye and I size myself up, surprised at the definition I can see beneath the surface of my shirt. The sun blazes overhead while I wait for a staff member to come and address me. I should be proud of how far I've come. Shading my face with my hand, an intern pokes his head out of the door, just enough to let his question out but not the air-conditioning.

"Jordan . . . what do you need?"

"Is Mike in there?" I look over my shoulder. "I didn't see his truck in the parking lot."

"Mike? No, I haven't seen him all day. I'm sure he's out surfing —the waves are firing. Can I help you?"

I think I need to take this a little higher up the ladder. "What about Ty?"

"Ty? Yeah, he's here. I'll grab him, but what should I tell him this is about?" The intern, no different than the rest of us, doesn't want to be left out of the loop.

I hold up the envelope with my letter inside. "It's time for me to go."

The door clicks shut and I grind my teeth. By now, it's more of a reality than a running joke that this facility is a lot like a gang. That famous saying "you're either with us or against us" has always been embraced as a line in the sand here that addicts don't have the freedom to cross. It's always all or nothing, and I understand why it has to be that way.

A client can't only partially relapse, or only somewhat walk out of the gate. We either do the right thing, or we don't. The moment it looks like someone's out the door is the moment clients and staff distance themselves from them. Anyone who becomes a threat needs to be cut off like cancer—it's too big of a risk to keep associating with an addict who returns to using. There is nothing worse than someone who goes down and takes others with them.

I'm not leaving here to relapse, in fact it's quite the opposite, but they won't believe that. Wanting to leave the program is something nearly everyone considers, but acting on that impulse is a step too far.

The door swings open and out walks Ty with Yvonne in tow.

"Mr. Barnes . . ." Ty begins, but doesn't speak further. He raises an eyebrow, waiting for an explanation.

I clear my throat and let out a quiet, relieving exhale. "Ty, first let me begin by saying how much I appreciate everything this place has done for me." He crosses his arms and drops his chin, keeping his eyes on me. "But as you know, I have outstanding warrants in Oregon that I have to clear up. I've tried everything, but they won't accept anything short of me turning myself in." I pause for a second. "*In person.*"

Yvonne taps her pen against her clipboard.

"I've written this letter to the Director. It's my notice of intent to leave the program and I'm hoping I can do so on good terms. It would be nice to be allowed back for continuing care and meetings. Also, I know this doesn't go without saying, but I am not leaving to get loaded."

I reiterate this to both of them as well as myself.

"You guys have taught me to do the right thing and that's all I'm trying to do. As a walk-in with warrants, I've always felt like I'm just hiding out in limbo. It's time for me to fly back to Oregon and turn myself in."

It was hard, but I've said my piece. I hold out my arm to hand Ty the letter. "Please, can you give this letter to the Director?"

"I'm not taking that. You've come too far and made too much progress here to just throw it all away like this."

"I'm not throw—"

"I'm not done." Ty drops his arms and leans forward on the handrail. "And neither are you." He looks behind me at the other clients who have gathered around, waiting for their turn to have their own needs addressed. "*Hui.*" He commands their attention. "A little privacy, please."

Even though the crowd has disappeared, Ty still drops his voice, talking to the inner me. "Jordan, we have watched you change. And heal. And grow. What you have done, coming from where you came from—it's not easy. Most don't make it this far."

His eyes lock on mine, and he waits for me to look up from the ground and make eye contact.

"Many don't even get this shot—you know that as well as I do."

He's hitting where it hurts and I think of Simon. I often wished he had the opportunity to be accepted into a place like this before it was too late.

"Jordan, you can make it, but I'm telling you, your work's not done. Not yet."

"Don't leave before the miracle happens," Yvonne adds.

My palm grasps the back of my sweaty neck. I feel like the miracle has happened already, because never in a million years would I have expected I would turn myself in. I'm torn inside, uncertain if I am making the right decision.

"Please. This is something that I have to do. I've made up my mind and already bought the ticket to Portland."

"Does your family know?"

I nod.

"You can't tell me that they are okay with it?" he says.

"No, they're not, but I think they understand. Everyone, especially my mom, knows that Sand Island is a safe place. She would probably want me to stay here forever if that was an option, but we both know that's not the point of recovery, right? Besides, these charges won't ever go away." I shake my head. "Ty, I made it through intensive, and now I need to make it through this. It's the only way to clear up the wreckage of my past."

"It's not the only way, but it sounds like your self-will has made your mind up for you. For the record, I think you're making a mistake." Yvonne turns around and heads back into the office.

Ty watches the door close behind her and turns back to me. "I can't tell you how many times we've both had this same conversation before." He wipes his brow. "To build a life rooted in recovery and self-discovery takes time. What can I say to persuade you to stay?"

"Honestly, nothing, because I believe this is the right thing to do." Again, I hold out the letter, shaky and unsure if this is the right step to make.

I'm looking into the eyes of a man who has helped save my life and asked for nothing in return except that I give this my all. Since the beginning, he has been nothing but kind, supportive and encouraging, so it hurts me to turn my back on him.

"If that's the case, then keep the letter, take it back to your bunk and sleep on it. You can find me or Mike tomorrow if nothing changes—we'll both be on duty. In the meantime, do yourself a favor and don't forget to pray. I mean it Jordan. This is too big of a decision for you to be making on your own."

"A man who stands for nothing will fall for anything."

MALCOLM X

31

IRON WINGS

"Care for anything to drink? Beer? Wine? Bloody Mary? Mimosa?"

"Ginger Ale please, and if I could, I'd like the whole can." I watch the stewardess pull out a drawer, her hand blindly locating the drink while her smile falls on the next passenger. She pops open the top and hands me a fresh cup of ice, passing it over the stranger sleeping next to me. I take a sip and let my head rattle against the window.

This is a trip I am making alone.

Upon filtering off the plane, I skip the carousel and head straight for the train. Everything I need is in my carry-on, including my Good Thoughts that my mom wanted me to have. Beyond that, I purposely didn't bring any baggage with me. No longer cheating the system, I purchase my ticket and proudly slip some bills into the fare box.

Rumbling into the city, I hate to admit that I haven't quite thought this plan through. Halloween is right around the corner, but I know this city is already full of monsters. My parents understood this and pleaded with me not to come back here alone, yet they hit a brick wall when I sunk my teeth into my heart of hearts, refusing any help. A damn fool, I had spent so much time convincing myself that I would conquer my demons that I failed to plan how I would surrender myself to the authorities.

My goal is to clear my record and handle my outstanding warrants once and for all. Initially, I thought I would walk up to the first police car I saw and stick my wrists through the window to be cuffed, but now, I'm second guessing that plan. My instincts tell me I'm better off handling these matters from inside a courtroom, not a jail cell.

I decide to go straight to the top and look for a pay phone to call the district attorney's office.

The gatekeeper on the other end of the phone filters my call. "Can I help you, sir?" she asks matter-of-factly.

I calmly explain my situation and that I flew up from a treatment center in Hawai'i to turn myself in, preferably to the courts.

"And what are your charges?"

As I explain, she cuts me off and stops me dead in my tracks.

"Sir, as we are discussing an alleged felony, I will advise you to seek counsel, if you have not done so already. You probably should not represent yourself in this matter. Do you know where the public defender's office is located?"

"No, I don't," I respond instinctively. I would never return to court to fight any case of mine and never needed a defense. I had hoped this whole process would be easier and shake my head as if the woman on the other end could see me. As she fires off the address to the public defender's office, I scrounge for a pen, a piece of paper and some change to make one more call as soon as we hang up.

The phone rings three times before I hear a familiar, "Hello?"

"Hey, it's me. Look, you were right. Things aren't starting off the way I expected them to, and the district attorney won't meet with me. I wanted to give you a heads up—I'm worried this could drag on. I'm wondering if you would be willing to come up here if it turns out that I need your help?"

"Yes, of course. My bags were packed before you even took off. Just say the word."

"Wow, you're a lifesaver. Thanks, Mom. I love you."

"Bradley?" The judge pauses for a second, awaiting a response. He looks up from his bench. "Paul Bradley?"

"I don't have any information about this," the district attorney says. He turns to the clerk beside him as the judge addresses them both.

"Mr. Bradley—what should we do with him? For acceptance and petitioning, he is supposed to be here for his arraignment. He's not here?" The judge's eyes dart up from his paperwork for a final call. "Bradley?" His pen casually scribbles away. "Bench warrant."

I sit back and wait my turn, watching as a few more cases get cleaned up and processed before the court. The deputy district attorney and court clerk shuffle through some papers and talk back and forth like gossiping in-laws. After the protocol is neatly processed and completed, I think they are finally reaching my case.

"Uh . . . so . . . shall I get started on this one?" The clerk holds up some paperwork, asking the judge for approval.

The district attorney nods in agreement and gives a heads up to the judge. "It's complicated," he whispers.

The court clerk proceeds. "I will be calling on Jordan Barnes, who is treated out of . . . *Hawai'i?*" Her lips curl up in a light-hearted smile.

I push off from the bench and flatten my shirt against my stomach with both hands. Making my way to the podium, I stand next to Ms. Whitaker, a supervisor from the public defender's office.

"Your Honor, perhaps we can have a sidebar on this?" she asks on my behalf.

Yesterday, I had arrived in court unannounced and waited patiently until every last defendant exited the courtroom. All eyes turned to me as the judge asked if I needed help. In a similar response to the district attorney's receptionist, he heard me out just enough to cut me off and refer me to the public defender's office. Following his advice, I sat across from Ms. Whitaker in her office, trying to decipher my options that led me back to here today.

"Sure, we can have a sidebar, but . . . I don't believe I have this. Is this an off-docket matter?" The judge's voice trails off.

"No, he's page two, line one, your Honor." The district attorney jumps in to help out as the judge flips through his paperwork, pulling his chin back to his Adam's apple.

"Why don't I have that?" the judge asks. He raises his palm to the court clerk. "Oh wait, now I see him."

"It's kind of an unusual situation, your Honor. If you recall, he came in yesterday at the end of the docket. The court looked at his warrant. He's been in extensive inpatient treatment in another jurisdiction—"

"Yes, I remember Mr. Barnes, I just couldn't connect the dots on paper. Uh, counsel, back here, please." The judge waves his hand toward his robe. "And Mr. Barnes, you may want to sit in on this as well?" He gives me a quick nod and doesn't need to ask me twice.

As the judge, district attorney and my public defender huddle quietly off the record, I listen intently to capture any glimpse of my fate. Any hopes I had of seeing these matters handled in a timely fashion dissolve as the judge states how he won't simply take my word that I've been in treatment. I don't see any sign of dismissal on the horizon.

The district attorney and Ms. Whitaker seem to discuss option after option until they finally break and resume back on the record.

"Okay," the judge concludes, "in order to proceed, I think it makes sense to meet back here tomorrow, along with any supporting documentation Mr. Barnes can obtain to back his claims."

I bite my upper lip and switch gears from expecting all charges would be dropped to feeling thankful I'm not being remanded into custody.

"I think we're off to a good start." Ms. Whitaker turns around in the hallway. "We can make this work, but I need you at my office tomorrow morning at 9:00 a.m. for S.T.O.P. Court Orientation. It's critic—"

"I've heard of S.T.O.P. Court," I say, "but I don't know much about it?"

"Sanctions. Treatment. Opportunities." She racks her brain and snaps her fingers. "And Progress. It's a successful and progressive division of the court aimed to reduce drug abuse and recidivism through treatment. Graduates can have their charges expunged and avoid felonies if they survive the probationary period, usually about a year. But you need to go through it before we can proceed any further."

"A year?! But I just did a whole ye—"

She levels her hand flat by her waist cutting me off. "We'll talk about it tomorrow, as one possible option. Now before you leave, make sure to check in with my assistant Sharron and follow her directions to a T. Do not be late tomorrow or I can't help you."

I watch as she scribbles down her office fax number, followed by a short list.

"I also need you to get in contact with your treatment center the second you leave here and have them fax me a letter with all of this information drafted on their letterhead. Do whatever it takes to get that letter on my fax machine by tomorrow morning." Our eyes connect to ensure I know what I need to do. "Help me help you."

Ms. Whitaker returns to her desk with the letter hot off the fax and reads it aloud:

Mr. Jordan Barnes was a participant in the Substance Abuse Rehabilitation Program offered by the Kline-Welsh Behavioral Health Foundation at its Sand Island Treatment Center. He successfully completed the counseling intensive unit level of treatment and secured full-time employment after transitioning to independent community living. Please feel free to call me with any questions.

-Yvonne, C.S.A.C., C.C.S., C.S.A.P.A.

Director of Operations

She sets the letter down on her desk. "This is perfect. I'm impressed."

"So, is that all we need?" I ask.

"Well, it's all the judge requested. But now I need to ask you, what do you need? What are you hoping to take away from all this?" She stares at the letter in front of her, trying to make sense of it. "I mean, why even come back here? I doubt they would have extradited you."

"This is just something I have to do. I need to do the right thing for the right reason. I have always intended to plead guilty because I am." I crack a knuckle against my palm. "I need to close this chapter in order to move on with my life."

"See, *that's* the part that confuses me," she says, leaning forward. "You pleading guilty to these felonies all but ensures that you will *never* move on from this chapter. You seem like a bright young man. Don't you understand that drug convictions will haunt you forever?"

I look at Ms. Whitaker and know she's right. I've considered the ramifications of having a felonious record long and hard. "Ms. Whita—"

"Please, we're not in court. Call me Lisa."

"Sorry, Lisa, but look—I have to do the right thing, regardless of the consequences. If I could enter S.T.O.P. Court, I would, but not if it means moving back to Portland for a year to see it through. We both know that wouldn't work, so my hands are tied, right?"

I sit up a little straighter and clear my lungs.

"Sand Island taught me to do the right thing. I can't fight the charges or lie in court."

I think back to Gordon from Sand Island, a program graduate with decades of sobriety under his belt. Even with his years of recovery, he still returns to the program week after week. He's one of the few who completed the program, then served his sentence. I can hear him yelling at the class how he stood in front of a federal judge many years ago and pled guilty to thirty years for trafficking and conspiracy because Sand Island taught him to do the right thing. Every legal mind in his corner advised him against it, but he was listening to a Higher Power.

"Jordan, let's be clear—I would never ask you to lie. But I think that there may be a way you can do the right thing and walk out of here with your head high. Judge Lopez is a reasonable man who wants to see every defendant succeed. I think you can plead guilty, do the right thing, get into S.T.O.P. Court *and* work it out so you can complete the program back in Hawai'i. It would be a massive exception, but let's not rule it out. Out-of-state cases are always handled on a case-to-case basis. My vote is to test the waters. Trust me, you've come so far—if it can be avoided, you don't want a felony on your record."

I have to admit, I like the sound of that. If I can make it out unscathed, I might as well try.

"You have a few hours to think about it before our court appearance later today," Lisa says without pressure.

As the elevator drops five floors, my heart sinks with it. Something doesn't sit right, as though doing the "right thing" and the "smart thing" might not always be the same. I've come so far, I am afraid of throwing it all away, but remember how Sand Island has ingrained in me that throughout recovery, we often have to do the things we don't want to. I guess if it were easy, then everyone would do it, and society wouldn't have such a widespread mess of addiction on their hands.

. . .

"Mr. Barnes, welcome back," the judge says. He looks at me before turning his attention to Lisa. "Ms. Whitaker?"

"Yes, your Honor. Mr. Barnes has been at my office, completed S.T.O.P. Court Orientation this morning, and I have been able to contact Sand Island Treatment Center in Hawai'i, where he did a significant stint. They faxed me some documentation like his intake and that sort of stuff for confirmation, so we were able to follow up on that."

"Okay, great," Judge Lopez says.

Lisa continues. "We were also discussing whether or not he wants to proceed and resolve this matter today, however after talking that decision over with his family, the preference is to not have a felony on his record."

"So he is interested in entering S.T.O.P. Court?" The judge glances at me and I smile with my eyes.

"Correct, your Honor. However, as an out of state client, we would like to advise the court that due to his length of sobriety along with his family, support group and home group treatment center being back home in Hawai'i, we would ask for the accommodations to ensure his continued success."

I can't get a read on the judge or which way he is leaning at this point. He thinks for a second before addressing me.

"Mr. Barnes, I appreciate and respect the fact you are standing before me today clean and sober. What you've overcome is amazing and you should be proud of yourself. You sound like you are living a healthy and happy life as a functional and contributing member of society. That is one of our main goals through this court, so I applaud you for that."

A light smile crosses my face.

"However," the judge says, "I cannot emphasize that last sentence enough: that is one of the main goals *'through this court.'* What you did, while noble, was take matters into your own hands outside of the jurisdiction and good sense of the courts. Do you see why we may have a problem here? So, Mr. Barnes, I ask you: what do you think would happen if every single person did that?"

I look to Lisa, who must see me out of the corner of her eye, yet makes no adjustment to acknowledge me.

"Well, let me tell you. There would be no criminal justice system. The world would be chaos."

I nod in agreement. The judge is right. I want him to know I agree with him and hear him loud and clear.

"Okay. Here is what we are going to do. Mr. Barnes, we will set you up with a staffing to see if we can coordinate this thing for you with the program in Hawai'i and myself. We will meet back here in one week. See you then."

I turn to Lisa as we walk away from the podium. "A week?!"

She makes me wait until we're out of earshot of the judge. "I know it may not seem like it, but he just did you a huge favor—normally, it's a three-week delay."

"So what do we do until then?" I look through her glasses and into a soft gaze that tells me this is where we part.

"We process you through my office." She holds the courtroom door open for me to leave. "Jordan, I'm just filling in this week for Eric. He's your actual public defender and will take over your case from here, but don't worry, he's been around much longer than me. You're in great hands. All you need to do is sit down for a police report review. He'll advise you of your legal rights along with those you will be waiving. Then, he will help you submit your guilty plea and you should be home free."

Home free. I remember the letter from Mrs. Rumbough.

Run. Home. Jack.

"You going to be okay?"

I don't answer her question.

Lisa leans in closer. "Jordan, are you going to be okay? Where are you going to go for a week?"

I think for a second until an answer comes to mind. "I don't know. Probably to the airport?"

"You're not running away are you?" she asks.

"No, not at all. I'm never running away again."

. . .

The train ride to the airport takes longer than I remembered. Perhaps this is because I'm not missing out on life passing me by today as I used to when I was dumbed-down on opiates. Back then, everything moved slower under the influence, and that's only counting what I'm able to recall.

I decide to camp out near the baggage claim and wait for my mother's arrival tomorrow. Every now and then, I move seats and swap clothes in the bathroom to change my appearance so security leaves me be. Even though I'm confident a week alone in Portland won't drag me down, I don't see a need to take the risk by floating around Downtown. My addiction takes no prisoners, and I have nothing left to prove other than showing old acquaintances in passing I'm doing well.

Finally able to relax, I wrap my backpack straps around my legs, kick my feet up and drift away.

There she is. I see her coming and jump up for a hug. The coat she wears is long and thick. Large brass buttons adorn the front.

"Don't you look a little rich, huh?"

"You like it? It's Ralph Lauren." She leans in close and does a half-twirl. "Bought it from Ross, half-off!"

I chuckle aloud and pinch her sleeve. "Why was this even there? Nobody in Hawai'i needs a wool winter coat?"

"Maybe for Mauna Kea? You know it snows on the volcano sometimes?"

"Yeah, but nothing like Mount Hood. Anyway, thanks so much for coming. So, did you have any luck getting through to them?"

A closed-lipped smile crosses her face, emphasizing her button cheeks. "No, I'm sorry. I don't think the district attorney wants to take my calls or meet with me because of how much we've talked about you in the past. I left him a message, but I'm not expecting a callback. You know that in my efforts to keep tabs on you, I often called him to see if you had been arrested recently?"

It's a depressing thought, knowing my arrests were the only indicator she had that I was still alive. "Yeah, you've told me."

"But what I haven't told you is that in a rare parent-to-parent moment, I once asked him what we should do if we ever found you?" She flashes a sad smile. "Off the record, he told me that if you were his son, he would get you the hell out of the city. He said that with their overcrowded system, addicts can always come back and face the music, but they can never come back if they're no longer with us."

"That's so true," I say. I know what she means. "Well, I've got an appointment with my real public defender today. Want to come with me?"

"Jordan, do you think I flew all this way to sight-see?"

The public defender's office is packed wall to wall with new cases. After signing in, I wait to be called in and have a seat next to my mom until we're both invited to the back.

I take a seat in the small office across from Eric. He's middle-aged and frazzled, with wispy white hair that he continuously combs back with his fingers.

"Okay, um . . . from what I can tell, I don't see any holes in your case." Eric skims over my police report once more. "So it's basically your word against the police report, assuming I can convince you to fight it. The good news it it's an old case—the officer may not even remember it." He reads a few lines from the police report and places it on his desk in front of me.

Years later and the report still makes my blood boil. Looking back, I knew that my property had been illegally searched, but I was surprised to hear Eric read out the fabrication that the officer penned. No respectable junkie would ever leave their needles sticking out of their kit in plain view to prompt reasonable suspicion, as the officer indicated. Still, I don't want this process to drag out. I'm in a dangerous city, and though I am confident in my convictions, I feel as though remaining in Portland is akin to playing with fire.

"Eric, regardless if I could win or not, I won't fight the case."

"Yeah you say that, but again, we're not talking misdemeanors here—you *need* to understand that." He taps his desk with each word and sighs as if he doesn't get paid enough to argue with me. "Look, felonies today are not handled as lightly in the courts as they used to be. The city isn't as lenient on heroin and cocaine charges as I think you're expecting." He studies me for a second longer, looking deep in thought. "I know that in a perfect world, you'd want to get into S.T.O.P. Court and make arrangements to go home, but to do so requires pleading guilty. The problem with that is if you relapse, the hammer drops and you're stuck with that conviction *forever*."

His words don't hit home like he expects. "Eric, I'm not worried about that."

"*'Not worried?'* Do you know how many of my clients have said the same thing and later regretted it?"

"Doesn't matter. I'm not going to relapse."

"Right, but the problem is that nobody plans to relap—"

"I'm *not* going to relapse."

He lets out a deep breath. "How can you be so sure?"

"Because relapse is not an option."

He runs his fingers through his white beard. "Okay. If that's what you want, let me see what I can arrange."

32

ALL RISE

"Is she another lawyer of yours?" the judge asks. It's immediately apparent that nothing slips past him.

"No, sir . . . I mean, your Honor." I can't help but smile. "She's my mother." I look back to her standing by the door. "She flew up here from back home to sit through the proceedings with me. She's also a huge part of my support group."

"Well, she's welcome to sit in if you wish."

"Thank you, I appreciate that," I say. I reach behind my chair and give her a thumbs up to call her off the sidelines. My team could make use of the extra player.

The judge's private chambers gets cramped quick once myself, my mother, my public defender and the district attorney all cram in. The judge has already gone above and beyond what I could have ever asked for by being willing to meet with us in private, and as much as Sand Island has ingrained in me that I am not unique, the courts concern over setting any precedence makes sense. We are all seated at his desk across from Judge Lopez, except for the district attorney who kicked back his chair to sit on the outskirts. He powers on his laptop, uses his crossed leg as a makeshift desk and casually types away behind me.

The judge begins. "As you are all well aware, we are here today to determine what to do with Mr. Barnes. As I previously stated, I cannot reward any behavior that has evaded warrants and circumvented the law. That said, Mr. Barnes, I understand why you may have felt the need to do so and feel you deserve the opportunity to explain yourself outside of court. I'd also like to know what you think the penalty of the court should be in your case?"

I can't believe he is asking me to judge my case. Mom shoots me a glance as if she's trying to transmit the right answer to me. I initially wished for the judge to dismiss all charges, but I know that for the life of me, it's not the right decision to ask for.

"Your Honor, I returned to Portland to clean up the wreckage of my past. I came here to do the right thing." A distracting keyboard clicks away behind me. "When I checked myself into treatment, I had no idea whether it was even possible to get sober —all I cared about was running from my problems."

I slow down my speech to choose my words wisely. Judge Lopez has given me the floor and allows me to continue. "I want to tell you that Sand Island Treatment Center is Hawaii's oldest rehab facility. It's the treatment center that an addict goes to when no other program wants them back. At times it felt like a jail, but I think that's exactly what I needed." I feel my public defender urging me to get on with it. "I learned to deal with my problems there in a healthy way, but it wasn't easy, and it took time. Now I need to deal with these charges. So, to answer your question, I would want my record expunged and am willing to work for it."

"Okay, so now that you've told me what you want, I'd like to know what you are willing to do?" Judge Lopez leans in. "And if you were me, what would you tell yourself to do?"

I don't skip a beat. "I would sentence me back to a year of outpatient at Sand Island, and allow me to move on with my life once I complete the program." I think back to Deborah. "I'll do whatever it takes."

Judge Lopez leans back. Even I didn't see my response coming. "And what's you're sober date again?"

"August 29th, 2011."

"And if I asked you to take a drug test today?"

"You got it."

I watch him think for a second and realize he's weighing my chances of success if I become one of the few exceptions. I know it in my bones—he cares deeply about those he so orders.

"Okay, here's what we will do—I'm inclined to allow you to enter S.T.O.P. Court and finish up your therapy at Sand Island. When we all head into court—" he checks his watch, "—in fifteen minutes, I will accept your guilty plea and sentence you to S.T.O.P. supervision. Your guilty plea will be my collateral that you will honor the wishes of the court and your supervised probationary terms. Then, once you obtain your clinical discharge from Sand Island, all findings of guilt will be cleared, and I will personally expunge all derogatory information from your record. Are all parties in agreement?"

I let out a quiet breath while the district attorney still types away.

"Thank you, your honor."

"And Ma'am," Judge Lopez turns toward my mom, "if you don't mind, could you please write down your name and address for me?" He slides a piece of paper across his desk. "In case things go south and I need to reach out to him."

"Oh, absolutely, your Honor," she says.

"Thank you. And with that, I'll see the rest of you in court in a bit." We all push back to leave, though the district attorney takes his time winding up his charging cable. The judge picks up the paper. "Oh, and *Jeri*, if you don't mind, might I have a quick word with you in private?"

After a real cigarette and the taste of freedom, I walk back into Adult Drug Court feeling like an oddity. The room looks like every other courtroom I remember, except the defendants remind me of a high school experiment where the students hope to control the agenda. The court room itself is orderly and clean, yet every defendant in the room is at some stage of addiction. A clean-cut father looking to override a lousy night's decision is seated next to a strung-out homeless street kid nodding out with his mouth open.

The judge walks in and everyone rises. The placard on his bench reads "Hon. Lopez." He has a kind face stacked behind square glasses beneath a full head of graying hair parted neatly to the side. As he talks, half of the room listens up while the rest are in their own world.

"This morning, as I was walking into the courthouse, I noticed how many wet leaves were on the sidewalk, slapped and spineless against the curb." He takes off his glasses and cleans them with his robe. "I'm used to seeing a healthy mix of color, but today, I noticed there were way too many brown leaves." His eyes scan the room as his face softens. "Most of you stepped right over them on your way in here, but I knew something was wrong. Once in my chambers, as I slipped on my robe for court, I called to my clerk." He pauses again. "I was advised that one of my cases had relapsed and overdosed. He will not be with us today, or ever again."

Mom places her hand on my knee.

The judge is friendly yet stern. I watch as he remands his first case of the day into custody after learning his orders to report to an employment agency weren't satisfied. The very next participant, oddly enough, is rewarded for passing her third drug test in a row. She is handed a gift card, which is a totally different approach from that of Sand Island Treatment Center.

Where I am coming from, no one gets rewarded for doing the right thing, and the duration of sobriety is rarely celebrated. It all feels surreal to witness, but the act shows its benefits. The same defendant is also being inducted into S.T.O.P. Court for the first time. After a haphazard round of applause that trails off, the judge hands her a coin and reads off the inscription for her. "The coin says 'change attitude, change thinking, change behavior, and you'll change yourself for the better.'"

One by one, addicts learn their fate and disperse until the room almost clears out.

"So now we have that out of state matter that is Mr. Jordan Barnes," the judge says.

My lawyer goes over the paperwork with me and asks me to sign off on my guilty plea. "This is the one where you tell the judge that he can hold this felony over your head, and when you graduate, your case gets dismissed, forever and without prejudice." My lawyer, Mr. Lee, winks at me and looks up to the court. "Your Honor, Mr. Barnes and I have prepared and gone over a petition to enter S.T.O.P., and also a petition to forward a plea of guilty to the court."

"Okay," Judge Lopez says, "and just so we're clear on everything, I will allow you to treat in Hawai'i, as pursuant to where you live, and pursuant to those terms, you wish to enter S.T.O.P. court, correct?"

"Yes, your Honor."

"Thank you, sir. I allow the petition, and understand that you also want to plead guilty today? Same thing, I'm not going to accept the plea, but we have to have your plea on the record. Is that also correct?"

"Yes, your Honor."

"Thank you, sir. Okay, so Jordan Prescott Barnes is your name. You're twenty-seven years old, you've gone to school up to and including . . . six years of college. Today, you are not under the influence of any drugs or intoxicants, and you are of sound mental and physical health, right?"

"Correct, your Honor."

"Thank you. And I see that Mr. Lee is your attorney, who should have explained to you that when you plead guilty as you do, you give up all of your trial rights, which are: the right to afford a jury trial, the right to have the assistance of counsel, the right to sit here and cross-examine those witnesses who testify against you, the right to testify, the right to remain silent and have the jury told if you decide not to testify they could not use your silence against you as an indication of guilt. You also give up the right to call up any evidence or witnesses who might be in your favor, along with the right to be proved guilty beyond a reasonable doubt. Do you understand the trial rights that you are giving up today, sir?"

"I do, your Honor."

"And you're not on probation or parole right now?"

"No, your Honor."

"Okay, let's see—and you are a U.S. citizen, correct?"

"Correct, your Honor."

"And today you are pleading guilty to unlawful possession of Heroin, a Class B Felony, which means that you can get up to ten years in prison and a maximum fine of $250,000, or both. Now, I saw you sign the document, but for the record, I need you to verify that this is indeed your signature?" He holds up my Sentencing Order.

"Yes, your Honor. That is my signature."

"Thank you, and when you signed that, you did so under your own free will?"

"I did, your Honor."

"Perfect. So you are pleading guilty today because in Mult-nomah County on the 25th of June 2011, you unlawfully and knowingly possessed Heroin. Is that true?"

"Yes, your Honor."

"Okay, so to the charge of Unlawful Possession of Heroin, you plead guilty today?"

"Yes, your Honor."

"Alright. Plea accepted. Welcome to S.T.O.P. Court, and of course, here is your coin." Judge Lopez reaches over his bench to hand me the coin. "Again, change attitude, change thinking, change behavior, and you'll change yourself for the better. Good luck to you sir and I wish you all the best. Oh, and for the record, I am going to need to receive a status update on the 14th of November."

What a weight off of my shoulders. As the clerk and district attorney take notes on their paperwork, my lawyer leans over his shoulder to address me.

"Well, I guess all the hard work was already done, so it's smooth sailing from here." He looks down on me as if the battle is over, and I realize how alien addiction may seem to the unaffected, even those knee-deep in their journey. I know I have a lifetime of work cut out for me, but for now, the court clerk Sharron brings it down to earth.

She hands me a paper with the simple instructions scrawled across it. It reads:

> Prior to the court date above, you must do the following: for a status update, make sure your treatment provider faxes the judge a treatment report a day or two before your court date. Failure to complete these tasks may result in sanctions. As long as you are compliant (i.e., doing perfectly) you will be able to remain in Hawai'i. You have a lot at stake (you don't want a felony on your record) so rock this. I know you will. Any questions, call me!

She signs her name and phone number with neat handwriting that tells me she still cares about her job.

I know I can do this. I look at the paper and realize this is my real ticket home. Free to go, I thank the court for their time and willingness to work with me. Mom is on her feet, clasping her hands to her chest, ready to bring her baby boy home.

"Oh, and Mr. Barnes, if we never see each other again, that will be a good thing." The judge smiles at me, squares up his stack of papers with his palms and calls on the next case.

I walk out of the courtroom with my mother, take a few steps and stop as she reaches in for a bear hug. This time it doesn't hurt.

"You are one lucky man," she says. "I hope you know that. Every step of the way, angels have looked out for you."

If she's crying, it's tears of happiness.

"Well, let's hope I'm still in their grace, because as of right now, the real work starts." I pause for a moment. "Mom, can you tell me what Judge Lopez said to you in his chambers?"

"You know, I'll only tell you because he told me I could share this if you asked. He told me that first and foremost, he is hoping that everything will go well, but it's ultimately up to you. He also wanted to share that he thought I seemed to be a very nice woman and reminded him of someone he knows, someone very special." She pauses. "In fact, I think that's why he asked me to write out my name before I left, to see how I spell it. He told me his mother-in-law is also named Jeri and we both spell it the same way." I admire her faith, too strong to believe in coincidences.

"Wow. Small world huh?"

She smiles back at me. "No, it's not. A small island maybe, but it's a vast and wonderful world where you couldn't make this stuff up. One day, I pray that you'll get it and thank God for watching over you." She pauses for a second. "Honesty, He's probably just as thankful to receive a break."

"You've always said that Mom, but people do change, and always in their own time." No one else in the corridor is smiling like I am. "I'm living proof. I mean, just look at me!" I take a step back to put things in perspective. "I've come a long way and will be the first to admit that I didn't do this alone. I'll never forget that I wouldn't be here today if it weren't for you and Dad, Sand Island, along with the help of so many others. And you may think I'm forgetting someone, but I know that He has been right here with me all along."

Beyond God, there's one more thing that has carried me through both the good times and the bad. I step forward, turn over her hand and carefully curl her fingers around my Good Thoughts.

"I want to say thank you for never giving up on me and for keeping these safe. They served their purpose when I needed them most, but we both know they have always belonged with you."

She opens her mouth to speak, but I cut her off and pat her hand.

"Mom, there's no reason not to take them." A wide smile

crosses my face and I gently place my hand on her back. "Today, there's a lot more where that came from." I take a step forward and lead the way with an endless smile. "Now, if you don't mind, can we please go home before these people change their mind? I think we both know I've got a lot of work to do."

PAU

AFTERWORD: A CLEAN SLATE

"Aloha! My name is Jordan. I'm a grateful recovering alcoholic and addict, and Sand Island is my home group."

It sort of has a ring to it, huh?

I suppose I don't say that as often as I used to back in intensive treatment, but the words still hold weight and take me where I need to go. Today, I do not drink or get high, and haven't since August 29th, 2011. (Okay, *technically*, my last hit was about a week before that when I returned to Hooper detox for the final time, but because I was highly medicated, I don't personally count that as clean time.)

Either way, it all comes out in the wash, but what matters most is that I have been clean for longer than I ever thought possible, and with the odds stacked against me. It is also worth noting that beyond detox, I have never been on any prescribed long-term regimen for opioid treatment, such as Suboxone or Methadone maintenance. This was a personal choice and it's important to note that recovery is full of them. And while it's not my place to say that what worked for me will work for anyone else, I do feel it's important to express that I was able to get clean without such maintenance treatments. I make this a point because I'll never forget thinking at one point that it was impossible to kick the habit unassisted.

After I plead guilty in S.T.O.P Court and was handed my sentence, I immediately reached out to Sand Island and humbly asked if they would have me back. This time though, with official court orders in hand, I had the law on my side along with a hammer waiting to fall.

I held my breath, but upon reviewing my mandates with Yvonne, she made a highly unusual accommodation and arranged a one-off outpatient schedule for me, but *only* because I was legally sanctioned to treatment by a judge. So with nearly a year of inpatient treatment already in the books, I moved into the Tentalow on my parents property and began the arduous journey of completing my second year of recovery as an outpatient client back at Sand Island. In addition to working full-time with my family business, I attended no less than two classes a week, submitted to random drug testing when asked and sat down for monthly one-on-one counseling sessions with Mike. All along, reports were being fed back to S.T.O.P. Court, updating them of my progress.

I knew it then and I know it now—I couldn't have asked for a better opportunity to be held accountable while transitioning to normal life. In retrospect, my second year of recovery as an outpatient client also reaffirmed that I was still just a pup, nowhere even close to out of the woods yet. That said, it's not lost on me that few are afforded similar direction and guidance while trying to recover from a seemingly hopeless condition, which makes me appreciate my vast support system more than ever.

I learned that the only way I would grow into my skin was with time and hard work as I carefully ventured into the real world and began to fend for myself. My confidence grew and my parents—supportive as ever—helped me out even further by loaning me an old truck that afforded me the freedom to travel around the island and branch out on my own. By the end of this year, I saw enough progress in the mirror that I became a firm believer that if you do the right thing, you get the right results.

In addition to satisfying the S.T.O.P. Court sentence, one of the proudest achievements of my life was receiving my clinical discharge from Sand Island, even though I should have known it would be immaterial. I don't know why I expected to receive a plaque, diploma or a shiny certificate after two years of being told that no one should be rewarded for *finally* doing the right thing.

The real prize though came shortly after graduating, when Judge Lopez honored his word, worked his magic with my guilty plea and expunged my felonies in the interest of justice. In effect, he handed me a clean slate that kick-started a whole new beginning for me. Faced with a second chance and then some, I held my future in my hands and for once in my life, I had the control to decide what to do with it, along with the appreciation to see its value.

With no outstanding warrants or felonies lurking in the background, I spent the next few years after leaving the program just *itching* to be pulled over by the police, if only to greet a cop as a free man with a smile. In time, I eventually gave up, and to this day, I have yet to have a run-in with the law, except on one or two occasions when I was victimized myself, or when I took initiative to report a crime as any law-abiding citizen would.

I have also never confirmed why the police were hunting me, though a part of me believes that they were hands that were guiding me in the right direction. To be honest, I have even questioned if police ever really were looking for me, or if it was all a setup by my friends who knew there was nothing left for me in Portland. I wouldn't put it past them, but unfortunately, I'll never know the answer since I don't know where any of them are since I've moved on with my life.

And so it goes.

Moving forward, I've been able to create the same future for myself that I had learned to dream of in early recovery and used my earliest motivation to regain control of my life, starting foremost with my health. The first immediate threat I needed to address was my diagnosis with Hepatitis C, which I thankfully cured following six months of antiviral treatment from Queens Liver Center here in Honolulu.

After signing a sobriety contract with the clinic and promising to abstain from drugs *indefinitely*, they prescribed me a take-home regimen that included pumping horrid injections into my stomach along with a complicated schedule of medications. But by far, the most painful struggle of the whole ordeal was taking blood tests to track the reduction of my viral load. I often maxed out the laboratories "two-spike" limit per phlebotomist as every technician in the building took a stab trying to spike a vein. It was an unholy reminder that some scars will never heal and some things will never go back to normal. So even though I am now technically cured, I will forever harbor traces of the Hepatitis C antibodies in my system and therefore can never be a blood donor . . . not to mention the fact that it's nearly impossible to draw blood from me.

And that's okay, because beyond that, my life is amazing today, especially since I remember where I came from. I have my family back in my life and I still work at the family business, where we have hired many employees from the same program that saved my life. In business, working with other addicts can either work for or against you, but the ones that "make it" make it all worth it. I have witnessed the promises of the program play out in more lives than I could have hoped for, and it's a beautiful thing.

I was also lucky enough to meet and marry the most beautiful woman in the world. Chelsea and I met a few years after I got clean, long after I started down the road of learning how to love myself. And while I have always made it a point to be open with her, she has learned so much about me through the process of writing this book that we are closer than ever. We even bought a home in the city I grew up in, which is a feat unto itself in the ridiculous Hawai'i housing market.

Sweetie, I love you, and I will always be here for you.

Dreams do come true and I'm not willing to throw them all away today. Not for a hit and not for a drink. Day in and out, I quietly protect my recovery and have to remind myself that, fortunately, I am not normal. For me, relapse is not an option, never has been and never can be.

My dad used to always say that life is too short to make all the mistakes yourself, so I've watched as other addicts trip, stumble and fall, and learned from their failures. It's safe to say that all too often the ones that go down are the ones that everyone assumes will make it, and the stakes are higher than ever.

I've been clean long enough to lose too many friends to the disease, including my older brother Jonathan who I found dead in his kitchen. A few weeks earlier, I had given him the original first draft of this book, but sadly, he didn't get the chance to finish it. The painful irony is that while I was pouring my heart and soul into this book in the hopes of helping others, my own blood was drowning in alcohol. I couldn't save him and the pain is still sinking in.

In retrospect, I now realize that because my addiction had side-lined our relationship for too long, I was willing to make an exception to the rule that I had no business hanging out with any alcoholic or addict that is active in their addiction. I instilled healthy boundaries so that we would never cross paths when he was drinking, but these rules were often tested and murky. This worked as well as it could, though he would never allow us to broach any discussion of his alcoholism. To his defense, I would never let him forget that we were no different because of our demons, only at different points in our journey. The truth is, I eventually gave up trying, and continued to hang out with him— along with the elephant in the room—until all that remained was the elephant.

I will forever carry the pain of his loss with me, but I refuse to let it break me—he would never want that for me. And as much as I hate being the one who found him, I believe Mike was right when he told me that discovering him was my Kuleana, *my respon-sibility*, because I was strong enough to do so and loved him unconditionally. I continue to work through this experience responsibly and am grateful for my support network, though as expected, it has not been easy.

I've suffered more than my fair share of tragedy in recovery, but the difference today is that I look for the lesson being taught instead of an excuse to get loaded. After my brother passed, a handful of family and friends made it a point to keep checking on me, vocally worried that I would fall away from them. I had to be honest—the loss of my brother is an open wound and brush with mortality that only strengthens my resolve, reaffirming the truth that I am on the right path because "There but for the grace of God, go I."

Relapse is not an option.

That affirmation has served me well over the years, and allowed me to carve out a life in recovery that is beyond my wildest imaginations. I've also witnessed the opposite ring true for too many of my peers who either returned to using and then subsequently to the program, prison or worse. Many of their deaths were pitiful in nature, surrounded by unanswered questions and families wishing they could have done more. I pray for those former peers of mine who withered away and left this world before the miracle happened, yet in the same breath can't afford to dwell in misery. Instead, I choose to celebrate the outliers, the opposite side of the spectrum.

Both Cavin and Eli were groomsmen at my wedding, standing by my side to celebrate the happiest day of my life with myself and my beautiful bride. Cavin is now off building canoes somewhere on the Big Island and paddling daily. Eli, now married, remained here on O'ahu and decided not to return to Maui. I haven't seen or heard from Austin since treatment.

After completing his Drug Court sentence and stint at Sand Island, Deacon got the hell out of Dodge and moved up to Montana. Before he left though, he made it a point to get a coverup tattoo on his elbow, proving that change is always within reach. He is now a foreman with a custom home builder and is madly in love with the woman of his dreams. Someday, they hope to return to Paradise, and he will always have a friend here.

Jared and I reconnected through social media years later after he was released from prison after serving time for filling fraudulent prescriptions. He paroled in 2015 and would later come out as gay, partially attributing so many years of drug abuse to a lifetime of suppressing his sexuality. He is now an agency operator of two rental car lots in the Pacific Northwest and though clean from opiates and Benzodiazepines, uses cannabis products recreationally as well as for medicinal reasons. He also drinks occasionally, and while not officially in recovery, is in a much better spot than when we first met.

Lucy, now married, has started a beautiful family and is raising her children in the Pacific Northwest.

Samajean is still an addiction and substance abuse counselor at Hooper Detox. She works alongside many of the same staff who saw me through my stay.

To this day, I've yet to meet a better acupuncturist than Eiji, though I haven't found a need to look any further after meeting him. Though a selfish part of me wants to keep him a secret, I find joy in sending referrals his way and later hearing how he continues to work wonders. He can be found at his clinic, Acupuncture Hawai'i Kai.

Haven continues to run the syringe exchange program at Outside In as she has for the last thirteen years, providing help and hope for those who need it most. She has successfully launched several programs, including the same Naloxone distribution program that allowed me to save Lucy's life and avoid a homicide charge. Haven championed the rapid drug-testing initiatives program at Outside In as part of an overall public health strategy, and even now, after so many years, the results of my false-positive HIV test remain an isolated anomaly. She is currently working on initiatives to reduce the harms of substance use and promote health in the community of people who use substances.

The staff at Sand Island are still hard at work and committed to changing lives one intake at a time. Mike is still chasing waves and I am honored to call him a dear mentor and friend. I turn to both him and Ty whenever there are significant ups and downs in my life, and the first stop I went to after leaving the scene of my brother's death was to Sand Island to process what I could muster. Ty met me at the gates and embraced me until Mike returned to help walk me through my next steps.

A couple of staff have also passed on over the years, proving to us clients that the ultimate goal of dying sober is not a pipe dream. Along with hundreds of other current and former clients, I paid my respects to Uncle Stan, James, and most recently Saunoa, showing their families what far reaching impact their loved ones had.

My program of recovery may not be exactly what was taught at Sand Island, but I also believe that is sort of the point. If I was pressed to give one piece of advice, I would say to keep an open mind, choose what works for you and then proceed with caution. For most addicts, recovery is uncharted territory, and because there is no cure, every path is different. Some paths are a ritzy walk in the park while others are a seemingly hopeless waist-deep stink pit. And while no rehab can guarantee an addict success, in hindsight, I am forever grateful that I didn't walk out of treatment smack into a mountain of debt. In fact, I had enough savings piled up to be able to breathe, which proved invaluable for anyone who is starting over from scratch. But regardless of the finances, if you ever find yourself in treatment, remember that you're likely there to save your life. Even if you're lucky enough to touch down in Hawai'i, you're not there for a vacation.

Remember, if you're anything like me, your best thinking probably got you to where you are, so if you don't know what to do, don't do anything at all.

I also like to remind addicts not to be afraid to try new things. If the goal of recovery is to live a long life and die sober, then the objective should be to make it a life worth living. Sobriety ought to be better than using, otherwise what is the point? I used my earliest years of sobriety to explore, literally, *hundreds* of new hobbies. Some stuck and many didn't, but with a new lease on life and an excitement to make it worthwhile, it was critical to find those healthy hobbies that excited me most. Here's a brief list of some of the passions that keep me excited and out of trouble:

- Underwater Metal Detecting
- Treasure Hunting
- Surfing
- Bodysurfing
- Diving
- Paddling (OC1 & OC6)
- Woodturning
- Beat Making
- Turntablism
- Record Collecting / Crate Digging
- Eurorack / Modular Synthesizers
- Playing 'Ukulele
- Thrift Shopping
- Sensory Deprivation aka Floating
- Mountain Biking
- Glass + Stone Art
- Board Games
- Chess
- Gardening / Aquaponics
- Backyard Chickens
- Backyard Archery
- Writing

(Additionally, there is an ever-growing list of fascinating hobbies that I hope to experience one day. These tend to require more buy-in and understanding from the wife, but I imagine there is a time and place for everything. Most notably, Flight School and Beekeeping are at the top of the list.)

In the years since receiving my clinical, I've practiced a treatment plan for myself that suits me well. It starts with the most fundamental building block that I learned early on in recovery: do the right thing, get the right results. After that, I still have to remind myself that in recovery, we often have to do things we don't want to do. I guess that's life.

A strong support group also makes all the difference in the world, and I'm aware that it's truly a privilege to have loving parents who never left my side. If you happen to know or love an addict who is struggling, I hope you never give up on them, regardless of how hard they push you away. Remember, that is often a tactic employed by a user to protect their addiction since our loved ones usually care enough to want the best for us.

I also believe it is a common misconception that a person needs to be ready to get help to stand a chance. I look only to myself, where I didn't believe it was possible. Yes, I was willing to walk into treatment, but I wasn't ready to get clean, and I did not get sober because I wanted to. I vividly remember believing the lie that detoxing off drugs was impossible and that a lifetime of sobriety was out the window.

Fortunately, I found myself settling in with a group of amazing people, all working toward a common goal that has rubbed off on me. Over time, I realized my life was too good to ever think of going back. I put enough distance between myself and what once troubled me to witness the promise of the program come to fruition.

And I've reaped the benefits as a result: I control my thoughts, my conscience is no longer dusty and I am no longer separated from my soul and suffering needlessly.

In short, I stuck it out long enough for the miracle to happen—I am alive in every sense of the word instead of fervently drifting away.

And that's how the promise of the program has played out in my life. Once that tide turned and I stopped fighting it, I was swept away by an unstoppable force which carried me to places I could only ever dream about. It's taught me to trust the process, and in turn, I now have functioning faith that has become second nature.

Of course there's been ups and downs, but I've ridden the wave for so long that it's finally carrying me and I'm able to enjoy the ride. That said, I still make an exerted effort to remain humble, knowing that even though these past years have flown by so fast, someone at Sand Island wouldn't miss the opportunity to remind me that one more year is better.

I think I'm finally starting to get it.

Tomorrow is *always* better in recovery, and we're not done yet. If the goal is to die sober, then the marathon must continue. It's a good life to lead and doesn't have to be overly complicated. There's a lot more where that came from, but to simplify the message, everything I've learned boils down to that black and white affirmation: there is no longer muddled waters that I may or may not find a way out of.

I am one hit away, and tomorrow will be the same story. I have a bearing and know where I'm heading. Following my mother's advice, I stand proud with a backbone and find strength in the truth and surety, that for me, relapse is not an option. And while I'm sensitive that many others work a different program, I have found that this works for me. If you're of a different mindset, please remember that recovery is as personal as it gets, so take what you can and leave the rest. That's what I've done, and it has served me and many others well. It's allowed me to not only protect what I have, but remain fortunate enough to give it away through service and sharing my experience, strength and hope, which is ultimately how we keep moving forward.

Imua.

ACKNOWLEDGMENTS

Mahalo Ke Akua—*God is good, all the time.*

Mom and Dad—I owe you my life. Thank you both for every-thing you have done and continue to do to support me.

I also want to take this opportunity to thank my mom for keeping such accurate notes and records leading up to me being found. Once I amassed the wherewithal to put pen to pad, we spent a great deal of time recalling and rehashing both happy and painful memories. Her records helped to fill in the gaps of my story and connect the dots. Many of the details she contributed were unbeknownst to me, and there were many more that I had buried somewhere along the way. Mom, it was not easy, but the good news is that I promise to never put you through that experi-ence again.

Hooper Detox, Central City Concern and Outside In—I would not be here today without your services and the compassion of your employees. Samajean (Hooper) and Haven (Outside In)—I was not surprised to learn that you both are still wholly committed to your work! Please know that your passion has fallout that reaches far and wide, likely more than you'll ever know.

In recovery, it truly does take a village to raise a child, and I will forever be indebted to Sand Island Director Mason Henderson for opening up his home and allowing me to receive the help I so desperately needed.

Mike "White Lightning" Coleman and Tyrone "Ty" Spears—thank you for always being here for me. Your mentorship, counseling and endless guidance means everything to me. I can never repay you, so I promise to pass it on. #Imua #YGI.

To the rest of my Sand Island 'Ohana: Allen, Auntie Mae, Carolyn, David A., David G., Duane, Deborah, Dr. Lai, Gordon, Mama Grace, Wes, Nader, Miss Cats, Kevin, Russel, Sutton, Tammy, Tony, Yvonne and everyone else including the interns and those who are no longer with us—the work you do is hard and selfless, but never thankless. My life is what it is today because you all paved the way and showed me it was possible.

Rest in peace to Uncle Stan, Uncle James and Uncle Saunoa—you each proved to me that not only is a lifetime of recovery possible, but it can be wildly beautiful. I thank God I was able to pay my respects to each of you in person, *clean and sober,* and it meant the world to me to tell your loved ones how large of an impact you each had on my life. Your legacy and life's work continues to live on through the lives of so many.

Judge Angel Lopez, S.T.O.P. Court and my public defenders, Mr. Lee and Ms. Whitaker—you all worked with me in my best interest to give me the one shot I needed to succeed. I promised you each that I would make the most of this opportunity, and I promise to keep my word still. You also recognized the strong support group I had back home and allowed it to work in my favor. I will never forget your kindness and hope I continue to make you proud. I can't thank you enough.

To Doug & Hollis, Diego & Kate, Will, Deb & Jeff, Justin & Emily, Jonathan, Eli, Cavin, Heather "Hobbes" Ashley, Jessie, Shelley and Kelly, Crystal & Steve, Ian, Chris, Chelsea, Coral, Kamille, Linsey, Jonas, Tara, Aunt Vivian, Kate & Dan, Kevin, Dan, Buzz, Walt, Tim, Eiji, The Wahine Book Club (Molly, Rebecca, Melissa, Andrea, Diana, Jordan, Théodora, Hanna, Florianne,

Mhairi, Lisa and Kate), Brian, Mr. & Mrs. Rumbough, Damian & Ashley, Jordan, Annie, Marisa and Kylie—mahalo to everyone for the precious gift of time and support, offering invaluable feedback to this project that challenged me to constantly improve.

Kate Wadsworth (www.KateWadsworth.com)—your talent as an artist knows no bounds. Mahalo for gracing this book cover and being such a pleasure to work with. I'm so happy with the final product that part of me wants to write another book just to work with you again.

To my editor Jessey Mills (www.JesseyMills.com)—your edits unveiled a world of confidence in my craft. You went above and beyond and I am fortunate to have found you. Thank you for all you have taught me and for helping me tell the story I was born to tell.

Hui!!! I owe a massive mahalo to my audiobook narrator Ryan Haugen (www.RyanHaugen.com)—I am so grateful that we crossed paths and that you handled production with such passion and empathy. You were a pleasure to work with and I can't wait to hear what you come out with next.

And to my wife Chelsea, who supported this project from start to finish, at much sacrifice and understanding—I love you with everything I have.

MAHALO NUI LOA

THANK YOU!

If you enjoyed this book, and feel inspired to share, please help spread the word by leaving an honest review on the book's page at Amazon.com, Bookbub.com and/or Goodreads.com.

More reviews means more exposure, which helps put this book and its message into more hands.

Mahalo for your support!

ABOUT THE AUTHOR

Jordan P. Barnes is a grateful alcoholic & addict in recovery and Sand Island Treatment Center is his home group. When he's not sharing his experience, strength and hope through writing or talking story, he enjoys bodysurfing, sound exploration and mountain biking. Jordan resides in beautiful Kailua, Hawai'i with his lovely wife Chelsea. Together, they are excited to grow their 'Ohana, beginning with their very first keiki due in December of 2020. Jordan has been sober from all mind-and-mood-altering substances since August 29th, 2011.

Learn more at www.JordanPBarnes.com

Join my Newsletter and be the first to learn about upcoming giveaways, interviews and new projects:
www.JordanPBarnes.com/newsletter

Get the latest deals and new release alerts by following me on BookBub: www.bookbub.com/authors/jordan-barnes

Correspondence:
P.O. Box 630
Kailua, HI 96734

info@jordanpbarnes.com

Let's join forces:

facebook.com/jordanbarnesauthor

twitter.com/jordan_p_barnes

instagram.com/jordan_p_barnes

youtube.com/onehitaway

goodreads.com/jordan_p_barnes

bookbub.com/authors/jordan-barnes

GOOD THOUGHTS INSIDE

THE TWELVE STEPS OF ALCOHOLICS ANONYMOUS

AA'S 12-STEP APPROACH FOLLOWS A SET OF
GUIDELINES DESIGNED AS "STEPS" TOWARD
RECOVERY, AND MEMBERS CAN REVISIT THESE STEPS
AT ANY TIME. THE 12 STEPS ARE:

1. We admitted we were powerless over alcohol—that our lives had become unmanageable.
2. Came to believe that a Power greater than ourselves could restore us to sanity.
3. Made a decision to turn our will and our lives over to the care of God as we understood Him.
4. Made a searching and fearless moral inventory of ourselves.
5. Admitted to God, to ourselves, and to another human being the exact nature of our wrongs.
6. Were entirely ready to have God remove all these defects of character.
7. Humbly asked Him to remove our shortcomings.
8. Made a list of all persons we had harmed, and became willing to make amends to them all.
9. Made direct amends to such people wherever possible, except when to do so would injure them or others.
10. Continued to take personal inventory and when we were wrong promptly admitted it.

11. Sought through prayer and meditation to improve our conscious contact with God, as we understood Him, praying only for knowledge of His will for us and the power to carry that out.

12. Having had a spiritual awakening as the result of these Steps, we tried to carry this message to alcoholics, and to practice these principles in all our affairs.

RESOURCES

IF YOU OR SOMEONE YOU KNOW IS DYING TO LEARN MORE ABOUT RECOVERY, HERE ARE SOME RESOURCES THAT MAY HELP:

Acupuncture Hawai'i Kai, Eiji Takeda
Honolulu, HI
www.acupuncturehawaiikai.com
808-389-0823

Addicts Ripple
www.addictsripple.com

Al-Anon
www.al-anon.org

Alcoholics Anonymous
www.aa.org

Co-Dependents Anonymous
www.coda.org

Hooper Detox
Portland, OR
www.centralcityconcern.org

503-238-2067

Narcotics Anonymous
www.na.org

Nar-Anon Family Groups
www.nar-anon.org

Outside-In
Portland, OR
www.outsidein.org
503-535-3826

Sand Island Treatment Center
aka Kline-Welsh Behavioral Health Foundation
Honolulu, HI
www.sandisland.com
808-841-2319

Substance Abuse and Mental Health Services Administration
(SAMHSA's) National Helpline
1-800-662-HELP (4357)

National Suicide Prevention Lifeline
1-800-273-8255

This Naked Mind
www.thisnakedmind.com

CPSIA information can be obtained
at www.ICGtesting.com
Printed in the USA
BVHW081514040123
655471BV00003B/29